TABLE OF CONTENTS

I0160648

Page 7   Foreword by Steven Payne Ph.D.

Page 9   Prelude – Rise of the Latin Hustle

Page 22   Chapter One – The Bully of P.S. 27

Page 31   Chapter Two – Expressway to Death

Page 42   Chapter Three – The Flames - Juvenile Delinquents

Page 66   Chapter Four – The Death of Mr. Letto

Page 73   Chapter Five – The Ghetto Brothers

Page 82   Chapter Six – Trouble in Paradise

Page 89   Chapter Seven – Back to the Boogie Down Bronx

Page 98   Chapter Eight – The Imperial Bachelors

Page 113 Chapter Nine – We Never Promised You a Rose Garden

Page 124 Chapter Ten – The Plan for Peace

Page 131 Chapter Eleven – The Court-Martial of Sgt. Cartwright

Page 137 Chapter Twelve – The Birth of St. Mary's Jam's

Page 173 Chapter Thirteen – The Death of Rubberband

Page 186 Chapter Fourteen – The 310 ½ - Stuck on Stupid

Page 198 Chapter Fifteen – Rocking the Lower East Side

Page 220 Chapter Sixteen – The Disco Bandits

Page 236   Chapter Seventeen – The Jive Five

Page 241   Chapter Eighteen – 1977 The day after the Blackout

Page 250   Chapter Nineteen – The Beat Down

Page 263   Chapter Twenty – Saturday Night Fever – The Sham

Page 267   Chapter Twenty One – Rock Masters – The Last
              Hurrah

Page 272   Chapter Twenty Two – The Birth of Faces

Page 300   Chapter Twenty Three – Working for the King

Page 311   Chapter Twenty Four – The Birth of Friday Night Fever

Page 336   Chapter Twenty Five – The Death of Bonds 1983

Page 342   Afterword, and Reflections of the 1970s

South Bronx 1960 My Siblings, Wilma, Maritza and I

I've loved music and dance since I was a very young boy, and everywhere I went, I took my Dad's small Radio so I could dance.

Events change history. Events make history. And the telling of events often also changes History. The truth usually lies somewhere between the telling of the facts and the re-telling over time as the false testimony of witnesses is proven and unproven. Some stories require unknotting and deciphering until a credible narrative emerges consistent with the individual and collective memories that comprise a cultural phenomenon, a war, or a meaningful change. In this case, a peace that kept an oppressed people intact and sustained its shared conviction that resilience was life's most enduring characteristic and that our culture would be kept safe from the racism and hatred of the oppressors.

This book is about my life and the story of how an extraordinary dance movement helped end gang violence in one of the most violent neighborhoods in the South Bronx during the early 1970s.

Finally, I can present the second edition of my book. A story about one life preserved somewhat intact by the grace of God, and the unconditional love of my family and friends, a good dose of street smarts, and a unique aptitude for survival. I am grateful. And now that I think back to the sufferings, conflicts, challenges, and sorrows, the woes and the hopes. I also think about all the people without whom this narrative could not exist and the tremendous difficulties, obstacles, and help I received. Sometimes not even knowing it was' help' I was receiving... that mysterious, inexplicable taken-by-the-hand-by-an-Angel type of guidance that navigated bullets and knives, envy and betrayals, and much more. I offer my eternal heartfelt gratitude to all of God's blessings from above and those he put in my life. I used real names in this book to validate my accounts by all those I mention in these pages of authentic history.

Please accept my apologies to anyone who may have been hurt or harmed by my actions, and I hope you understand I acted without malice.

May your lives be filled with love and happiness, and may the best things find their way into your lives, as they have found their way into mine.

Peace and God's blessings always be with you all the days of your lives.

Dedication

This book is dedicated to the memory of my father (Eduardo "Eddie" Estrada), who I lost July 6, 1998, and to my mother (Maria Estrada), who I lost on Oct. 8, 2021. Despite my initial shortcomings, the unconditional love they always gave me was and continues to be endless. They never stopped believing in me, and thanks to their teachings, and by the grace of God, I am still here today to share my story with the world.

I am also dedicating this book to my daughter Lindsay pictured here with me, who has been the greatest gift in my life since the day she was born. I love you with all my heart!

In loving memory of all those I've loved and lost throughout my life's journey, this is for you.

Our Story has never been told, nor have we ever gotten credit for the many significant contributions Puerto Ricans have made throughout the years. Especially within the Latin Hustle Culture we created and the Dance Cultures of New York City dating back to the 1950s when we came here in significant numbers. The Puerto Rican influence has been suppressed for far too long how. However, I now firmly believe our time to be heard and our stories told has finally arrived.

-- Willie "Marine Boy" Estrada --

Mom, Wilma and I - Puerto Rico 1956

An American/Puerto Rican Story

Foreword by Steven Payne Ph.D.

The Bronx's dynamic history of cultural creativity over the past century has few parallels. Our borough has been a primary incubator for such worldwide sensations as doo-wop, mambo, Latin jazz, boogaloo, salsa, hip-hop, break dancing, and graffiti. In recent years, thanks to a variety of documentaries, books, and other media, The Bronx and its people are beginning to receive credit for some of these innovations—mainly hip-hop and everything surrounding it. Yet even with hip-hop, credit is still often only given to a handful of individuals. Citizens of this country have long been obsessed with myths of individual brilliance as if creative or technical inventions owe nothing to the broader human communities, social settings, and histories from which they emerged. We live in a type of society—capitalism—where a few individuals benefit tremendously from the collective labor of all, so it should be no surprise that these types of myths have so much holding power. History, in the truest sense of the term, aims to dismantle long-cherished myths and, as far as possible, reach a more realistic conception of the world, no matter the consequences.

I write these somewhat abstract reflections because the main thrust of Willie Estrada's memoir is not myth but *history*. The more mythological approach to the past focuses only on individuals and leads us to believe that these individuals single-handedly invented a culture and the various components that comprise it. When phrased in this direct manner, of course, such myths sound absurd. Certain individuals, no doubt, contributed more than others to the rise of cultural phenomena like hip hop, and their contributions should be honored, but human culture is a messier and more collective affair than myths of individual excellence suggest. Rather than emerging from one person or site or having a direct line of descent, cultural phenomena arise bit by bit, in multiple places, on different timelines, and take years

7

to come together into a single movement or art form. Formerly marginal or little-emphasized moments within a particular cultural movement can suddenly take center stage, and aspects that once seemed central can fade into oblivion. Human culture is incredibly complicated, and we leave out so many factors and actors when we fall back on easy myth-making.

Taking a critical, more historical approach to human culture forces us to pay attention to complexity. Willie's book exemplifies this approach because it reminds us that there was no predetermined reason that hip-hop had to take the exact form or reach the prominence that it eventually assumed. Many distinct, only partially related cultural phenomena played into the eventual formation of hip-hop in The Bronx, and Willie's book helps us get into one of the most fascinating of these that is often overlooked. As readers will learn, one of Willie's main topics is the development and rise of the Latin Hustle during the early 1970s. Indeed, by the time a few hints of what would become hip-hop were popping up in The Bronx in the mid-1970s, the Latin Hustle was already in full swing. Like hip-hop, the Latin Hustle was a cultural phenomenon formed by youth in the South Bronx. Basements, community centers, and small neighborhood venues scattered throughout Mott Haven and Hunts Point served as sites of cultural innovation for the primarily Puerto Rican teenagers like Willie, who gave birth to the dance. Willie highlights the many beautiful ways that the music and dance of the Latin Hustle impacted the lives of countless teenagers and young adults in the South Bronx during this period of time.

Because he was a central participant in the rise of the Latin Hustle, Willie, by telling his own life story, also helps recover this lost Bronx cultural moment. Bringing this history to light enriches our understanding of the variety and brilliance of Bronx culture and allows us to contextualize later Bronx cultural phenomena like hip hop. Without the prior emergence of the

Latin Hustle in the South Bronx of the early 1970s, in all likelihood, B-boying would not have become a part of hip-hop culture, at least not in the form that it did. For example, before it was called B-boying, the dance that became a central part of hip-hop culture was known simply as "Rocking, or Uprock," how it later became known as Bboying is a mystery. This is not to say that the Latin Hustle and hip-hop are directly related or that the Latin Hustle derives its historical importance only because of hip-hop, or vice versa. The Latin Hustle was and still is its own brilliant thing that just so happened to play into the broader cultural landscape of the South Bronx, out of which hip-hop eventually emerged. Moreover, as Willie points out, in the Bronx neighborhoods where the Latin Hustle was king, gang violence experienced a sharp decline. This was at a time, 1973–1975, *after* the short-lived Hoe Avenue gang truce of 1971 and *before* hip-hop became the widespread phenomenon that it eventually became. During the days of the Latin Hustle, members of rival gangs could gather peacefully in community centers like St. Mary's Recreation Center. Indeed, although various factors played into the disappearance of most Bronx street gangs in the mid-1970s, Willie argues convincingly that the Latin Hustle— more so than hip hop, which had not yet taken off—was one of the primary reasons for this development.

This means that the South Bronx cultural history during the 1970s is even more intricate, dynamic, and multi-racial than popular documentaries like *Rubble Kings* suggest. The Bronx of the 1970s contained multiple shifting focal points of cultural creativity, the Latin Hustle being one of the most important of these. The various nodes of cultural innovation, like early hip-hop itself, often involved the full spectrum of the working-class residents of our borough: people of African descent, Latinos, Asians, and even a few white "leftovers" (as we call ourselves in the Boogie Down).

Willie's story, therefore, although first and foremost a story about the remarkable creativity of Puerto Rican teenagers, is also a story that belongs to all of us who call The Bronx home, and I am honored to introduce it.

Dr. Steven Payne

Dr. Steven Payne and wife Rachel with Author Willie Estrada at an event with students from Fordham University, 2021

Prelude: Rise of the Latin Hustle

During the 1950s, Puerto Ricans came to the United States in great numbers searching for the American dream but faced discrimination and the biased rejection of prejudice instead. People tend to see the wrong side of things, and many paint ugly pictures with an ever-present stigma attached to us as people. They fail to see all the savagery we had endured during the early conquests of the Island people. Or that slavery was forced upon us for over 400 years by the Spanish Empire, referred to as "The Conquistadores." People don't know our true story, only that we differed in colors, behavior, and desire to retain cultural identity. We would not relinquish all this even as we tried to assimilate ourselves into an unfamiliar world that also terrified us. Since World War I, Puerto Ricans have fought and died in every major war alongside mainland Americans. This fact did not make a difference to all those Americans who rejected and disrespected us and continued to doubt our courage and bravery. We became known as "Spics" because many of us did not speak English at this time.

I was just a boy during the early 1960s. Still, I remember well how tightly knit the Puerto Rican community was. I witnessed the disparity and the separation, or I should say, division among our people during the latter part of the 1960s. It is something that I have always attributed in part to the War in Vietnam. What supports and makes my statement evident is that there was a night and day difference in how the Puerto Rican community treated each other once our Vets started coming home.

After surviving the horrors of war up close and personal, these young men, still kids in the eyes of many, were now afflicted, and most came home mentally damaged and drained of the love that once held us together as a people. Where there once was pride, there was now the rage, and hate replaced love.

However, somewhere inside remained the heart of passion, armed with a new type of resilience, but hope was all but gone from their eyes. Resentment and anger dominated their lives. Many took the hatred this country made them exude and projected it with rebellion and disobedience, which led to war among our people. We divided ourselves from one neighborhood to the next, a hatred not of our own making. Faced with the economic meltdown in New York City during the 1970s, the South Bronx was the most brutally hit, and divide and conquer tactics rained brimstone and fire, which blinded us with bellows of smoke when chaos ruled the streets. Although sorrow and despair were in abundance, the resilience of our people remained strong, as did our indomitable spirit.

During the late 1960s, upon their return from the horrors of Vietnam, there were no parades nor fanfare to welcome our young soldier's home. Instead, people shouted at them and cursed them with chants of "Baby Killers" and several other derogatory names. Many veterans felt shame for something imposed upon them that they had not sought. They came home to gang wars raging on the streets of the South Bronx, and needless to say, they fit right in and often became the most violent among all gang members. They came home trained killers and had no hesitation or remorse in inflicting death and destruction on an already broken community, in the wake of a senseless war, with their hearts and spirits partially broken. Music and dance seemed to soothe the savage beast raging inside them, and yet as they danced, you could see the warlike gestures emulating what resembled a fierce battle on the frontlines of Vietnam. Invisible Bazookas were pulled out of thin air, followed by hand grenades. At the same time, another simulated machinegun fire and yet another fixed the bayonet to his invisible weapon or simply pulled a knife, and aggressive stabbing motions ensued.

All this being done to the rhythmic drums with the music's hypnotic transformation of reality, steadily embraced by euphoria.

Those are the things I saw Vietnam Vets doing at the Royal Javelins clubhouse during the late 1960s. The dance I saw resembled a ritual, as though intended to pay tribute to the brothers they lost in Vietnam. Many years later, the form of dance I saw became identified as what we refer to today as "Outlaw Rock." It was the first form of Rock Dance created by the Puerto Rican youth living in dysphoria and amplified by the long-standing and continued oppression of our people living in Puerto Rico and the South Bronx.

As gang violence continued into the early 1970s, a new form of Rock Dance was developed within the Puerto Rican community. However, it had become more of a tribal dance of sorts, and it boasted fancier moves and a whole new look and feel. In the early 1970s, as teenagers, we frequented a local club called the 310-½ off Prospect Ave in the South Bronx, and we fine-tuned our dance as we danced together in peace. However, the disruption of violence and chaos of the surrounding neighborhoods was always close by and waiting to unleash hell at any given moment. There was something new on the horizon, and by late 1972, after protests from our elders, who did not like us dirty dancing with their teenage daughters. By 1973, the dance born as a result of our elders' protests to "dirty dancing" or "Fresqueria," as they would put it, had already gone through two versions of an elementary five-step dance to a more intriguing six-step dance. However, it was still a bit robotic and stiff during its early days as a six-step dance. It had gone from being called "The Rope Hustle to the Push and Pull Hustle" to the "Hustle" and finally "The Latin Hustle." By mid-1974, the first six-step Latin Hustle became much fancier. It had lots of spins and fancy footwork, and gang members turned dancers led the way alongside the attractive young girls who enticed gang members, and other boys like to dance with them at **St. Mary's Recreation Center**. Unlike some gangs, the Imperial Bachelors protected their neighborhood despite all the nearby violence caused by other divisions of one of the most significant gangs in the South Bronx.

13

St. Mary's Recreation Center served as a beacon of hope and provided refuge in one of the most violent neighborhoods in all of the South Bronx during those tumultuous years.

The staff and center manager **Rita Pasquelaqua** helped us navigate those turbulent days with counsel and genuine love. It helped immensely that the President of our gang, **Henry DeSosa,** also worked at St. Mary's. One could say we had the coolest Gang Club House in New York since **St. Mary's** boasted a swimming pool, a basketball gym, karate, and boxing gyms, as well as a host of other activities such as Pool and Ping Pong tables, which worked to keep us off the streets, and out of trouble.

Our gang was different than any other gang I had ever been affiliated with: we weren't troublemakers. Instead, we fiercely protected our neighborhood. For example, **St. Mary's Park** had no lights at night during the early 1970s, and during the night, the park became a death trap for unsuspecting victims.

Women were dragged into the park and raped; men were robbed and, at times, killed, while criminals seemed to get away with murder. In 1973, when I became the Warlord of the Imperial Bachelors, we decided to start protecting our community by patrolling the park at night and hiding in wait for someone to attempt to rob, rape, or kill. Soon after that, the park became safer as a result. The Police called us, Vigilantes, but the people called us Heroes, and we liked that title better.

"Ghetto," "disenfranchised," "hood rats, "uneducated animals" are but a few of the descriptions applied to residents of the South Bronx throughout the years. I am a product of my environment, but I am none of those things, and neither are any of the people who grew up alongside me. Poverty-stricken, oppressed, abandoned, and angry is how I would describe us, and it was not by choice that we lived under that stigma. Instead, it was a purposeful intention caused by the prejudice and indifference of those in power who simply did not care about us. Fictional movies like "**Fort Apache the Bronx**" and "**The Warriors**" scratched the surface of the problems concerning actual events and why these things happened. However, for us, the reality was much uglier. As a direct result of our oppression, during the late 1960s, Gang Wars were raging on the streets of the South Bronx, and violence was at an all-time high with no end in sight. Ignorance and stupidity, however, were in abundance. It was a time of great despair and sorrow, and hope was all but lost in the fires of abandonment as intended by the local government, who purposely neglected the Puerto Rican and Black communities, already living in poverty and despair.

Imagine, if you will, living in a neighborhood where the buildings around you are set on fire by gang members and the very people who live in those buildings. Landlords had over 36,000 buildings burned down within ten years to collect insurance money on their property.

Between the fires, which left nothing but brickyards that resembled post-World War II Berlin in their wake, and the rebellion of the inhabitants, the South Bronx, had also become a place where even the police, supposed to protect you, abused and brutalized us instead. However, what bothered me the most was that they seemed to take delight in demoralizing us, and it was evident by the way they treated us, which made us hate them with a passion.

As a kid, I looked up to Police officers, and I always felt safe when they were around patrolling our neighborhood, but that all changed when I grew older and witnessed the savage and unjust beatings of injustice at their hands.

Life took on a different perspective, and I also had to learn how to fight at a very early age, as my environment was extremely violent and volatile, and chaos ruled the streets and the schools we attended. Gang membership was a must in those days because survival on the streets was much more challenging if you weren't a part of one, and many times your life depended on fellow gang members coming to your aid. By 1971 there were more gangs in the South Bronx than any other borough, and senseless and cruel violence was rampant.

It wasn't until a gang leader Cornell "*Black Benjy*" Benjamin, from a gang called the "Ghetto Brothers," was violently killed by three rival gangs, as he attempted to make peace between them, that those gangs started talking about peace. On December 7, 1971, the gang meeting I attended at the Hoe Avenue Bronx Boys Club produced relative peace for the gangs involved in Benjy's murder. The Ghetto Brothers and the three gangs who killed Black Benjy: The 7 Immortals, the Black Spades, and the Mongols. The truth is that not all the gangs made peace that day. However, Benjamin "Yellow Benjy" Melendez made a great effort and tried his best to bring peace among rival gangs.

Music and dance in the form of jams with live music were their primary weapons of choice during the late 1960s and continued well into the early 70s, notably in light of Cornell *"Black Benjy"* Benjamin's death. Yellow Benjy had become the most prominent spokesman in advocating for peace among the gangs. Still, it was a slow process, and it was evident he needed help from other leaders, which as a result of not all the gangs making peace, never really came about that year.

In 1973 Henry DeSosa was promoted to Supreme President of the Bachelors by his predecessor Black Tony because he was going to prison. Before he left, he instructed Henry to make peace among our rivals at a time when the South Bronx went from nine gang-related homicides in 1971 to fifty-four in 1972. By mid-1974, Benjy's ideology was implemented by the new Supreme President of the Imperial Bachelors, Henry DeSosa. St. Mary's, the center, served as headquarters for the gang leader and its members in a building that became a neutral ground for many of the residents of the South Bronx, including rival gang members, so long as they didn't wear gang colors. Peace did not come easy, especially since some gangs were still hell-bent on self-destruction, and words of peace and harmony were never a part of their vocabulary. Regarding the most violent gangs, such as the Savage Skulls and several others, reasoning with them was often futile.

Music and dance were already a part of the gang scene, and slow dancing or grinding with the girls had become very popular at gang parties and house parties. However, most people do not know that the first five-step Hustle was created because of objections by parents and our elders to slow dance grinding and doing a very provocative move called the "500" at house parties. The first 6 step Hustle was born in late 1973, and while it had turns and spins, which its earlier versions did not have, it was a bit robotic and stiff in the beginning, but it would soon become a thing of elegance, grace, and beauty.

Young people continued dancing very closely to slow songs, but mostly at hooky parties and makeshift basement clubs where young people congregated to skip out on school and dance with no parental interference to worry over. By the mid-1974, the new 6 step version of the dance had been developed further and became fancier with lots of elegant turns and spins, and it became known as "The Latin Hustle."

We were born from the ashes of a burning South Bronx, when violence and death reigned supreme in the land of broken promises, at a time when love and hope were almost lost. In the summer of 1974, The Imperial Bachelors hosted Latin Hustle parties, which brought many young people from several boroughs to the South Bronx to dance at St. Mary's Recreation Center every Tuesday and Thursday night. I firmly believe it was music and dance that spearheaded the peace process among several gangs of the South Bronx in our territory that year. It seems to me that the contributions of the Puerto Rican people have always been minimized for some reason. The beauty of our culture has spanned the globe, but nobody attributes it to that from which it came. Be that as it may, nothing will ever dishearten my people because we are among the most resilient people on the face of the earth and have proven that many times over during our long history of living under the cruelty of oppression. As our plight continues and our resolve gains momentum, the great walls of disparity that once kept our stories hidden have begun to crumble as our stories have taken on a great new life of their own. We will not be denied from a history that is rightly ours, and soon the indignities brought to bear by our oppressors will be revealed, as we exclaim in one loud voice. Here is what happened to us, and here are the contributions we have made over the years; now, hear our Roar!

Some think complete peace among the gangs of the Bronx was established at the gang peace meeting at the Hoe Ave Boys Club in 1971, after the brutal killing of Back Benjy.

However, as mentioned earlier, most simply do not know that there were nine gang-related murders in 1971, but in 1972, the NYPD had recorded 54 gang killings. Those numbers dropped to thirty-eight in 1973 and fell dramatically in 1974 to 8, with only 2 in 1975 and not one gang-related murder recorded in 1976. According to police and records, the street gang unit kept from 1971 to the latter part of the 1970s.

By mid-1974, it was the Imperial Bachelors who made the most significant efforts for peace amongst several neighboring rival gangs by creating a venue where we could all dance the Latin Hustle together in harmony, and gang colors came off in recognition of that unspoken truce.

The Imperial Bachelors hosted Latin Hustle and Rock Parties during the summer of 1974 at St. Mary's Recreation Center.

While our contributions have been many, the credit has been non-existent for the most part. That said, I intend to bring forth some of the hidden pages of lost history from a time long gone, but not forgotten, that belongs to the Puerto Rican people and other Latinos alike. The ironic part is that many Puerto Ricans who live stateside are not aware of the history of our people. In all fairness, neither was I until I took it upon myself to learn our real history contrary to the narrative offered by the United States. The official story left out many of the details of our oppression on the pages of history.

Who were our heroes, what did they do, and what happened to them? The answers will both surprise and shock you, but they will also give you a sense of hope and pride. They will also teach you about the importance and the power of our resilience for over 500 years.

This story is one of resilience perseverance, and, most importantly, it is about the power and beauty of music and dance. It is also about the love that binds us all together as people. Although the struggles continue, so does our search for freedom. I started writing this story when I went back to school to study computer technology in 1987. I started writing this book because the origins of the Latin Hustle had never been documented until now.

It was developed and nurtured during the most violent days of gang wars in the early 1970s. I felt it was such a compelling story; it deserved to be told by a gang member and leader and one of the original pioneers of the Latin Hustle. I went through several versions as I attended school; however, after I graduated and began working in the computer field, I also settled down and started a family. Although this story always remained close to my heart. Life happened, and between work, and my family obligations, writing became extremely difficult, so I put my pen down in 1990 and concentrated all my efforts on my career to better provide for my family.

As fate would have it, nineteen years later, in 2009, I was contacted by my old friend, Hollywood Film Director **Franc Reyes,** who introduced me to **Fabel Pabon**. He was very excited to meet me, but I didn't know why until he told me he and **Mr. Wiggles**, a member of the **Rock Steady Crew**, had been looking for 1st generation Rock Dancers to clear up some discrepancies over the history of Rock dancing in New York.

He went on to tell me that some dancers from Brooklyn had been claiming that Rock dancing was created in Bushwich, Brooklyn and that the Bronx had no 1sts generation Rockers.

He got my full attention the minute he said that, and I told him they must be high on Crack. I explained to him how rich our Rocking history from the South Bronx was, and that I had battled dancers from Brooklyn and the Lower East Side during the 1970s, and described their style of Rock to a T, and how our style was a lot more stylish than what they were doing during those days. I, of course, had no idea that style of dance was still around. For that matter, I had no idea young people around the world were also doing the Rock style of dance, and the Latin Hustle was also being done.

Fabel asked me if I knew any other 1st generation Rock dancers from the Bronx, and when I told him I knew them all, he started doing his happy dance, or at least that's the way I imagined it since we were on a 3-way conversation with Franc. He invited me to bring someone else to interview to help him correct some history lost in our absence. Fabel invited us to speak on a forum where all the Brooklyn Rockers were in significant numbers, but he warned me that he was taking me into the belly of the beast as he put it and that they would be a bit rude. When he introduced me to those who had been making claims that they created Rocking in Bushwick, they were a bit surprised by my arrival, but it didn't take them long to act like complete jerks with me. I was trying my best to share our history. After a short while, lousy behavior and doubt on their part were apparent. Yet, most of them were too young to be part of this dance culture during the early 1970s.

I continued to educate them, and eventually, they came to terms with the fact that the Bronx not only had 1st generation Rock Dancers, but that we were among the very best throughout New York City, during a time when it was the Latin Hustle that reigned supreme.

21

Fabel and his friends had been looking for us to help them correct Bronx dance history. However, I noticed that it was not the only part of history that had been changed in the absence of truth. They say, "The truth shall see you free," so here is our truth about a part of history that has never been told correctly. Our story begs to be heard by those searching for knowledge during those violent years of gang wars. People want to know how peace was born in one of the most violent neighborhoods of the South Bronx in 1974.

This is the coming of age true story of a young man and his friends during the most violent days in the history of the South Bronx, before the birth of Hip Hop. A young gang leader and his crew helped transform their neighborhood by hosting dance parties and creating peace through the power and beauty of music and the dance called **(The Latin Hustle)** as the Bronx burned down all around them. Though many lives were lost on the road to peace, this art form helped to prove that the indomitable human spirit has the power to prevail despite the most impoverished circumstances in life.

Willie Estrada, a former member of the world-renowned "Latin Symbolics Dance Company" and former gang leader turned dancer in the name of peace, love, unity, and having fun!

Willie Estrada and Millie Silva Performing at St. Mary's

THE DANCING GANGSTERS OF THE SOUTH BRONX

A TRUE STORY BY WILLIE (MARINE BOY) ESTRADA

CHAPTER ONE: THE BULLY OF P.S. 27

As a kid, I grew up and still live in one of the poorest and most violent urban areas of the United States, the South Bronx. Allow me to take you back to the years of my youth, a time when violent street gangs ruled the mean streets of New York City, and death was waiting around every corner. There are over eight million stories in New York City; this one is mine.

The year was 1971, and I was in the tenth grade in one of the worst High Schools in the South Bronx, Morris High. Violence lived within those halls, and it took courage to attend school daily. During the time, either you were in a gang or protected by one for your lunch money, or you'd get robbed for anything you had as payment. If you protested or gave them a stern look, they would beat you pretty badly in most cases, especially when they were big in numbers and you were alone. Gangs thrived on fear, and they were always looking to make a bigger rep for themselves. Even when they beat someone within an inch of their life, they had no remorse. The more savage the beating, the more feared they would become, and if you squealed on them, they would beat you worse or kill you. Those who weren't in a gang wouldn't dare wear nice sneakers or cute clothes to school, or if they did, they wouldn't be wearing them for long.

If we saw someone running down the school hall bleeding and crying, wearing nothing but a t-shirt and underwear, we all knew a gang had robbed them.

Smaller gangs sometimes beat up or mess with the wrong person, like someone from a more prominent gang, but retaliation would be swift and brutal. It didn't happen often, but when it did, the school would become a war zone, and the smaller gangs always got the worst of it. During those days, there were no metal detectors, and gang members always brought weapons, mostly 007 knives, to school and used them for the slightest altercation. Teachers worked in constant fear, especially if they tried to interfere or report gang activity, and some paid with severe beatings. There was no order or discipline, so daily chaos and mayhem ruled the school environment. I had to learn how to fight when I was very young simply because I refused to be a chump or a victim. I guess I got that from my father, a good man who earned his respect the hard way, as he too had learned how to fight when he was young.

He taught me this, "Never let anyone pick on you just because you're smaller. Show them you may be small, but you have a big heart. Even if you get beat up, they will respect you from that day forward." He also said, "If anyone ever hits you, you, hit them back harder, don't be a victim, or you'll go through your entire life being one." Gang members made your life a living hell, especially if you were a coward. It was one of the main reasons most kids joined gangs in the first place. The first time someone bullied me was because of a girl I liked. The year was 1967, I was in the 6th grade, and there was a pretty girl named Jasmine, who was my younger sister's best friend.

Jasmine had a crush on me; only I never knew it because she never told me, nor did my sister, who was her best friend.

Every school has a bully that preys on the weak; we call our bully Big Nicky. He didn't discriminate; he bullied everyone smaller than him! On one fateful day, the prettiest girl in the school told the biggest bully that I was her boyfriend when he asked her to be his girlfriend. I wish she had told me how she felt before she told Nicky I was her boyfriend because that would have made things easier for me. Right after I saw them speaking as I looked on, Nicky started walking towards me with a mean look on his face and asked me if Jasmine was my girlfriend. I, of course, said, "No." because she wasn't, but Nicky thought I was just a coward, so he slapped me in the face hard, right in front of the entire student body. I had never been slapped, nor had anyone ever made me so angry, so I instinctively made a fist, and gave him a mean look, then I asked him why he hit me. He said, "Because you lied to me, chump, she told me she was your girlfriend! That brought a big goofy smile to my face, and I looked up at him and said, "She did?"

I knew that even if I did know how to fight, which I didn't, I would have to fight Nicky and the two flunkies he always had with him! They wanted me to fight, but I did nothing and walked away in shame, with my pride shattered and a deep hatred for Nicky. I vowed that I would learn how to fight, and someday I would get even with Nicky.

That very same day, I knocked on my upstairs neighbor's door, who was a boxer, and I asked him if he would teach me how to fight; he asked me, "Why?"

So, I told him what happened, and he then asked me, "Why didn't I ask my father to teach me."

I told him I did not want my father to think I was a coward for not fighting back. He understood and agreed to take me to his Gym, providing, of course, that my mother permitted me to go. Here I was, eleven years old, and already had the desire to fight for my honor, but to be honest, I wanted to make up for the embarrassment Nicky caused me. Carlos trained me for the next few weeks and was surprised at my determination and progress in a short time. I never told anyone that I was learning how to box to win the heart of the prettiest girl in school. However, I could not find the courage to talk to Jasmine while she still thought I was a coward; I figured I would soon show her by my actions that I was not. I found myself avoiding Jasmine at all costs, and even my sister asked me why I was avoiding her and told me that she wanted to talk to me.

Nicky was always around, making it impossible to speak to her since I was not ready to take him on yet. As much as I wanted to talk to her, I had to redeem myself in her eyes first. My sister told me I was just stupid and that Jasmine did not care about what happened. She did not understand how I felt about it, but she would soon. After two months of training, Carlos told me I was ready to test my skills. He set up a match with a boy taller than me. The Boy's name was Tony, who Carlos told me was a novice but good boxer and was just taller than me and not to be afraid and stay on the inside since he had more reach than me. He looked like a pretty tough kid, but I was not scared; I was determined!

He figured if I could do well against someone in the ring, it would boost my confidence.

Carlos always taught me that a quick stiff jab would set up a powerful right cross. Keeping this in mind and that Carlos told me I was a natural-born fighter, which also provided confidence, I was finally ready to step into the ring to conquer my fears. Right before the fight started, he told me, "Use your speed, and make-believe he's Nicky!" The match was to be three rounds, but it only lasted two. I had won the fight when they stopped it due to a bad nosebleed. When I got back to my corner, Carlos gave me a big hug. He said he knew I would win and had even placed a bet on the fight. He then told me something I'm glad he hadn't told me before the match.

He said, "The kid you fought has only lost one fight, and he's been fighting since he was nine." He was eleven now and gave me a black eye to remember him. "Wholly cow, are you kidding me?" I said out loud, "Does this mean that I'm ready to pick a fight with Nicky?"

"I am sure you are ready," said Carlos. He remembered that I told him Nicky always had two cronies with him. "But don't get into a fight with all three," he said. "Wait for an opportune time when you know he can't back down and has to fight you one-on-one and knock his fat ass out!" Carlos was very proud of me and assured me that I was ready! I could not sleep that night, especially since I had told my sister that I would kick Nicky's butt the next day. I wanted to do it in front of Jasmine, so I asked my sister to ensure she was in the schoolyard after lunch. The following day, I sprung out of bed, had my breakfast in record time, asked my Mom for her blessings, as we Puerto Ricans always said "Bendicion" before we left the house, and ran off to school.

(Bendicion means, "give me your blessings.) I told some of my friends what I would do and asked them to watch my back. They all told me I was crazy, but none of them knew how hard I had been training for the past two months! All they saw was the black eye I was sporting courtesy of Tony, the boy I had fought the night before. They all thought Nicky had given me that shiner because Nicky was always telling Jasmine that if she did not become his girlfriend, he would kick my ass again. My sister made sure Jasmine would be at the schoolyard, and I could not wait to redeem myself, and the butterflies in my stomach were not from fear. When the moment of truth came, Jasmine was in the schoolyard and guess who was sitting next to and talking to her; you got it; it was Nicky. I went over to them and asked Nicky what he was doing talking to my girl.

I told my friends after this day, Nicky would no longer bother us. They saw the look of determination in my eyes, and all agreed that Nicky's two cronies, Sammy and Junior, would not interfere. After asking Nicky what he was doing talking to my girl, he turned around and said, "Are you talking to me, chump? It looks like someone already gave you a black eye; you want another one?" "That's right. I'm talking to you, and the only chump here is you. And by the way, I knocked out the guy who gave me this black eye!" Nicky saw the evil eye again, only this time it was staring him down in a brutal and threatening way, which said."I'm going to kick your ass." For the first time in my life, I was in control of the situation, as I saw a hint of concern in Nicky's eyes. Of course, I couldn't back down this time, so I pressed the matter further. "Get away from my girl now!" "Come and make me chump," he replied.

Nicky stepped towards me, and as I took my fighting stance, he pulled his hand back to smack me again. I stepped in like Carlos had taught me and hit Nicky with a quick stiff jab, which snapped his head back, followed by a right cross to his chin.

Down went Nicky, to everyone's cheers! I said, "Get up if you can, chump." Nicky got up, holding his chin, opened his eyes wide, and made a loud grunting sound, trying to intimidate me. It didn't have the effect he hoped for; a lunging right-hand right to his nose put Nicky down again. This time it was me who bloodied his nose. I started bouncing on my toes like a boxer, telling him to get up and get some more with the entire schoolyard yelling, "Fight, Fight, Fight." I then told him, "If you get up again, I'm going to give you a black eye to go with that bloody nose!" Yes, I was full of confidence and cocky now, can't you tell? Nicky stayed down and thought about it before waving his hand as if to say, "No Mas," (No more) while holding his nose with the other, then bowing his head in defeat. His days of bulling us were over! That was a great day for all my friends and the entire school. My favorite part was all the cheering, I felt like a real hero, and I guess in a way, I was, at least to my classmates and, most importantly, Jasmine's eyes. I had won the fight, and all my classmates gathered around me with my biggest fan, the prettiest girl in the school.

Right there and then, I asked Jasmine if she would be my girlfriend in front of the entire student body. To no one's surprise, she said, "Yes!" "Hooray," yelled all the kids as Nicky got up and walked away in shame. I looked at his two friends and asked them if they had a problem with me.

They both looked at me, and one of them said, "I don't even like Nicky!" Everybody started laughing, including his two cronies.

When I got home, my father saw the black eye I had gotten the night before. "Who did this to you?" my father asked. "Papi, I knocked the guy out who did this to me!" I had not told my father that Carlos had trained me to fight. My younger sister Maritza put her two cents worth, "Daddy, Willie beat up the school bully, and everybody was cheering for him." "You did?" asked my father. "Yes, Papi, I beat him up good!"

My dad gave me a big hug, which did not come easy for him because although my father was a good man, he was never an emotional man. I had only ever seen him cry once when his mother died. One thing's for sure; I will always be grateful to Big Nicky. Thanks, Nicky, wherever you are, thanks to you, I learned how to stand up for myself! I cannot emphasize enough how much I would need to be brave in the coming years; not only that, but I am glad I learned how to fight at a young age, mainly because I lived in the South Bronx! I call them the crazy years, the gang era. I loved boxing and got good at it, but it was kickboxing and martial arts that I came to love most as I grew older and still practice to this day.

My Dad was a hard-working Master Carpenter but also a dapper musician.

My dad and Uncle George were what you might call "Crooners" since they had soft romantic voices.

Music and dance are in our DNA!

CHAPTER TWO: EXPRESSWAY TO DEATH

After that ordeal with Big Nicky, I got popular with practically the entire student body and the teachers. It was then that I started realizing that standing up for myself was starting to make a significant impact on my life in ways I had only imagined, and I liked it! The cool crowd took a liking to me, and that included Kike, a kid even Big Nicky didn't mess with because of his older brother Tony, who was <u>in</u> an older gang of thieves. They were from 150th St. and into robbing the freight trains that ran down the block close to the buildings where they lived. The opening in the brush with a makeshift platform at the end of the block in a wooded area infested with rats and bugs, which nobody ever went into, was the perfect place to break into the trains and steal whatever was inside.

I started hanging out on that block with Kike, who introduced me to Julio, his brothers, Henry, and their gorgeous sister Ana, who got bit by a rat for following us into the empty lot the day I met her. Julio and I became the best of friends in a short time, and we hung out every day. We called one of his older brothers Tony Expressway because he always sang that song, **"Expressway to your heart."** Expressway stole a small sports car one day and started teaching us both how to drive while driving everyone else on the block crazy in the process. It had a standard transmission with a stick, but we learned how to drive. We drove up and down the same neighborhood and almost ran over a few kids a couple of times before we got good at driving it. Driving was fun, but the real adventure began when they started using me as a lookout when they broke into the freight trains in broad daylight. It was scary but exciting at the same time.

The adrenaline rush I got from being a part of their civil disobedience was too much fun to pass up. If mom ever found out, she'd have my head for sure. I also liked the part where they would come back with boxes filled with all sorts of goodies. They never knew that would be in the trains they broke into, but we always knew when it was a freezer car because there would be meat inside. So if anyone ever saw a couple of kids running down the street with a frozen side of beef, and I'm talking <u>about</u> the whole leg here, everyone knew they had stolen it from the freight trains and were off to sell it to the Butcher. The train cars were very long, and they always stopped there because the front of the train was already in the train yard, a few blocks away. There were several openings like the one on our block, so the freight train company security always had their hands full trying to catch thieves before they got away with whatever goods they had stolen. I guess they got tired of getting robbed all the time, so the NYPD got involved as well and started setting up stings to catch us at different locations. They had already arrested several guys at the site by the old Lincoln Hospital. That was the hottest spot because it had the biggest opening and had lots of ways to escape when the guards came to try and catch them.

The people in our neighborhood loved us because we'd share everything with the entire block whenever we stole food. I never realized just how poor we were back in those days because <u>I never considered it</u>. However, it always felt good to share, especially when we handed packs of meat or cereal to the elderly and got the look of appreciation along with smiles we got from them. We were the Robin hoods of our neighborhood during those days.

Every time we hit the trains, we'd gather and have a party to celebrate the day's take. Expressway, whose real name was Tony, would sit us down in a yard in the middle of a brickyard, where a building once stood, and would tell us stories. "Playing Robin Hood and stealing from the rich and giving to the poor is our way of getting back at our white oppressors," or white devils as he called them. The younger kids never really cared about what he preached about – since they were too young to give a shit. But since he was older, they listened. The older guys always agreed with him, as they built barn fires and drank cheap wine in the middle of the brickyard. They would sing Expressway by the Soul Searchers, Tony Expressway's favorite song. It was cool hanging out with the older guys, and while I didn't know it at the time, it would also prove dangerous.

After a couple of weeks, Tony picked a new lookout, and I started going into the train yard platform to help carry out boxes and take things for my family. On my second trip to the yard, we opened up a train that contained lots of cereal boxes, including my favorite, Captain Crunch. I grabbed a box of Captian Crunch, hid it behind some tall bushes behind a tree. As I started walking back to get more, I saw the cops coming from all directions, so I ran back to the tree where I had hidden my box of Captain Crunch. It was too late to warn everyone, so I just stayed out of sight while all my friends got caught, handcuffed, and thrown into a police van that pulled up. The new kid acting as our lookout was a goofball who didn't pay much attention to who was coming and going and didn't see the cops coming, so he never warned us.

I waited among the rats scurrying around me for a long while to make sure there were no more cops around, hoping I wouldn't get bitten but too scared of getting caught to worry about them until the police were gone. After I was sure they were gone, I stepped out from behind the bushes and onto the street to ensure nobody would see me taking the box I had hidden. The coast was clear, so I grabbed the box, and off I went down the other street just in case they happened by again. When I got home with the box, mom asked me where I got it and told me, "Don't lie!" I panicked because I knew mom had psychic powers, and she would know it if I did lie, and I'd get punished for a week or more.

I told her how I had escaped while all my friends got arrested, and I bowed my head in shame for stealing.

She was strict, but she didn't want my father to find out, or he would be angry with me, and while he never hit me, there is always the first time.

This was the type of freight train broken into during the mid-1960s. The Robin-hoods, as I called them, were good kids for the most part. I am not making excuses for our actions, but poor people do crazy things out of desperation when you continuously oppress them.

My sisters, Maritza, Wilma, cousins Danny, David, and Robert in Crotona Park during the 1960s. RIP Danny and David always in our hearts.

My family came to New York in 1958 when I was two years old, and I grew up speaking both English and Spanish. We were naturalized citizens of the United States but never treated as Americans. Instead, we were oppressed and mistreated, even though our families were hard-working and decent people. It was one of the reasons my generation rebelled against the establishment when we started coming of age during the latter part of the 1960s.

She told me she didn't want me hanging out on 150th St. anymore, or she would tell my dad what I had done. She reminded me that I had a lot more freedom than my sisters because I was a boy, but if I messed up again, I would have to stay home, and for some reason, she didn't punish me. There she stood with a look of disappointment on her face, and she shook her head with discontent but didn't say another word. My parents were very old-fashioned and believed that our people needed to do things the right way to be accepted by a society that Tony said hated us. I couldn't say that to mom, but that's what I thought while she spoke. I realized the things Tony always talked about made sense to me, and it was like an awakening for me, yet it made me sad to think about it. The good part was that most of the kids who got caught were all minors and were brought home the next day by their parents.

The following day Kike came to school and told me he had a problem with a kid from P.S. 5, which was on Jackson Ave. on the corner of 149th St. He gathered a few of us. He told everyone we were going to meet the kids from P.S. 5 at St. Mary's Park during lunchtime, and we were going to fight against them in a rumble. We usually played stickball in the afternoons, but we would use our stickball bats for something else on this day. That park area we chose to fight was out of view from the schools we attended, which is why we chose it. When we got there and saw all the kids from P.S. 5, I was scared but didn't let on.

I had never been in a fight like this, and for that matter, my fight with big Nicky was the first time I had ever fought.

The other kid who was the leader from the kids going up against us was taller than Kike, but he was brave nonetheless, which was evident when they both started taunting and talking trash. I forgot to mention that the other kids had baseball bats while we had stickball bats. Our advantage was that our sticks were longer, which meant we had better reach. Not that it made me feel any better, mind you, because I was still scared. After they were finished with the insults and the screaming back and forth, the other kid told his friends to attack, and he led the way. Kike and the other kid were the first to swing their bats. The rest of us just watched as opposed to fighting, so I guess we were all just as scared to get hit in the head with a bat. After a short time of watching them hit each other, there was a loud crack when the kid's bat made contact with Kike's head.

Kike went down, but before the kid could hit him again, I swung my stickball bat at his head, and there was a second crack, this time coming from my stickball bat, making contact with the kid's head. After that, I just started swinging my stickball bat wildly, and my friends all did the same. Since our stickball bats had the reach, they didn't have the guts to engage us further, especially after their fearless leader went down like a sack of potatoes and started crying. We rallied around Kike as they ran off, but he was hurt and started saying he saw his mother coming.

We walked further into the park to give him time to regain his senses, and we could all return to school. Kike was lucky; the only damage inflicted was to his pride, but we kept telling him the kid got lucky when he slipped.

He just kept saying his mother was coming, but none of us laughed, and after a short time, he regained his senses and started asking us what happened as he held his head. We told him he slipped, and the other guy took advantage and hit him in the head with the bat. Henry then said to him that I stepped in and hit the other guy in the head with my stickball bat, and we beat the rest of them up, and they ran off crying. He was happy to hear that, but a bit embarrassed that he had lost the fight against his rival.

The following day I was with Kike and his older brother Tony Expressway and a few other guys who were up to no good, breaking into a shipment of trains filled with goodies. Even though my mother had warned me to stay away, I couldn't help myself; I wanted to be a part of the Robin Hood crew even if I couldn't bring anything home so mom wouldn't find out. I knew I could leave whatever I got in Julio's house for safekeeping. When I was coming out with a box of goods, and Expressway and Kike were coming up behind me, I was approached by the kid I had batted in the head and his older brother. The kid pointed at me and told his brother I was the one who hit him in the head and gave him the big lump. He immediately started punching me in my face with no mercy for the fact that I was just a kid. Tony dropped the box he was carrying and hit the guy in the back of the head, and he let me go as he fell to the ground. When the guy got up, he pulled a knife on Tony; that's when everything went wrong because the next thing I knew, Tony pulled a 007 from his back pocket and stabbed the guy several times, as the rest of us looked on in horror.

His younger brother started screaming for him to wake up, but he was dead since he wasn't breathing. Tony had killed him while defending me, but there was no time to think about that; we all started running after Tony threw his bloody knife into the wooded area while his little brother continued to scream as he wept. When we got back to our block, I was in shock and couldn't believe what had just happened, but Tony shook me and told me that I couldn't tell anybody what he had done.

I promised that I wouldn't, but eventually, I told mom because I was terrified, and I had never seen anyone killed in front of me before, and she also told my father. Tony got caught the following day anyway, but I wasn't around to see when they came for him because mom wouldn't let me come out after that day. Dad was also scared of retaliation, so even though he was the super of the building we lived in and the one adjacent to it, my father started looking for a new place for us to live. It was a sad time for me, but I knew it was the right thing to do because it was my fault that kid was dead, and I knew sooner or later they would come for me too.

It was a sad farewell to all my friends, but I never got to say I was sorry to Tony Expressway, who got life in jail, and I never saw him again after that day. But I would never forget him, or that tragic and senseless way that young man died and for what?!

Police Car In front of my building on Wilkins Ave

This location was where the freight trains once ran through; although they removed the tracks many years ago, the memories will always be with me.

There is still a wooded area there, but the only ones who go there now are the junkies who built that makeshift shack below, so they could have a place to shoot up heroin.   The Graffiti below is reminiscent of those days.

Our neighborhood drug addicts no longer have access to the tracks, so they shoot up on the streets, much to everyone's dismay, right in front of the kids walking to and from school.

CHAPTER THREE: THE FLAMES:

(Juvenile Delinquents)

1968, the Vietnam conflict was raging, and many of the older teens had been drafted to go to war. While they had their war going on, there was also a war raging on the streets of the South Bronx. Those of us, who were too young to serve, were left behind to fight for ourselves. The streets were our teacher because let's face it, our parents could do only so much since they could not control what was going on on those mean streets. The older guys who were supposed to serve as mentors were just not around. When some of them returned from Nam because of injury or time served, they were screwed up in the head, and many of them were now drug addicts. I was almost 13 years old when my father moved us into a new apartment away from the dangers of my old neighborhood, but it only had two bedrooms, one for my parents and the other for my sisters, while I slept on a cot in the living room. I guess that's what happens when you move out from one hood to another in a hurry, but it was like out of the frying pan and into the fire for us all.

My courage was tested on my very first day in my new hood. We had moved from a neighborhood where my family knew everybody, and a lot of my family lived in the same area. To a place where we knew nobody, keeping in mind that this had all happened because Tony Expressway had killed that kid. This new place was a nightmare for me, It seemed very hostile, and I was not too fond of it, yet I still felt safe because there was no fear of reprisal for what Expressway did.

However, when we moved in on a Saturday morning, one of the local gang members decided he would test me early. "Yo, what gang you in, punk?" My response was, "You see a punk, slap him."

I guess that response came from my experience with Big Nicky and the results of that encounter. We were still in the process of moving our things into our new apartment. When out of nowhere, a kid slaps the box out of my hands. My father, who was just coming back down to continue moving in our belongings, saw what happened. He told the kid, "Hey, what's going on?" My father didn't want any quarrels with our new neighbors, not on our first day anyway. My father was not one to look for a fight; he would always try to avoid a confrontation if he could, but I have never seen him take any shit from anyone either.

The kid was surprised at my father's intervention, so he said, "Nothing." He whispered, "I'll see you later, punk." and he ran off. I have two sisters. My older sister Wilma 14, and my younger sister Maritza 12, were born one year apart in the same month. They had also seen what happened from the window of our new apartment and came down to ask me why he did that. "Because he's a moron," I told them. "I guess I'll have to deal with him later." "We haven't even moved in yet, and already you're getting into a fight." My older sister Wilma said. "Hey, I didn't do anything to that guy; he started looking for trouble without me saying a word to him!" My father said, "See what you can do to make friends with the kids around here." From the looks of it, that was not going to be easy. "OK, Papi, but don't expect miracles."

The very next day, I was running an errand for mom, and as luck would have it, I bumped right into that idiot kid who didn't like me. Only this time, he wasn't alone. It turns out he was part of a young gang called The Flames, and he was with about five other gang members. The Flames consisted of young teens whose older brothers were in a much bigger gang called The Royal Javelins. They were part of what we called "The Third World," which the gang world was called back in those days. Gangs ruled the Bronx through violence, and fear, and anyone who got in their way, got the living daylights beaten out of them or worse. Almost everyone feared these gangs, and the cops were useless in trying to stop their rampage throughout the city, especially the South Bronx, which had more street gangs than any other Borough.

Many cops feared the gangs because of how senselessly violent they were, and they always retaliated against those who even looked at them the wrong way! Anyway, I was confronted with six gang members, and my dad was nowhere around to intervene this time. My heart was beating fast, and although I was scared, I showed no fear in my eyes because I knew that would only make it worse for me. I decided I had to confront this kid. If I was going to survive in this new neighborhood, I also knew I would have to fight sooner or later. "Hey, what's up, guys? My name is Willie, and I just moved into the neighborhood. What do you guys do for fun around here?" The other kids were receptive to me and started to introduce themselves. The kid I had the confrontation with was not as receptive at all. "Yo, you owe me punk." "Why don't you give me a break? I just moved in here."

"Yea, give him a break Jayjoe, he can be one of us," said a kid they called little Louie. "Why should I give this punk a break?" said Jayjoe. From behind, Jayjoe came a voice and said, "Because I said so!" Suddenly, the ranks broke open, and Jayjoe's Cousin Raymond stepped into the fry. "Why are you looking for trouble with someone who just moved into our neighborhood?" Raymond asked, "Because I don't like him!" Jayjoe responded. "Well, since he lives here now, you have to settle this according to our rules." Raymond was someone who these guys respected. "You either fight, or you play chicken. Which will it be, Jayjoe?" "Ok, let's see what this kid is made of; let's play chicken." Said Jayjoe. "Chicken? What's that?" I asked. "You'll find out soon enough!" Said Jayjoe. "Let's go up to the roof, and we'll show you." All the other guys were pumped up; let's go, let's go. So up to the roof, we all went.

Raymond was my age and complexion, and it didn't take a Rocket Scientist to figure out that he was the leader of the Flames, and even though I didn't know it yet, we would soon be best friends.

Once we got to the roof, Jayjoe took charge and told me I had to do everything he did. If I didn't, I would get thrown off the roof of the building! "Does that mean that you have to do everything I do as well, and if not, do we throw you off the roof?" All the other kids started to laugh, and so did Raymond. "I like this kid, said Raymond; he's got guts." Jayjoe was not amused and said, let's get started, and you'll find out! Jayjoe began by running on the edge of the roof and jumping to the adjacent rooftop, which had a six-foot gap that went straight down six floors. I followed and found it to be fun and yet scary.

Is that the best you can do? Can I make the next dare, I asked Raymond? Raymond replied, "It's only fair. Go ahead, make your dare." I choose the roof on the far end of the rooftops. It had a broader gap between the two parallel rooftops. It didn't have the first jump's advantage, jumping from the roof's edge onto another lower rooftop. This rooftop had a two-foot wall you had to clear to attempt a leap onto the other side. This is the one I'm going to jump, I said. All the other kids told me I was crazy and should not attempt to make that long jump. I was convinced this was the jump I would have to make to get Jayjoe to accept me as more than just his equal.

"Shit, if you can make that jump, you can be our new War Counselor!" Said Raymond! "I'm going to hold you to that, Raymond," I said. "Go for it, then if you got the balls!" All the other kids thought I was crazy and kept telling me not to do it. I went over to the wall; I would have to clear and inspect the tile on the edge of the rooftop wall. I realized that if I were going to make this jump, I would have to take a running start and leap from the top of the wall, which meant I had first to make sure it wasn't loose. It was a long way down, but I wanted to make this jump. I was lucky I checked the tiles before I jumped because they were loose. I took off the loose tiles and cleared the top of the bricks of all debris. This was it, my moment of truth, I had to do it, now or never! I took a practice run to visualize my footing and speed and think about what I was doing one last time.

I took a deep breath, almost as if it were my last, and ran very precisely step after step, with my heart beating faster and faster with each step I took.

Until finally making what was a terrifying jump off the wall of the roof's edge and landing on the other side. I landed with distance to spare and my heart in my throat. I had never jumped so high or so far in my life, nor had I ever been so scared. After I landed on the other side, I looked down at what could have been my other landing place. I saw lots of clotheslines from one building to the next with clothes hanging from them, and at the bottom, I saw lots of garbage and old appliances.

When I looked up, I could finally hear the cheer of all the other guys on the other side. "You did it; you did it!" Everyone had a big smile on their face, everyone except Jayjoe, that is! Your turn, Jayjoe. I said with a big sigh of relief on my face. "No freaking way. You are crazy, man!" I looked at Raymond and said. "Well, Raymond, I guess we're going to have to throw Jayjoe off the roof; that was the deal, right?" Raymond looked at me and smiled, then he turned to all the other guys and said, "You guys heard our new member, grab Jayjoe, let's throw him off!" Of course, he was only kidding. As it turns out, Jayjoe was Raymond's cousin, so he was only having a little fun. Jayjoe's response was, "If anybody touches me, I'm going to punch him in the face." Everybody started laughing at Jayjoe; he was so upset he went downstairs by himself. I told the other guys I would meet them downstairs, and I welcomed everyone to join me by jumping over to where I was. Most said they were not as crazy as me, but Raymond said he would only make that jump if the cops were chasing him! I believed him when he said that. When we all got downstairs, Jayjoe was waiting for us.

He turned to me and said, "You've got balls, man, and everyone seems to like you so that you can be one of us. The name of our gang is The Flames. Mostly junior high school kids, who were not old enough to be part of the bigger gang, "The Royal Javelin's," whose President was Big Louie, Raymond's oldest brother. Raymond had five brothers and two sisters and many family members who ran the neighborhood.

It was a big family, all living in the same neighborhood. He had more uncles and aunts than I could count. Usually, you had to go through a line of initiation, with guys on both sides of the line hitting you as you passed them, called a Gauntlet or Apache Line. I had proved my courage by jumping from one rooftop to the next and did not have to walk the Apache Line. I started to hang out with the guys every day. We mostly played sports, like softball, football in the snow, and basketball with a wooden milk box as the hoop. However, sometimes we got into trouble with other young gangs and went to war with them, which we called a Rumble in those days. Most of us attended a Junior High School named JHS 136, which was on the corner of Prospect Ave and Jennings St. It was a tough school filled with young gangs from different neighborhoods, so needless to say, we didn't always get along! There were still fights after school, and usually, it was gang-related because when you mess with one, you mess with them all.

One time in particular, after one of our guys got into a fight with a rival gang member, he beat the guy in a fair fight and later got jumped by the other kid's gang. That meant war, so I made the frame for a zip gun in the woodshop and then broke the antenna off a car to use as the barrel, which would fire 22 caliber bullets.

I used a nail with a wooden piece at the top used with a rubber band, which you could then pull back and let go to fire it. That afternoon we all went to Crotona Park to fight with a rival gang.

I took the zip gun with me, and when we got there, one of our gang members named Little Willie asked if he could see the gun. When I gave it to him, he shot at some guys walking towards us from the rival gang. We all scattered and started running back home to our neighborhood; Little Willie was the first one to run, so we started calling him Chicken Willie after that. He did not like the name and protested, to no avail, the new name stuck. A short time after we got back to our block, about twenty guys from the rival gang walked right up to us on the block. They started selling wolf tickets and thought they were all tough guys. One of them had a real gun and started waving it around. He told us he knew we had a zip gun and that we were no match for them. Suddenly, Big Louie came out of nowhere and slapped the guy with the gun, and took it from him.

"What the hell are you doing in our neighborhood, punk?" Louie asked as he pointed the gun at the guy's head. Louie, if you remember, was the president of the Royal Javelin's and was no joke; he was the real thing, a bad SOB. The guys from the younger rival gang were all scared shitless. They all knew who Big Louie was, and they were all terrified of him.

The guy Louie took the gun from was trying to explain to Louie that we had gone to their turf and taken a shot at them. We told Louie that the reason we had gone over there was that one of them had punched one of our guys in the mouth at school the day before. So Louie turned to the guy, cocked the gun, and put it to his head. He said, "Why did you punch one of our guys in the mouth, asshole?" The guy started crying and telling Louie that it wasn't him and to please not shoot him. So Louie smacked him in the face and told him to never come back on his block again. He said, "I'm keeping your gun, and if you ever come back, I'm going to shoot you with it. Now get the hell out of here." Louie then kicked the guy in the ass as they left, and we all started laughing. The guy just kept walking with his head down, as his pride had been tarnished, because he started crying right after selling wolf tickets. Louie told us to shut the hell up and stop laughing. We all shut up. Louie then said, "Okay, who was the little smart ass who took a shot at those guys?" Everybody pointed to Chicken Willie and said, "He did."

Louie looked at Willie and said to him, "Don't ever do something so stupid again, without me knowing about it. Suppose I had not been here? One of you could have gotten shot!" Willie agreed not ever to do something so stupid again, and Louie told us to behave and not bring trouble to the block again. Jayjoe slapped Chicken Willie on his head and said: "Yea, don't ever do something so stupid again!" We all started laughing again and making fun of Willie. That was the end of an eventful day that we would never forget.

There would be many more such days in store for me in my new hood, and that was only the beginning. The next day was a good day for me. You see, I was still trying to prove myself to all my new friends, and that day I would have to prove myself against Jayjoe's cousin, a kid they called Crazy Junior.

Junior was taller and heavier than me, and they called him Crazy Junior because he was born with a learning disability, but he also looked and acted crazy most of the time.

He was like a cartoon character; only he was real. He didn't have good reasoning skills, so getting into an argument with him was a no-win situation because no matter what you said to him, he would always have a stupid come back, and if you made him angry by getting in the last word, he would get violent. Well, on that particular day, I got the last word in, and Crazy Junior did not like it very much. He said. "Don't mess with me. I'm crazy. I'll kick your ass!" While most of the other kids in our little gang were afraid of him, except his cousins, I decided to stand up to him, mainly because Jayjoe was instigating us to fight.

Now, Junior was most definitely stronger than me but not as quick, nor did he have my skills as a boxer. With that in mind, I ended our fight with one hard punch that knocked Crazy Junior right through the window of his uncle's grocery store. His uncle Paco came out of the store and was mad as hell. He asked in a loud voice, "What happened? Who broke my window?" Everybody in the neighborhood knew Paco, he was a no-nonsense kind of guy, and nobody messed with him.

He is also Jayjoe's uncle, so Jayjoe told him what happened and how I had punched Junior in the face and knocked him through the window. Paco looked at me and asked me why I hit him? I told Paco that Junior tried to punch me, so I punched him first. Paco said my father would have to pay for the damages because it was my fault for hitting Junior first.

What was I supposed to do, let him punch me in the face? I don't think so! Sure enough, when my father got home, Paco told him what happened, and my Father paid him for the window. I thought my father would be mad at me for having to pay for the window, but when he got me alone, he said he wished he had been there to see it.

He started laughing and told me that it was the best ten bucks he had spent in a long time. He turned to me and said, "Now they will respect you, but that doesn't mean you should continue getting into fights. I don't make that much money, and windows are expensive." I cracked a big smile, and he returned it with a smile of his own. Junior did not mess with me, nor did any of the other kids from that day forward. The next day, everybody had heard about the fight I had with Junior and how I had knocked him through the window. I was finally one of the guys because, from that day forward, everyone in my neighborhood knew me, but most importantly, they knew I was not a punk.

After a while, I was comfortable in my new environment and enjoyed the different games we played. Of course, some of those games were a little crazy, like a game we played called Run, Catch, and Kill.

The game's object was to choose-up sides, and once the teams were even, it was one team's turn to be the hunters, and the other team was the hunted. Both teams had a home base, and there was an object or objects that we, as the hunted, would have to retrieve from the hunter's base to become the hunters. As the hunters, you got to track down and beat up the guys on the hunted side.

Trust me; it was no fun being the hunted because, more often than not, you went home with a bloody nose or worse. And then, there was our other main point of focus, girls! One of the games we would play daily was backyard softball. We called it backyard baseball because our field was the backyard behind our buildings and the buildings on the other side of our block.

The guys from the other side of our block were not allowed to play there unless we let them or played with us. When we played, sometimes the girls from the other side of our block would come and watch us. Among them was a beautiful girl named Adela. Her brother was younger and hung out with us sometimes. He liked me because I was always cool with him, not just because he had a pretty sister. Anyway, he told me one day that his sister Adela liked me and thought I was cute.

I asked him to invite her to watch us play the next day to talk to her. Adela was a natural beauty, with long black hair, beautiful almond brown eyes, and a great smile, not to mention a beautiful body! When I woke up the following day, all I could think about was meeting Adela and getting to know her. We always started playing in the afternoon after lunch. I had played in that makeshift backyard field a few times, but I had never hit a home run until the day Adela came to see me play. It's funny because she wasn't there when we started playing, and I asked her kid brother where she was, and he told me she was getting pretty for me. I said, "For real, you're not kidding me?" He laughed and said, "I'm not joking; she's nervous and wants to look nice so that when she meets you, you'll like her too!"

He pointed at me and said, "You look nervous too." "Shhhh, don't tell your sister that." So he promised he wouldn't.

I told him if he did, I would not let him hang out with us anymore, so he promised not to say a word. Now, keep in mind that I did not know that much about girls, and even Jasmine, who was my first sweetheart, never gave me more than just a peck on the cheek. The 2nd inning ended, and I was finally getting up to bat, and when I looked up, I saw Adela sitting over the 3rd baseline. She looked beautiful and was wearing a short yellow dress, which all of the guys noticed right away and started whistling at her. She blushed but managed to look at me as I approached the batter's box and smiled at me. Now, all the guys already knew she was there to see me, so they all started saying things to me like, "Don't strike out, get a hit."

Little Louie patted me on the butt and said, "Hit a Homerun for her!" Of course, I had never hit a home run before, as all I ever wanted to do was get on base. You have to remember that I had never played softball before moving to my new neighborhood. This was all new to me, but I loved playing baseball.

I was determined to at least hit the ball as hard as I could so I could impress her. My first swing was a foul line drive into the fire escape near the first baseline.

I was so nervous, but I wanted to impress her so bad I could see it in my head. I took a deep breath, and when Little Louie pinched it right down the middle, I hit it as hard as I could. To my amazement, I had hit it over the right-field homerun maker.

Nobody was on base, but it didn't matter; I had hit my first home run, and Adela was there to see it. I'm pretty sure the pitch was perfect on purpose because little Loue wanted me to get a hit so that I could impress Adela. I did one better and hit a home run. He never said anything about it, but I knew.

As I ran around the bases to everyone's cheers, I looked over to Adela, she was also clapping and cheering, and the grin on my face turned into an ear-to-ear smile. As I rounded third base, close to where she was standing, I looked over to her and winked. She responded with a big smile, and then she blushed again.

She was a bit shy, but I could see that she liked me and I knew she knew I liked her. It was a great feeling; I still carry it in my heart until this day. As a kid, there is no greater feeling than having a pretty girl like you and having her there when you do something extraordinary.

It doesn't get any better than that in my mind. Well, at least back in those days and at that age, it didn't. When the game was finally over, we won it by one run. Everyone knew the difference in the game was my home run, which made me even more proud of having hit it with Adela watching.

Her little brother Mikey came over to me and told me Adela would meet me by the exit on her side of the block; she didn't want the other guys around because she knew they would tease us. She played it off like she just left. Of course, everybody knew better because they saw her little brother come up to me and whisper something in my ear and then saw me walking towards the other exit, which led to her block.

I tried to be discrete, but it was so obvious, and to be honest, I was so happy that she wanted to meet me; I didn't care what the guys were saying. I started walking towards the exit, where the end of the tunnel led to her block. There she was, waiting at the top of the short stairwell. My heart pounded faster as I got closer, and when she greeted me with a big bashful smile, my heart completely stopped for a second, and I was in heaven as I looked into her beautiful almond-colored eyes for the first time from up close.

All I could do was say "Hi," and when she said hi back, she followed with, "I liked watching you play, and my brother told me that the home run you hit was for me." For a second, I thought he had told her it was the first one I had ever hit, and I wanted to tell her myself that she inspired me.

I didn't know he had told her that I hit it for her, so I told her, "It was the first one I ever hit, and the only reason I think I hit it is that I was trying so hard to do good, just because you were watching me." She started laughing, and then we laughed again when she told her little brother it was past his bedtime, so he would go away and let us talk. He didn't mind because, after all, as I found out later, he had told her that I said that I liked her. Afterward, he followed by telling me she liked me and wanted to meet me after having told her the same thing.

I started calling him Little Cupid after that day. As I walked and talked with Adela, who was my age but attended a Catholic School and wasn't allowed to have a boyfriend, I came to realize how amazing she was and unlike any other girl I had ever known. Of course, I had not known many girls, exceptionally as smart and pretty as Adela.

We had to sneak around to see each other, and she became a regular at our daily games to watch us play. This was not always a good thing because then I felt that I was still expected to do well since she was watching, and of course, I didn't always do well. Then came a day which I will never forget because it was the day I got the nickname "MOON HEAD."

I had been doing well ever since Adela started coming to almost every game to watch us play. After a while, I made the top of the order because I got on base a lot. So, on one beautiful Saturday afternoon, as I led off, I got on base, and our shortstop Hector hit a popup after me, so I stayed on base as I knew it would be a sure out.

The next batter was Jayjoe, and he hit a line drive right into Big Louie's glove. Again I stayed put.

Our power hitter, Big Louie's brother Charlie, was the next batter, just a year younger than Big Lou. I decided with two outs, and knowing Charlie's power, I would take off as soon as he made contact because he already had two strikes, and I wanted to get a head start to try to score from 1st. Charlie had just said, "This Ball is going to the moon," which meant he was going to roof it, which he often did, and it was considered a home run.

As soon as the ball was pitched, I ran without looking where the ball was going because I thought Charlie would hit it to the roof for sure. To my surprise, Charlie hit a line drive, which hit me right in the head, which knocked me down, and I was out.

Everybody laughed, but Charlie was pissed with me for not looking where the ball was going; he started screaming at me and calling me names. At the end of his barrage of name-calling, he said, "You, you Moon Head!" I was trying to say I was sorry. I just thought he would roof it, and I asked him not to call me that name. The name stuck, and I was known as Moon Head from that day forward. I spoke to Big Louie about it one day, and he shortened the name to Moonie, which was a bit better considering that I had become such a good hitter. That and because his younger brother Mickey had the biggest head in the world, the name suited him a lot better.

Adela was the only one not laughing that day, and when the game was over, she told me that she would never call me that because she loved me. "You love me? You're not just saying that to make me feel better?" It was the first time a girl had told me she loved me, and I had ever told a girl I loved her too. "I'm not just saying that. I do love you, and I told my mother about you, so she wants to meet you." I swallowed hard and said to her, "What did you tell your mother?" I told her I love you and that you were my boyfriend!" "Wholly shit, she's going to kill me!" "No, she won't, she has seen you when you come around and try to talk to me after school, and she has asked me about you before, and my brother told her that out of all the guys, you were the nicest and that he likes you!"

Little Cupid had gone to bat for me, and in that instant, I knew he was a true friend and had genuine feelings for me. So I asked Adela when she wanted to meet me, and certainly not how I looked and smelled from playing all day.

She told me she wanted me to have dinner with them that night and that Adela's father was not to know anything until she decided the time was right because he was very strict with them. Her father was in Puerto Rico, starting a business out there, and came back like once a month to be with his family. Lucky for me, he was in Puerto Rico, which gave her mother time to give me a once over and meet me, so she could get to know me first and then put in the good word with her husband. At least that's what I was hoping she would do.

I went home and told my mother that I was having dinner at Adela's house, which my mother liked because she was a good girl. She permitted me to go and told me to make sure that I behaved myself to make a good impression on Adela's mother.

They always wanted me to do the right things and never liked the fact that I hung out with so many of what they considered to be "BAD BOYS."

I was very naive and even gullible at times because when I was younger, as you recall, I hung out with the girls a lot, mainly because of Jasmine, my first love. By the time we moved away from my old hood, Jasmine and her family had already moved years before. I never saw her again. I often wonder what happened to her and how she turned out, but I guess I will never know. When I got to Adela's block, I was nervous and hesitant to go upstairs. I imagined her father being home and waiting for me with a bat to scare me out of wanting to be his daughter's boyfriend. Little Cupid was looking out the window, telling me to come up. He could see that I was nervous and said: "Don't worry, it's ok." I asked him to meet me at the door, so off he went to open the door.

They lived on the second floor, so if it got terrible, I could always jump out the window (at least that's what ran through my mind as I was going up). To my surprise, Adela's mother, Maria, opened the door, and I froze like a deer in headlights. Maria greeted me with a smile and a warm "Hello, I'm Maria Adela's mother."

The look in her eyes told me she was sincere, which made me feel comfortable right away. I extended my hand and said, "Hi, my name is Willie. It's nice to meet you," she asked me to come in and sit down. Oh, it's time for the grilling, I thought, but as it turns out, she was a sweet person and just wanted what was best for her daughter. She started by telling me how much Adela had spoken of me, and it was all right. She said her daughter had a schoolgirl crush on me; in those days, they called it "Puppy Love." She talked to me about not making mistakes and how she would eventually tell her husband about me if things went well. I wasn't looking forward to that and wanted to change the subject, so I told her that my mother was also named Maria. It worked because she was delighted and started asking questions about my parents, what they do, and things like that.

By the time I was done telling her about my parents, Adela had come into the room, so I got up and said hello. I also thanked her mother for inviting me to dinner and that I was thrilled to be there with them. I had won Adela's mom over in a matter of minutes, and it didn't even hurt. I had thought because both Adela and her brother had both told me how strict their parents were that I would be meeting the dragon lady, but Maria was as lovely as she was beautiful, which I forgot to mention.

I could see where Adela got her good looks. I figured out that it was not so much that they were strict, but that they were old-fashioned in their ways, just like my parents and their parents before them. It was a Puerto Rican thing, and in those days, our family values were much higher than those among Puerto Ricans today. The truth is that Puerto Ricans have a long and proud history. Yet things started taking a turn for the worse by the late 1960s. Our ancestors were probably rolling over in their graves because of the family values they had to establish long before we were being discarded and disrespected by the youth of that era. It was a sign of the times, and our elders knew things would be much worse before they got better.

As the evening progressed, Maria turned to Adela and said. "You were right; he is nice, and he seems to be very respectful, so it's OK with me that he be your boyfriend. Adela came over to me and said, "Did you hear that?! Now we don't have to hide anymore. Or, at least not from my mom anyway."

Maria started laughing but reminded us to beware of her father at all times. Adela hugged me like she was never letting go. Now, all we have to do is not let your father find out, but we didn't have to worry about it while he's in Puerto Rico. Life was blissful for a while. Adela and I were inseparable and often kept me out of trouble, from even going to rumbles with rival gangs. Gang violence, however, was a way of life during those crazy days living in the South Bronx. You couldn't just run away from the violence because it was all around us. As I think about it now, I understand it so much better than I was a kid because violence was just as evident as the poverty levels when we were young.

When I was younger and before the Bronx started to burn, it thrived, and I wonder how many people knew how much the Vietnam conflict affected our lives during the late 1960s to mid-1970s.

Gangs from the South Bronx and other urban areas from New York City were populated by returning Veterans from that conflict, and many of them came back stone-cold killers. Fifty Thousand plus didn't come home at all; many came back with disabilities, without arms or legs and strung out on drugs or just plain crazy from exposure to chemicals as well as the horror of war itself. Upon their return to a society that hated them for the most part, many called them baby killers, and they didn't have a clue that these boys did not volunteer to do those things. But ordered by a Government that found them to be expendable, nor that they had led them to death and despair as a result of that horrible war. Yes, the gangs lashed out with the most dangerous gangs comprised of those returning Vietnam Vets who were all kids when they left and came back morally afflicted and extremely dangerous.

I took the time to ask some questions of a returning Vietnam Vet one day, and my first question was, "What was it like fighting in Vietnam?" He turned to me and just said, "You never want to experience war; it is horrible beyond words!" I could tell he was reluctant to speak about his experience, and the look on his face said it all. That look became like a frozen stare for a short while, and then tears came from his eyes, and as he wiped them from his face, he snapped out of it and said, "You think it's terrible here because you lost a couple of friends to gang violence. Well, over there, I lost just about every friend I had ever made in a matter of days.

I saw my best friend blown up by a booby trap bomb, and there were pieces of him everywhere." He went on to tell me his friend was one of the bravest guys he ever knew and could still see his smiling face right before he got blown to bits. He told me his friend loved history and shared something he never knew. He said Puerto Ricans had been in every major war the US had fought since World War I. He considered his friend a hero, and he told me Puerto Ricans had had lots of heroes in many conflicts and wars for over a hundred years. I guess that was his way of changing the subject and generalizing conflict and our involvement throughout the years. I don't remember his name, but I do remember that he was older than me, but not by much. I don't know whatever happened to him, but I do know I will never forget the look in his eyes as he shared his story with me. What I took away with me that day after he shared several other things was that war was, at times, a stupid but necessary evil.

He said the Vietnam conflict fell into the category of being more like a conflict that was part of the Cold War with Russia and that they were arming the Vietcong.

That's when he told me it was why he got high on drugs so that he wouldn't be afraid all the time. I didn't understand what he meant by that at the time, but years later, I would come to comprehend the significance of what he said to me that day, and it has always stayed with me, even today. I will never forget the sadness it brought to me as he told me his story. The thought of young men dying in the name of freedom, in a war nobody cared about, seemed senseless to me. Those horrible days also spilled onto the streets of the South Bronx upon their return home.

It didn't matter what color you were to fight side by side in Vietnam. Once you return home, that's a different story altogether. However, the bonds forged during the horrors of war last forever. True Brotherhood comes to those who fight side by side to survive. The altar of freedom comes with a price paid in blood!

"WAR IS HELL!" (General William Tecumseh Sherman)

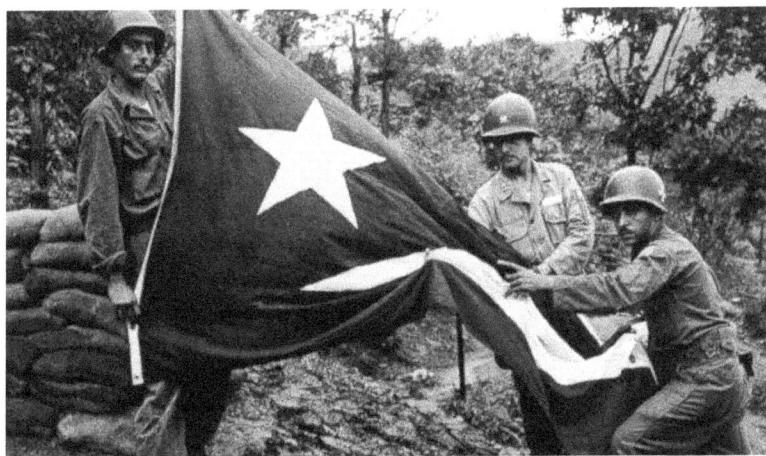

Puerto Ricans fought and died in every major war since World War I. Pictured above is, The U.S. Army's 65th Regiment called... (The Borinqueneers).

CHAPTER FOUR: THE DEATH OF MR. LETTO

The next day I was hanging out with Raymond and a few of the other guys, and an older guy named Carmelo, who was always begging for money to buy beer, was also with us. As we were walking down the street on Intervale Ave, which was right around the corner from our block, he asked a guy we knew named Flaco for a quarter to buy a quart of beer. The guy looked at him and told him he would shoot him if he asked him for a quarter again. Carmelo asked him again since he knew he was only kidding, but Flaco took out his gun, with a crazy look in his eyes, and aimed his weapon at Carmelo, but then moved it to the side, trying to scare him he fired the gun. Carmelo jumped to the side and got shot in the chest. He fell dead right there in front of our eyes. My neighborhood was crazy and violent, but I had never seen anybody get killed by mistake over asking for a quarter. It was sad to see a person die right before your eyes, but it wasn't the first time for me. From what I was told, someone burned down the building where Flaco lived that very night to get even if you could call that getting even since several people were hurt and displaced.

In the coming days, I found myself spending more time with Adela just to stay out of trouble. Still, one afternoon there was a problem with the Turbans. When Louie, his brothers Charlie and Raymond, and David, AKA Mr. Letto, were close to the main Javelin Clubhouse, they got into a shootout.

Nobody got hurt on our side, but one of their guys got hit, so the following day, David purchased a new rifle with Raymond, and they went into an abandoned building to test it.

Raymond said he had some things to do, so he left David alone to continue testing the rifle. After trying the weapon, he came out of the building and spotted the Turbans. David got into a shootout with them, but he was outnumbered, and they killed him in cold blood.

David was dead, and the neighborhood mourned, yet another brother lost to gang violence. David was also Miriam's boyfriend (she was Jayjoe's older sister), so needless to say when she found out, she went crazy. When Adela found out what happened, she came looking for me, started crying, and told me she was glad that I was with her when that happened. It's crazy because earlier that day, a junkie stole a women's purse, and as he was running away from the lady, she ran after him screaming, and he tried to hitch a ride on the side of the number 11 bus, but he fell off, and his legs were crushed under the back tires of the bus. When the lady got there, as he was screaming in pain, she snatched the bag from him and hit him on the head with it. She said, "It serves you right for being such an asshole!" Then she walked away. We all saw the whole thing go down right before our eyes like it was a Hollywood movie.

We were all laughing about how much stuff happens in our neighborhood and had no idea what would come that very afternoon.

After David's murder, Big Louie came down and told us to make ourselves invisible for a while, while he assembled a war council at the Royal Javelins main clubhouse on Vyse Ave.

We were going to war, and I wanted to go with them to avenge David's killing. Adela begged me not to go.

She was crying, telling me she didn't want me to die. I had a lot of anger inside me, the type of passion that gets one into trouble, so I paid no attention to her. When Louie got back, he told us he had also met with leaders from the 7 Immortals and the Savage Nomads and that they decided to go to war with the Turbans, and they were setting plans in motion after things calmed down a bit. There were just too many cops investigating the killing, and they knew that things were only going to escalate. They didn't count on the Turbans sending out a squad to kill Louie and his family at his home. They knew killing David, who was not only our War Lord but Big Louie's best friend, that Louie would not take the killing lightly. They knew he would come for them. The following day there was a knock on Louie's door. When his father asked who was there, they started shooting right through the door with his entire family inside. The family included his little sisters and brothers and his mother and father. Everyone ducked for cover, and thank God nobody was hit. Louie and Charlie had hidden a couple of guns in their parent's room since they always found them when they were hidden in their bedrooms. They returned fire right through the door.

Soon after that, Louie was ambushed by a couple of guys from the Turbans when he was alone, and they took some shots at him, but Louie was armed and returned fire. He recognized one of the guys shooting at him, whose name was Husky, and had also been one of the guys who killed David. Nobody got to hit that day, but the war was on, and there would be no prisoners taken. The following day big Louie met with father Tony, the warlord of the 7 Immortals, again because he wanted to make sure the immortals would be with us and decide how, when, and where we would hit them.

Father Tony also confirmed that the Savage Nomads would also be with us, but it was an uneasy alliance for Big Lou. It turns out we had beef with them at some point, but as the old proverb goes, "The enemy of my enemy is my friend," which was big Lou's mindset at the time. We were all teenagers but were armed to the teeth when we all got together on Wilkins Ave and made our way towards Charlotte Street to confront the Turbans. When we got to Minford Place, in significant numbers, there were cops there who directed us towards Charlotte Street., which was a bit suspicious to us, but we had no idea they were setting us up to be ambushed. Not that we knew or cared about it at the time because we were in significant numbers, we were headed straight towards an ambush in the middle of Turban territory. Not sure how the Turbans did it, but they had allies in the NYPD, unbeknown to us, but it was too late to turn back because when we got to the middle of the block, all hell broke loose.

I was standing next to Raymond when it happened, he had a 9mm, and I had a zip gun, and just about everyone with us had weapons, but we were shot at from above. It was an ambush set up by the Turbans who knew we'd be coming, and they got help from the NYPD in steering us right into harm's way. It was like a scene from a James Cagney movie, with a hail of bullets raining down on us from above, coming from windows on both sides of the street. One soldier after another went down from gunshot wounds. Watusi, Apache, Mejico all were wounded but alive. Father Tony wasn't so lucky; he got shot and was lying there bleeding to death right in front of our eyes. Everyone was running away from the hail of bullets while those of us caught in the crossfire were hiding. We fired back without looking at what we were shooting at for a while.

I am saying to myself, "I should have listened to Adela; she's going to kill me if I get shot." Raymond told me to keep my head down because he knew all I had was a zip gun, which was hard to load while raining bullets. Not Ray; when he ran out of ammo, he just loaded another clip and continued shooting while keeping his head down. Suddenly, a car rumbled down the street and came to a screeching stop. It was Clive from the Royal Javelins. He told us to get in as he fired at the building and then sped off with us safely inside. I never got a chance to thank him properly, but Clive had saved our lives that day, and that is something I will never forget.

We got back to our turf; we went up to the roof where we had a pigeon coup and should see anyone coming from all sides of the streets. The bird coup had a hidden compartment where we would hide our guns, except for me; I always took my zip gun home. Louie was livid when we got to the roof, and he started saying that the cops set us up so we would get killed in the ambush. We all agreed that they steered us into harm's way on purpose, and Louie wanted to declare war on them too. I admit Louie was a bit crazy, but none of us thought about shooting at cops and bringing the entire police force down on us. Louie screamed at us and reminded us that several were shot, and Father Tony was dead. He lost his life fighting alongside us, so now we had two deaths, we had to retaliate. We all agreed we needed a better plan in the future, but I told him I was never going back into that block again; it would have to be on different grounds. They all laughed at me when I said that, but I didn't give a shit; that was the scariest day in my life. We were all lucky to be alive, was the way I saw it, and I wasn't looking to tempt the hands of fate.

A few days later, Louie spotted the guy who shot and killed David as he was walking around the corner from where we lived. He asked me to come with him, and we hid in the hallway of a building on Intervale Avenue and waited for him. When he passed in front of the building, Louie shot at him but missed with the first shot, and the guy started running in between the cars, and Louie missed several more times. He was like a Jack Rabbit, very quick and elusive, and he got away.

As we ran out the back stairwell into the backyard, I was asking Louie how he could miss, and Louie turned and said, "The guy had luck coming out his ass." We started laughing but kept running to the safety of our block. When we stopped running, Louie grabbed me by the shirt and told me if I told anyone that he missed, he would kick my ass. A couple of weeks later, the guys' luck ran out, and he was killed. I don't know by whom, as I wasn't there, but God forgive me, I was glad he was dead.

I realize being happy about someone's death seems cruel, but in my eyes, he deserved to die for all the killings he was responsible for having committed. Husky was a stone-cold killer who had no remorse and a reputation that made him feared amongst his enemies in the South Bronx. David was 17 years old when shot down over something that I still do not understand to this day. However, as ugly as it was, gang wars and violence were commonplace in 1971, and the killings were as brutal as they were senseless and cruel. The mentalities of the youth from those days were surreal, but for us, it seemed normal because it was all we knew. We didn't grow up in those days with expectations of being a Doctor or a Lawyer, and hope was just a word.

Keep in mind that when our people migrated to the United States in significant numbers during the 1950s, they mainly were Factory workers, laborers, carpenters, and plumbers.

Although mothers and fathers wanted a better life for their kids, their biggest expectation was that they would live to have grandchildren someday.

Rango Created the original Royal Javelin Gang Colors during the late 1960s.

My Replica Imperial Bachelors Colors.

CHAPTER FIVE:

THE GHETTO BROTHERS

(The Murder of Black Benjy, Road to Peace)

A few weeks later, Black Benjy, who was the Peacemaker of the Ghetto Brothers, was sent to try and make peace between 3 warring gangs. He was severely beaten and then stabbed to death on December 2, 1971, as he was trying to make peace between them. Senseless killings were the order of the day during that short yet violent era. The Ghetto brother's President Karate Charlie wanted to go to war, but Cornell's mother said her son died trying to make peace, and she wanted his legacy to be that of a peacemaker. She said enough blood had been spilled, so they decided to listen to Black Benjy's mother and try to make peace instead. I can't even imagine how hard it must have been for the Ghetto Brothers not to go to war with those who killed Black Benjy. I guess Black Benjy's mom got through to them because they called upon all the gangs of the Bronx to come to a peace meeting they set for December 7th, 1971, at the Hoe Ave. Boys Club. Big Louie told everyone we would be there, but he had no intention of making peace with the Turbans at that meeting.

Let me just say that during the mid-60s to mid-70s, gangs had turf wars. In other words, they would fight for supremacy over any given area of the South Bronx where they lived. Sometimes bigger gangs absorbed smaller gangs because they were just too close to the more prominent gang's turf. Gangs from those days had hit squads, usually comprised of the craziest guys in the gang, who went out to either kill a rival gang member or just beat the shit out of him.

That, of course, depended on the gravity of the offense. There were select smaller gangs which the bigger gangs would not bully. They were older and more violent most of the time, and a good percentage of them had recently come home from Vietnam. At the same time, some gangs had young leaders with younger members under them. The truth of the matter is the gangs ruled the streets of the South Bronx during that era. The Turbans were not as big in numbers as the Royal Javelins, but they were older and had military training, so they were also deadly. That's not to say that the Javelins did not have Vets as well, but they soon found themselves dead or in jail. Big Louie was a young leader at the age of 17, but he was fearless and a bit crazy, if you ask me.

The leader before him was a guy we called Sammy the Beast. He went to prison for killing a gang member from a rival gang and why Big Louie became President of the first division Royal Javelin's when Sammy went to prison.

In retrospect, I sometimes think that young Urban Latinos and Blacks mostly populated the front lines of Vietnam, and those who came back to the streets were even crazier than before they fought in Vietnam.

When the day of the Peace Meeting came, we did not take weapons, but we wore our Royal Javelin Colors with pride. There were already hundreds of warriors out in front of the Boy's Club. It was a bit scary walking amongst our enemies in such close proximity. To be honest, I thought there would be a free for all, and everyone would just start beating the shit out of each other.

There was also a significant police presence, not that they could ensure anyone's safety, nor do I think they would interfere if there were a rumble. Sometimes, I believe that's what the police wanted us to do, kill each other off. I still think that statement is true to this day.

They hated us; we hated them. However, the hate was for different reasons. The amount of prejudice against minorities by Police Officers from those days was always present. They treated us like animals, so we did not disappoint them, yet when we were in significant numbers, they feared us and did not mess with us, as they usually did. We had gathered with the threat of all-out war looming over our heads. And yet, the fact that so many came to represent sent out a powerful message to the world. If all the Bronx Gangs had united that day and made war on the cops because of how very abusive they were, all hell would break loose throughout the City. The eyes of New York and the Nation were upon us that night, not that I understood it, during those youthful and violent days of my life.

They provided mediators; however, gang leaders did most of the talking that day, and while many say that total peace was made that day, I beg to differ. For example, Big Louie never made peace with the Turbans, and the violence between us continued for some time. They kept in mind that some gangs continued to be a menace to society well into the later 70s. Big Louie went to a meeting with Ruben (the Supreme President of the Royal Javelins), and they got into a fight because of what Louie said at the meeting about not granting the Turbans peace.

Big Louie punched Ruben in the face, told him he was no longer a Royal Javelin, called him a coward, and walked out. I came to know later that Big Lou was also angry with Ruben because he ran out on him during a rumble with another rival gang a time before that. When I got home after the meeting, Adela was upset and didn't want to talk to me, so she walked away.

At that moment, I knew we could never really be together because once her mother found out that I was a gang member, she never allowed me to see her daughter again. We still sneaked around, but it was not long before I got the worse news of all; Adela's father was moving them to Puerto Rico, where he had brought a house and opened a small business. We did not have a lot of time left, so we tried spending some time together. However, things were never the same after that day. Adela knew in her heart that it was not meant to be, and even though she stilled loved me, I was under too much peer pressure to be the boyfriend she wanted me to be.

I also knew that she was leaving me, not of her own choice, but she would soon be gone, and it bothered me. I kept myself occupied with the guys and our sports. I broke it off with Adela before she left and told her I had found someone else. Of course, that wasn't true, but I felt that it would help her forget me, which, of course, wasn't what I wanted either. The day she left, I cried inside, but I did not allow my tears to flow. I was too strong for all that crying thing now, and I didn't want my friends to see me cry because I knew they would make fun of me.

Adela's tears ran down her face as she said goodbye, but I was strong and told her that I would never forget her, and I wished her all the happiness in the world.

After she was gone that night, I thought about her and pictured her face as she cried, as she was saying goodbye. I had confessed to her how much I would miss her, but I wanted to make it easier for her, making her cry even more. After all, was said and done, I knew I would never see her again, so I finally put my guards down, and I cried myself to sleep thinking about my first love and how much she meant to me. Would I ever see her again? I doubted that, and while it was hard to fathom never seeing her again, I knew the next day would bring another adventure. A couple of months passed by since Adela left for Puerto Rico, and I found myself thinking about her less because we had more pressing problems within the neighborhood to contend with after that.

Since the peace meeting, things had calmed down a bit, but there was still violence among some gangs, especially at school. One afternoon after getting home from school, I got back to find cops in my house because my mother had been attacked with a butcher knife by a guy who tried to stab her while attempting to rob her. As it turns out, my mother had defended herself by hitting the blade out of his hand with her purse when he tried to stab her and started screaming for help. The guys who were usually playing dice on our front stoop came to her aid, and she told them she recognized the guy who did it. She said to them she had seen the guy who tried to stab her playing dice with them in the past, and you could tell she was terrified although she fought him off.

The senseless and cruel killings were escalating, but this time the violence had almost claimed my mother's life. That's when my father decided it was time to go, and a few days later, he told us he was moving us to Puerto Rico. Adela popped into my head right away, and it brought a smile to my face for an instant, but I couldn't get over the look of fear in mom's eyes, and it made me angry. I also thought about the kind of life I would have in Puerto Rico, the place where I was born, but I knew nothing about it at the time.

The thought of leaving all my friends behind and never seeing them again weighed heavy on my mind. Even though all the violence and the hardships we shared, I had come of age in this neighborhood. I learned so many things about myself, life in general, and just how unfair the world was. I learned about love, hate, and indifference, but most importantly, I learned about friendship and the importance of brotherhood. I couldn't blame my father for wanting to move us out of that neighborhood, mainly because my mother was almost killed for her gold chain, but I was sad nonetheless.

Anyone who thinks, or says that there was complete peace after that gang meeting at the Bronx Boys Club, must have been living in a dark bubble with no windows. The way most of us saw it, and as a direct result of the Bronx gangs not all making peace on December 7th, 1971, the violence continued for a few more years. Yellow Benjy was always visiting rival gangs regularly in his pursuit of making peace, and that is something we can all be thankful for.

It didn't come without a certain amount of danger in regards to his life, but Benjy was fearless in that regard.

Putting his safety aside, Benjy entered extremely volatile neighborhoods, to say the least, just to speak with other gang leaders. Joseph Mpa, affiliated with the Black Panther Party from Boston Road, was a considerable influence for Benjy. The Puerto Rican Socialist Party taught Benjy about structure and organization in early 1971. As far back as the late 1960s, the Ghetto Brothers were doing jams at Crotona Park, and bringing people together in peace and unity was always their message.

They were a gang; unlike the rest, they didn't believe in using weapons because they were Martial Artists who used their skills only when necessary and always preferred peace. Martial Arts skills were taught to most of the Ghetto Brothers by Karate Charlie, whom Benjy had given his Presidency to for a short while in 1971. However, after the death of Black Benjy, Charlie disappeared and wasn't seen for many years afterward.

As it turns out, Charlie wanted to go to war with The Mongos, the Black Spades, and the 7 Immortals responsible for Black Benjy's death. Yellow Benjy stopped him in his tracks when Charlie approached the 2nd Division Ghetto Brothers, who were from 158th St. and Trinity Ave, to prevent an all-out war. Black Benjy died while trying to make peace; why would anyone want to soil his legacy by continuing with the same mentality which claimed his life. In the end, he died for peace, and I can't think of a better way to go out than by dying for something he believed. This is why today, I frown at those who say the Zulu Nation brought peace to all the gangs of the South Bronx in 1974.

Yellow Benjy and the Ghetto Brothers first used the ideology of bringing people together through the power of music and dance during that era and playing live music for the masses who came in peace. It was not that it was a new concept, mind you, but The Ghetto Brothers were the first to use it during those violent days when we were killing each other for stupid reasons with cruel intentions.

In 1971, the Ghetto Brothers became the first gang to become an organization, and they also released their first album that year. Advocating for peace also came from the President of the Imperial Bachelors, spearheaded by Henry DeSosa, Tato Rivera VP, and Willie Estrada Warlord. They were given instructions by Black Tony, Supreme President of the Bachelors in 1973, to try and make peace with our enemies.

He said he was tired of seeing our people killing each other and told us how cruel it was. He gave us that directive right before he went to prison. He chose Henry to take over his position as Supreme President because Henry was an educated man who often spoke to Tony about the senseless killings. The peace effort for us officially started during the summer of 1974, at St. Mary's Recreation Center, on 145th St. and St. Ann's Avenue. The Latin Hustle was the dance that brought many Puerto Rican gang members together in peace to our neighborhood during the summer of our youth. For the record, peace was made in different neighborhoods by different gangs at different times, but St. Mary's was the place that helped set a new standard for bringing people together in peace in one of the most violent neighborhoods in all of the South Bronx.

The Ghetto Brother band "Street The Beat" - RIP Benjy

During that era, there were more Puerto Rican gangs than any other ethnic group in the South Bronx, but none like the Ghetto Brothers, who were mentored by the Black Panthers and the Puerto Rican Socialist Party, who taught them how to organize and create their organization in 1971. That same year they released their first album entitled: Ghetto Brother Power.

Saved from six feet under

To Benjy Melendez, all the world is a John. "John Lennon was my main man," he explains. "When he died, I started calling everybody John."

Leading a Beatles-inspired group called Street the Beat is another way Melendez keeps Lennon's legacy alive. A band of five (Melendez's brothers Robert and Victor, Manny Cortez and David Silva), Street the Beat's perfect harmonies belie their distinctly unharmonious past.

Long before forming the band in 1980, Melendez headed the Savage Nomads, one of New York's most notorious gangs. "Those were sad and violent times," admits the 32-year-old singer, who claims to have once commanded an "army" of 2,000. I knew I'd be six feet under if I continued much longer. The Beatles' message of love was our inspiration to change."

Though famed for their Fab Four covers, the label-shopping band plans to record its own material. "If John were here," says Melendez, "I know he'd say, 'It's time you went on to be yourselves.'" —*M.K.S.*

Benjy (c) keeps the peace with Street the Beat.

2/11/85 US Mag.

CHAPTER SIX: TROUBLE IN PARADISE

The day of our departure for Puerto Rico had finally arrived, and I had my final goodbyes to say, which were extremely sad for me because this was the place where I had come of age and had my very first absolute best friend. When we landed in Puerto Rico, it was sweltering. Even though I had been born there, I remembered very little about my country, as I was only two years old when I left for New York.

The first thing I remember about getting there was seeing my grandfather, whom I had not seen since I was two years old. He was a wealthy political figure in Puerto Rico and once owned the best custom furniture-making warehouse in San Juan. He was old and had lost both his legs to diabetes, so he had become a grumpy older man, whom I had never really seen smiling much. His brother Pedro, my aunt Judy and her daughter Evelyn lived in the same house. Pedro, his older brother, had once lived in the shop that got burned down by my grandfather's mistress after being scorned. Back in those days, grandpa didn't believe in banks, so he kept all his money hidden under the floorboards, and he lost everything when his mistress burned down his woodshop, and my great uncle Pedro was almost killed. (Hell has no fury, as a woman scorned!) After he lost everything, he also lost his legs, and he became a very bitter older man, who never really showed me any love, but I took it all in stride. Especially since I never wanted to be there, to begin with.

My first day of school in Puerto Rico was a bit hectic. I couldn't read Spanish very well, didn't write it very well either, and everyone called me Newyorican.

I hated that. But, the worse thing was after having finished 9th grade in New York, I was put back in the 9th grade due to not reading or writing Spanish very well. As if that wasn't bad enough, kids would make fun of how I tried to read in Spanish, and I knew sooner or later I would blow. The best part of being in Puerto Rico was meeting new friends from my town, especially the pretty girls.

I was waiting with great anticipation for the arrival of my Mini-Bike. In the next town, a group of guys had Mini-Bikes and would ride together and cause havoc throughout the neighborhood. After a while, everyone in my community started calling me. Willie Motora, translation, (Willie Motorbike), and it was like my right of passage, I think.

One day at school, as I was trying to read, the students started laughing and making fun of me, and I got irate. I started cursing at them in English, calling them assholes and stupid sons of bitches. The teacher came up to my desk and struck me hard with his yardstick ruler on my forearm. He told me to shut up and started walking away like I had to fear him. I picked up my chair and threw it over his head, and it bounced off his desk and hit the blackboard. Then I cursed at him and told him if he ever hit me again, I wouldn't miss the next time!

He freaked out, told me I was crazy and commanded me to go to the principal's office. I gladly left, and he followed behind me. Once there, he told the principal, a woman, what I had done, and that he wanted me expelled or suspended.

I wasn't afraid because I didn't like that school anyway, mainly because everyone made fun of me. Once the teacher told the principal his side, she asked me why I did it.

I explained to her that if he were a good teacher, he would not let the other students make fun of me, as I tried my best to learn how to read and write in Spanish. I told her he hit me with his ruler because I was screaming at the other students for making fun of me, something he should not have done, and put a stop to it. How will someone learn if the teacher allows the other students to make fun of that person, I asked her?

Needless to say, she understood my reasoning; however, she still had to suspend me for my behavior in class. I told her I didn't care and that if the shoe was on the other foot, and I was in New York, and someone trying to learn how to read English, I wouldn't make fun of them. I also told her that my classmates didn't like me and always called me Newyorican. They also said things like I should go back to New York because I wasn't an authentic Puerto Rican. She asked me if I knew the students' names, but I told her that's not how we do things in New York; we don't rat on anyone. She took pity on me and said she would put me on the Security Patrol Squad when I came back in a week. I would have authority over students; if they cut class or did other inappropriate things, I could report them and get them in trouble. That brought a big smile to my face. Revenge would be sweet; it was all I thought about the week I was out of school.

Meanwhile, I kept hounding my mother about how much I hated school in Puerto Rico and that I wouldn't do well and probably keep getting left-back. Finally, the day of my return to school had arrived, and as instructed by the principal, I went straight to her office to report to get my new schedule and get assigned to the Patrol Squad.

She put me in a class where the teacher spoke English and taught an English class to help him teach the students. When the principal gave me my badge, I put it on; it felt good. It was now time to patrol the area for students cutting classes. Most of the students who were my tormentors in the class were looking at me as I walked out of the principal's office with my badge on, and you can see in their eyes as if saying to themselves, "Oh Shit, here comes trouble!" They all thought I was crazy anyway, so imagine now that I was wearing a badge. There's a new Sheriff in town! I looked at them with contempt. All those who made fun of me were going to pay. It wasn't long before I found my first victim, someone I especially didn't like, so it was a pleasure to write him up for cutting class while on school property.

That was a big one for me because now, all of a sudden, he wanted to be kind to me. "Ha, fat chance, buddy," I told him. I was writing him up, which meant he had to attend after-school detention for a week. None of the other security patrols had ever written him up because they feared him, but I didn't have that problem. Especially after I threw a chair at a teacher, they all knew I was a bit loco.

I have to admit, I loved the idea of having power over the idiots who made fun of me. I wrote the student up and told him to tell his friends that I was coming after all of them. (Theme from the good, the bad, and the ugly.)

Before long, they all stopped messing with me and calling me Newyorican. Instead, they all tried to befriend me, and in a while, I did make some friends. The Principal's idea had worked.

I didn't know that was her intention until after a few weeks had gone by; she called me into her office to get a progress report from me. I still did not like attending school there, but it had become more bearable. I had lots of adventures in Puerto Rico, but I also had a couple of near-death experiences there as well.

We lived in Bayamon with some family for a while, and I met some of my cousin's friends during our summer vacation and started hanging out with them. One day they told me they were going swimming in a river with a waterfall, so naturally, I went along. I had been diving off the rocks into the water and having a great day with the guys, but big trouble was lurking nearby.

The guys hadn't told me that the field we crossed through was private property. As we were leaving, the owner saw us coming out of the field; he screamed at us and told us he would shoot us if he ever caught us on his property again. Yes, we were all scared because we knew he meant it, even though we weren't trying to steal his cows or livestock. He was very protective of his property and a bit crazy.

As we were leaving, I realized that I had left my basketball jersey on the fence by the river, so I ran back down the side of the hill through his property and got my basketball jersey. As I was going back up the hill to where my friends were, I heard a shot and a bullet zipping through the tall grass weeds close to my position. I immediately stopped and put my hands in the air, but the guys started screaming at me, telling me to run or he would kill me.

As he got closer, I realized he was aiming at me again, so I started running up the hill again, and all of a sudden, bang, another shot rang out, and I fell, but it was more like somebody pushed me from behind, and I heard the bullet pass right over my head through the tall grass. I got even more scared and started running again. Suddenly, boom, a louder shot rang out, and this time it was his son shooting at me with a shotgun. Again, someone pushed me from behind, and I heard the pellets zipping by over my head; I got up and started screaming. "Don't kill me, don't kill me."

Yet another shot rang out as I got closer to the top of the hill where the barbed wire fence was, as I made it to my friends. I didn't know that the owner had gotten into his car with his son and started driving towards us. Lucky for us, a man passing in his car saw what was going on and blocked the road, allowing us to escape on our bikes. I had barely escaped with my life, especially when they were both shooting at me. Every time I fell, I heard the bullet(s) go past me right above my head. I believe it was God or a guardian Angel pushing me so that I wouldn't get shot, and I've felt that way about it since that day.

What else is there to say about Puerto Rico, except I had lots of crazy adventures there, but New York was my home, and I was happy to be coming back here.

I will admit, I got into trouble a lot on purpose, and created chaos all around me, which is the main reason my parents caved in decided to move us back to New York. My father had gone ahead and found us a three-bedroom apartment in the South Bronx, then he sent for all of us, minus my dog Blackie, and my mini-bike, which I had sold.

I found out years later; my dog had been taken to the mountains and abandoned because he bit my little cousin. I left Puerto Rico heartbroken after losing our lifelong pet Blackie, who was more like family to us.

Our family house in Puerto Rico (above) was Abandoned by my cousin Evelyn a few years ago, shown below.

CHAPTER SEVEN: BACK TO THE BOOGIE DOWN BRONX

When we got back to New York in mid-1972, my father moved us into a newly renovated building on 145th St. between St. Ann's Ave and Brook Ave. A few blocks from where I attended grade school when I was a boy. But most importantly, right down the street from St. Mary's Recreation Center. It was only five train stops away from the hood where I came of age, and I went back often for a while. I also attended Morris High School and had to take the bus to get there. But, because it was so close to my old neighborhood, I saw lots of my old friends daily, and we raised hell, like always. We got into many fights, hung out every morning, smoked weed, and drank Swiss-Up, which we called "Bum Juice" before going to class. As you can imagine, I was not a very good student. I hardly did any classwork or homework because I was too stoned to concentrate and didn't care about school anyway. To get the unruly kids to the classrooms, the school started a unique program called the "Mini-School" for delinquent students and had some sort of talent. Music and Art were the order of the day.

It was how they got us off the streets, hanging out in front of the school and into the classroom. (Or class of retards as other students called us). The new teachers were much like the students, a little crazy. One teacher, in particular, Mr. Dinare, allowed us to smoke cigarettes in the back of the classroom, but he would also smoke pot with us. We weren't stupid; we just did not like being told what to do all the time, so you can say we were rebels with a cause.

We learned how to play instruments, and my preference was the trumpet, which I got pretty good at. I was also an artist and could draw anything I saw up close. During lunch, we would open the windows to the mini-school, which was on the last floor, and we would play music for all the students below. Everyone would start dancing and clapping as we played, and we sounded good. However, once the Principal got wind of it, our lunchtime jam sessions came to a halt. Just one more thing to piss us off! We started getting unruly again and even smoking weed and drinking bum juice, again, in the back of the classroom. So they shook things up again and separated some of us, and some even got expelled. I was lucky because I was never as unruly as the rest, and I knew when to chill. They put me on the Safety Squad and gave me a badge, and I became a sergeant in the school's safety patrol. I did well in school for a while, and a couple of teachers always encouraged me. They noticed that I was pretty bright and more respectful when I was not with my friends. They got me involved with helping others, and I liked that. It made me feel important. Everyone knew me, and they knew I didn't take crap from anybody, so they respected me for the most part, but for me, the worst was yet to come.

After a while, I stopped going to my old neighborhood as I met some new friends in my new hood, including Tony, who would become my new best friend. He lived in my building on the second floor, and I lived on the 4th. He moved in the same week as we did, and we were among the first families who moved into the newly refurbished building. A member of the Brothers of Satan moved into our building with his parents and two brothers. His name was Moses Martinez, and he was cool, as were his brothers.

I started hanging out with them and some of their other friends, who were also in the gang. When in Rome, do as the Romans. The cool part about meeting Moses is that he was an excellent Rock dancer, and he started teaching me in the hallway of our building. My new environment was full of surprises, and I was beginning to feel like I belonged to something special. By special, I mean, I was living in a new neighborhood that was coming up, while everything else around us was burning and continued to burn in many places around the South Bronx. Yes, many abandoned buildings were all around us, but St. Mary's Recreation Center stood out like a beacon of light and hope for us. While it seemed that I could not get away from the gangs, at least I had more productive things to do in my new hood, not only gang banging but learning how to dance Rock. A short while after I moved into my block, I met Willie Rivera, AKA Willie Whip. Willie and I also became friends, and he was an Imperial Bachelor, which was the gang's name from St. Mary's. Tony, Willie Moses, his brothers Willie, Gus, and Moe's best friend Tarzan (whom I later learned was my 2nd cousin).

I got close to Willie Whip pretty fast because he started practicing with Moe and myself in the hallway of my building almost every day. We practiced in our hall since nobody bothered us because they knew better. When we weren't hanging out with the rest of the gang, we would practice together, and I started getting good at Rocking. I wasn't a member of the Bachelors yet, but I was hanging out with them regularly.

The President of the division at St. Mary's was named Henry De Sosa, and he worked at the center.

Working there was a way of doing more positive things with his small army of gang members, and I liked that.

I wasn't forced to join them, but I was in the center every day because I always enjoyed going there as a kid, and it's where I learned how to swim. They had all kinds of cool things to do, a game room with pool tables and ping pong tables, chess and other games, a Boxing Gym, Martial Arts and Basketball Gym, as well as photography classes. They had everything I enjoyed doing and a great staff of people who cared about us. I can go on and write an entire book on my experiences there alone, but I'll just share some of the juicy parts with you guys. The hood we moved into wasn't as danger-free as my parents had hoped, actually the opposite, but we had a much bigger apartment, and I finally had my room to sneak girls in at night. I continued going to Morris High and regularly hanging out with my boys from Wilkins Ave. Tony was in Benjamin Franklin High School, in Spanish Harlem, and my sisters and I all went to Morris High School.

One day, some dude from my block got fresh with my older sister, and she kicked him in the groin and ran. When I found out this dude named Crazy Tony got fresh with her, I went looking for him in the center, where all my boys hung out. I found him, and when I approached him and asked him why he was bothering my sister, he told me to screw myself, so I punched him in the face and knocked him on his ass. I told him if he got up, I would hurt him. He stayed on the ground for a while, and I told him if he ever messed with my family again, I would beat him real bad.

He also had an older brother who was into Kung Fu and was supposed to be a little crazy. Later that day, as I was walking by the playground on the side of my building, I saw Crazy Tony with his brother (whose name I don't remember) staring me down.

I was alone, but that didn't matter to me. I didn't like people staring me down like they would kick my ass or something. I went over to them, and I asked his brother if he had a problem with me. He looked surprised that I even came over, as there were two of them, and he figured I would be afraid. He just thought wrong, I didn't fear anyone in those days because I could fight, and I had to assert myself even when I was scared. He gave me a hard look and asked me why I punched his brother in the face. Since he looked like he was punking out of a fight, I told him that his brother got nasty with my sister. I also told him that I would break his head open if he did that again. His brother got a little tough with me, so I got closer and asked him if he wanted to fight me too.

I took my stance and told him, "Come on; let me see what you got." I realized he knew some Kung Fu, but I didn't care. The look on my face told him I was as serious as a heart attack, and he quickly backed off. However, since he decided to get tough, I told him. "If you ever go near my sister again, I'm going to beat the shit out of you both!" The next time I won't be alone. You're messing with the wrong family." By that time, everybody around the neighborhood knew I was not only a little crazy, but I also loved to fight, so he decided that he didn't want any part of me and just walked away, tails tucked between their legs.

I always got a rush when I was about to fight, but I was still glad when I didn't have to. Rita Pasquelacua, the Center Manager, called me into her office the next day; she heard that I punched Crazy Tony in the face and asked me why. I told her what happened with my sister, and while she understood, she frowned on my attacking someone in her Center. However, instead of suspending me from entering the building, as she often did to others, she gave me some responsibility as a volunteer in the swimming pool as a Jr. Lifeguard since she knew I was a good swimmer. She intended to provide me with more responsibility and keep me out of trouble, which had worked in the past with me. She cared and would go out of her way to help keep me out of trouble. Unfortunately, I was still surrounded by a lot of peer pressure, and just like in my old neighborhood, sometimes the shit hit the fan. One day I had a conflict with one of the gang members because he disrespected me in front of people, but because I was not yet a gang member, they had his back, even though they liked me.

The brickyards are no longer there, but the memories of those days will be with me FOREVER! The South Bronx is still, to this day, THE LAND OF BROKEN PROMISES!

On the lower left side at the Cypress Bachelors clubhouse is my boy, Johnny Sanchez, at the Cypress Bachelors clubhouse during the early 1970s.

Tony and I had become great friends, so we decided to invite my boys from the Royal Javelins to play Basketball against the Cypress Bachelors to make peace between the two gangs. My plan worked as I knew it would, since I was close to both gangs by that time, so it made it easy for me to bring two rival gangs together during a time when they sometimes had conflict at Morris High School. There was always a wild card to deal with on occasions, and on this occasion, after a good game between us, the wild card was Henry's older brother Chu Chu, who was the leader of the Renegade Bachelors. Most people in my neighborhood were afraid of him because he was crazy and consistently hostile. Still, he caught me by surprise on that day when he instigated an argument over making peace with the Royal Javelins.

As it turns out, they had jumped him at school a couple of years earlier, and he was holding a grudge. It was time to bury the hatchet, and preferably not in my head, which Chu Chu was threatening to do when I spoke out in the name of peace and offered resistance, especially in light of having made peace with them that day. Chu Chu did not like that I had confronted him, which he took as a sign of disrespect and pulled a knife on me right in front of St. Mary's Center. My boy Tony Febles tossed me his 007 with a 7-inch blade after Chu Chu tried to cut me, and I was unarmed. Chu Chu thought he could intimidate me by lunging forward even though I had a bigger knife; he didn't know I would use it. Chu Chu thought wrong, I stepped forward while he was coming at me, and I sliced his chest open with a quick slashing motion he did not expect. When he looked at his wound and noticed he was bleeding, he became enraged with anger, which he thought would scare me, but he was wrong again as I lunged at him again, only this time with stabbing motions. At that point, Chu Chu decided I had come too close, and he turned and ran from me as I chased him down the street, screaming at him that I would kill him the next time. He never bothered me again after that day, and we would eventually become good friends. It was a crazy way to make friends, but this was more about respect than anything else, but it wouldn't be the last time I had to fight someone to gain respect during those days.

Chu chu would later that year invite me to work security with him during the Fania All-stars concert at Yankee Stadium on August 24, 1973. We worked by the stage area on the field, and they stored boxes of Budweiser Beer under the stage, so needless to say, we both got a bit drunk, to put it mildly.

It was my first concert, and I will never forget the day I got to see all the Fania All-Stars greats perform right in front of me, on the field at Yankee Stadium.

The Fania All-Stars were comprised of the Greatest Salsa Artists of ALL TIME.

Yankees Stadium, Fania Allstars Concert 1973

CHAPTER EIGHT: THE IMPERIAL BACHELORS

I decided to join the Imperial Bachelors, so I would not be an outsider anymore; that way, if I had a dispute with anyone, it could be settled with a one on one fight without anyone else jumping in or getting hurt. Once I joined, things got a bit better, and since I was now a gang member again, I was protected and could always depend on my boys to watch my back. After a few months and a few fights with other rival gangs, everyone knew I had heart and was a good fighter. One day, there was a buzz going around at the center about our supreme president.

Black Tony went to prison and came to see us because he turned over his position as Supreme President to the President of the 1st Division Imperial Bachelors President Henry De Sosa. Black Tony told us he was tired of seeing our people killing each other over stupid shit and gave our division the task of bringing peace into our territory. As it turns out, Henry had already spoken to Black Tony several times concerning the same thing, and Tony also knew Henry was brilliant and trusted his judgment. The thing is, our Warlord Julio had just gotten locked up as well and was already in prison.

Supreme President of the Bachelor's Henry DeSosa RIP

That meant there was an opening for the warlord position because our warlord was now in prison. However, you could not become a Warlord unless you proved yourself as the best fighter, or at least that's the way it was for us. I was chosen to fight to be Warlord and had to fight everyone else who wanted to be Warlord.

The only one who gave me competition was a crazy Bachelor we called Cowboy, and he and I were good friends.

He was bigger and stronger, but I had superior fighting skills, and I beat him with a flying dropkick to the chest, which made him flip over backward; and I jumped on him with my knees, pinning him down, and he gave up. He had had enough because he knew he was now at my mercy; I could have easily punched him in the face. After I beat everyone, I asked Henry if I was the Warlord now, but he told me I had to fight him as well. I looked at him and told him I wouldn't fight my President. He came over to me and slapped me so hard I saw little stars going around my head, as you see in cartoons. "Either you fight me now, or we all kick your ass." I looked at him, and as soon as I said I wouldn't fight him, he swung at me again, but this time I stepped back and put my hands up in a fighting stance.

"I don't want to hurt you, Henry," but he didn't want to hear that. He attacked me again, throwing several punches at my face, which I ducked. "Fight me, or we'll all beat the shit out of you!" He said again. It seemed I had no choice, so the moment Henry attacked me again, I hit him as hard in the solar plexus. Henry was a big guy, but even the big guys fall when you knock the wind out of them. I didn't want to hit him in the face, as he had done to me, out of respect for him. I wasn't looking forward to having everyone beat the shit out of me either, so I did what I had to do.

Henry could not go on, so I asked him again, "Am I the War Lord Now?" He was still winded but said in a low voice, "Yes, you are the Warlord now." That is how I became the Warlord of the Imperial Bachelors in 1973 at 17 years of age.

As the Warlord of the gang, I was excited because I could decide when we fought and with whom. I was tired of all the senseless violence, and I now had the chance to do something proactive for our community. The park where St. Mary's Recreation Center was located was called St. Mary's Park, and at night, you couldn't or, better said, shouldn't walk through it due to all the muggings, rapes, and murders that took place there.

These crimes usually happened at night because there were no lights in the park. It was easy for a predator to hide in wait during those days until some unsuspecting person walked into the park. If we saw someone getting attacked, we usually stopped it sometimes before it began. After I took over as Warlord, we patrolled the park every night, looking for anyone in the park trying to commit a crime. There were many trees for predators to hide behind, as did we at times waiting for them to strike, and it was pitch black at night, which was why it was so dangerous to walk through. However, unless you caught someone in the act, it was hard to determine if that person was walking through the park to rob, rape, or kill someone.

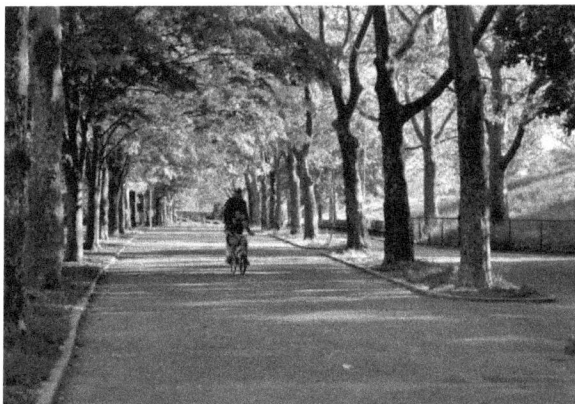

We started hiding behind the trees, usually on high ground, to see more and determine who was walking into the park to commit a crime or if someone was just stupid enough to be walking through the park to take a shortcut. We had caught and beaten the shit out of several guys trying to commit crimes, and after a while, many people knew not to commit crimes in our park. It wasn't long before some police officers who were both former Marines by the names of Sergeant Stamp and Sergeant Rico came into the picture. We called them "Batman & Robin" because they were very gun-ho and became famous in our neighborhood for being badasses. They got to know us because they knew it was us helping to keep the park safe, so they never gave us a hard time about it. They also wanted to keep me out of trouble and even came to my house to know my parents, who always offered them coffee. They knew I was a good kid at heart and didn't want me to get lost in the streets. They were both former Marines and sometimes told us stories about fighting during the Vietnam conflict and how it wasn't a popular war, and when they came home, nobody cared, except their families, of course. I remember the night they saved my life as though it was yesterday. I was with the guys in St. Mary's Recreation Center, and it was my turn to go for the beer as we were having a little pool tournament. I had my colors on, which on the back read, "War Lord Imperial Bachelors," and I wore them with pride.

Keeping in mind that I was only seventeen years old, and yet I was fearless as I walked down the street alone in my neighborhood, where everyone knew me. I was called over to an unmarked police car, and Sergeant Stamp & Ricio, AKA Batman & Robin, were sitting there undercover.

They knew another division, namely the Cypress Bachelors, had killed two members of the Savage Skulls, and they also knew they would be out for blood. They told me to watch out for myself because even though they knew it wasn't my division, the Savage Skulls wouldn't care and would kill any Bachelor they found on the streets.

I told them I would be careful, and I walked across the street, and as I got to the next corner, I was confronted by about 30 or so members of what I knew to be The Savage Skulls. They didn't have their colors on, but from their MC Boots and Raggedy Outlaw way of dressing, I knew they were Savage Skulls.

They surrounded me and asked me if I was a Bachelor, and I knew they were going to hurt or kill me, but I said, "Yes, I am; what's going on?" They told me some Bachelors murdered a couple of Savage Skulls and asked if I knew anything about it? I pointed at Ricio & Stamp and told them those two cops just told me the same thing, but my division had nothing to do with it. When they saw Ricio & Stamp looking at us and getting out of their car, they told me to take my colors off because the Skulls would be coming to find Bachelors, and they started running down the block and away from the Cops. I decided it was time to turn back to the company of my friends, but I knew had it not been for Ricio & Stamp being there, I would probably not be here telling you this story today. As I approached Ricio & Stamp, they asked me what had happened.

I told them they had confronted me about the two killings and that they said they were Bachelors, but I suspected they were Savage Skulls.

They asked me why I pointed at them, and I told them to save my hide because I knew they would not attack me if they knew you were cops. They both laughed and told me I was lucky they were there. I agreed and said I was going back to the Center and forgetting about the beer. Yes, I was scared when they confronted me, but they never got to see me shake, and the look in my eyes was not that of someone scared but instead of someone who was a Warrior. It's a survival technique and works simply because the aggressors always respect courage in the face of overwhelming adversity.

However, I suspect Batman & Robin had just saved my life, and there was no doubt in my mind. I got back to the center and told Henry what had happened. He called everybody together for a war council with the Cypress Bachelors to discuss the killings that went down and how they brought the heat down on us. He was angry because he was the Supreme President, and they had not told him what was going on. Keeping in mind that our division was trying to keep the peace, and they had declared war without his permission, so needless to say, there was some damage control to do. As it turned out, there was no reasoning with the Savage Skulls, and war with our brothers was the only solution since they wouldn't listen and who could blame them. It was a war nobody could ever win, even if they killed one of us, and we would kill two of them. And so, the violence continued for a while longer. All I can say is that all hell started breaking loose, and the year before, we saw a record number of murders regularly. But things were about to change.

Our division did not get involved with all the battles, but we fought to protect our neighborhood.

Batman & Robin passed by the hood more frequently and would come by to see us regularly. We continued to patrol St. Mary's Park at night and kept our neighborhood safe from predators. As a direct result, the muggings, rapes, and murders in St. Mary's went down because of our efforts to keep our park safe.

It seems Batman and Robin liked me because they knew I was not a troublemaker. They started talking to me about joining the Marines and told me they felt I would make a good Marine. I was having too much fun, so I didn't entertain the idea initially. They said that joining the Marines would help make me a man, considering I was only 17 years old. They were merely planting a seed in my head so that I would consider it. As time went on and things got a bit better, I started spending more time dancing with Moses and Willie Whip. We started going to more house parties in our neighborhood, and we started doing a new social dance, which would later be known as the Latin Hustle, which allowed us to dance with a girl. But don't get me wrong; we danced slow songs with the girls on every occasion. Grinding with the girls was a big deal for us.

However, parents did not like us grinding with their daughters, which is why the new social dance, which, as I said, would later be known as the Latin Hustle, was being developed amongst ourselves at parties. We always managed to get into fights at parties, especially outside of our neighborhood, for some reason or another.

Sometimes, we had party crashers from other neighborhoods, and fights ensued.

It seems that Puerto Rican testosterone levels are always higher when we want to impress girls.

Especially when the girls we are trying to impress belong to someone else. I knew that Wars had been started over women long before our time. However, we also created a few of our own during those days. Let's face it; we were young dumb, and full of cum. I'm not sure who said that first, but I know for a fact that it was true for most of us.

I tried staying focused on school, but we always had problems there. The results are often chaotic when you put so many gang members from different neighborhoods into one building. Another word that comes to mind is stupid, which is how I would describe the environment at Morris High School, and many considered it the worst High School in the South Bronx. If you got into a confrontation inside the school, you can bet your bottom dollar there would be a fight when you got outside. One of the main reasons you had to be part of a gang was that if you didn't belong to a gang, you were not protected and would be fair game for a pack of wolves.

Our President, Henry, was always trying to keep the peace, but that was a tall order back in those days. We had problems consistently, but I managed to stay out of trouble as much as possible. All I wanted to do was hang out and party with the girls. The thing I loved the most, which helped me escape from the day's problems, was getting together with my friends to dance.

By the time 1973 came around, we were hanging out at 310½ regularly and dancing all night long.

Willie Whip and I were practicing a lot more, and while we did not enter any contest, we were getting ready. As it turns out, we never got to enter a competition in 1973, as I got suspended from my senior year at Morris High School and joined the Marines. I might as well tell you how that happened. As you all know, I was not a bad kid, but trouble always had a way of finding me. The same way Rita Pasquelagua kept me out of trouble at St. Mary's, the Principal of the school I attended in Puerto Rico used a similar method in giving me responsibilities. The Dean of Morris High School tried to keep me out of trouble by putting me on the Service Squad. One day while I was doing service duty at the cafeteria, lunch was almost over, so I was lying back on one of the lunch tables.

I was not bothering anybody, just relaxing, mind you. A pretty girl I knew named Rachael came over to me, and without warning, she poured a dish full of creamy potato salad over my afro, and everyone started laughing. When I realized what she had done, I started going around and putting everyone's leftover potato salad on a plate, and when it was full, I started chasing her around the lunchroom. As it turns out, we started a food fight, and all you saw was that nasty ass potato salad being thrown all over the place while I chased Rachael around the cafeteria. When I finally cornered Rachael, and she had nowhere to run, I raised my plate of potato salad back to let her have it. Right when I was about to let go, a loud voice behind me said, "Estrada, Stop!" I recognized the voice and froze in place like a statue.

It was the Dean, and as I turned to see him, by the look on his face, I could tell he was pissed. He told me, "Throw the plate in the garbage, and both of you come with me right now!"

I thought to myself, damn, I'm in for it now. The Dean had given me a chance after chance to clean up my act, and I blew it again. As we were walking to his office, I was trying to explain to him that she had started the whole thing by pouring potato salad into my hair. He didn't want to hear it and told me to be quiet. I couldn't talk to him, so I asked Rachel why she had done that? Now we are both in trouble. She didn't answer me. She just had a smirk on her face, and this time the dean told me to shut up, which I didn't like. When we got to his office, he took her in first. She turned around and stuck her tongue out at me as she went into his office. When she came out, the smirk was gone, and she was crying. She told me the Dean suspended her for two weeks. I said, "Good for you!" She didn't respond. I was angry for getting me in trouble with the Dean since I had not done anything to her, or so I thought.

When he called me into his office, I told him what had happened and explained that I had not done anything to her. He told me he knew why she did it, but that did not excuse me from acting the way I did. He told me I was supposed to be setting an example to others, mainly because I was in the Service Squad. He then said he was suspending me for two weeks, and I told him it was not fair since I had not hit her with the salad. He went on to say that I would have, had he not caught me in the act. What he told me next really surprised me. He told me she did that because she had a crush on me, and I never paid attention to her.

Rachael was a pretty girl with long black hair, but I never knew she liked me. I didn't care at that moment.

All I cared about was my midterm tests coming up, which I would miss, and I would have to attend summer school. I told him if he suspended me, I would drop out of school. He told me it was up to me and that it was his responsibility to punish me as well. I was not happy about that. I was highly pissed as I stormed out of his office, cursing up a storm. I caught up with Rachael on the way out, and I asked her why she couldn't just tell me that she liked me. She got upset that the Dean had told me and said: "I don't like you; why do you think I poured potato salad on your head?" I didn't get girls back in those days, and I probably still don't; it's like you can never make them happy because the minute you do, Kabong, they do something mean just because they are P.M.S.ing or something. Thanks to her, I said we would both miss our midterms, and I was not planning on going to summer school and was dropping out.

She stopped dead in her tracks, turned around, and told me that I couldn't do that. I asked her why, and she said she was sorry, that she knew it was a stupid thing to do, but her friends dared her to do it.

Well, if they dared you to jump off the Brooklyn Bridge, would you do it? That was how I responded to her. "You're so stupid. I did it because you never paid any attention to me, and I do like you, which is why I don't want you to drop out!" Well, if you can tell me now that you like me, why couldn't you just do that on a dare, as opposed to pouring that smelly ass potato salad on my head?

She looked down, and again, she said she was sorry, and I usually would have forgiven her. I was so angry I couldn't even continue talking to her. I told her I would never speak to her again and that I would never come back to that stupid school, and then I walked the other way in anger.

Yes, boys are stupid, but it's more of a macho thing for us Latinos; it's pride mixed with stupidity, which makes it worse.

I didn't want to hurt her, but I was angry and wasn't thinking straight. Had I known that I would never see her again, I probably wouldn't have been so mean to her. Some things stay with you, and as a direct result, I have never forgiven myself for saying such mean things to her when all she wanted all along was my attention.

When I got home, I immediately told my parents what had happened. I also told them I was quitting school and joining the Marines.

As you already know, I had gotten the idea from Batman & Robin, officers Ricio & Stamp, who had a significant influence on me because they wanted to see me do something positive with my life. Although I was hesitant because I loved dancing and knew I would miss my friends, I knew I would end up dead soon if I stayed on the streets much longer. I spoke with my cousin, whom we all called Tarzan, and asked him to join with me on the Buddy Plan, which meant we would take basic training and get deployed together, so at least I would not be alone. Ismael Quiles was his name; we called him Tarzan because he was a good diver and a great athlete. We decided to enlist together and went to the recruiting station on Fordham Rd in the Bronx.

We both passed the entrance exam, and on the day we were going to swear in, a Captain interviewed us both. He asked me if I smoked weed, and I said no. When he asked my cousin, he told the Captain he smoked marijuana on special occasions, and that's when we got the bad news.

He told Tarzan the Marines could not accept him because he was a drug user. I was very upset when he told me that he would not be going with me because it meant I would be alone. I was sworn in that day and told I would be taking my basic training on Parris Island, S.C. All my friends were sad that I was leaving, but they wanted to give me a great sendoff, so they threw a going-away party for me at a friend's house in the Projects. I dropped a tab of Acid that night and started bugging out at the party. I almost fell out the window of the 16th floor of the Projects where my friend lived. Believe it or not, the one that pulled me back in was my cousin Tarzan, who was flying high himself.

The neighborhood I once lived in became a heap of ashes. The sad part is, nobody cared!

The picture below is Wilkins Ave; I lived in 1301, the first building on the left. It all burned down a short time after we left. All the other buildings down that strip suffered the same fate but were eventually rebuilt.

From left to right: Cabeza (RIP) Moses Martinez, Willie Estrada, and my cousin Ismael (Tarzan) Quiles was shot in the head and killed in 1988 by a drug dealer right in front of his 5-year-old son. We always remember you with great sadness for the senseless way you died! (RIP)

CHAPTER NINE:

WE NEVER PROMISED YOU A ROSE GARDEN

It was a cold and windy morning in February when I left the Bronx for Boot Camp in South Carolina. I had never flown alone, so I was a bit anxious because I didn't know what to expect when I got there. When we landed in South Carolina, I had to take a bus to Parris Island, and several other recruits came from different parts of the East Coast whom I guessed I would be going through Boot camp. I was not very happy to be there because I thought I had no friends there, and Tarzan was not with me. When we were getting on the bus, the bus driver started yelling at us, and for me, that made it real. At any rate, I never liked being yelled at, and it was evident on my face, so he just yelled at me even louder. On the road to Parris Island, I began to regret joining the Marines, but I knew I had no choice now, so I just sat back and closed my eyes and thought about what I had left behind.

I was a young ghetto kid, and at 17 years old, I had no discipline. I knew I was in for a rough time, and I wasn't happy about it. I gathered strength by saying that I would represent the South Bronx and my people with courage and honor, but I would not be taking any shit from anyone. Or so I thought. When we got to Parris Island, Drill Instructors (D.I's) waited for recruits to arrive.

The minute I stepped off, all hell broke loose, and the yelling started again. "Move faster, you maggots. Your little ass is mine now." I thought to myself, oh no, it's not!

I started giving the D.I.'s attitude from the minute I got off that bus, something which would prove to be futile and detrimental to my health, as well, and my limbs. The first thing they made us do was form ranks, and they started calling out our names one by one. There were about 30 of us on that bus, enough men, or boys in my case, to make up a Platoon. "You are now members of Platoon 314. My name is Sgt. Toomey. You will address me with a Yes Sir when I speak to you. No is not an option; you belong to me now."

After his little speech, he introduced us to Sgt. Ryan, who looked just as mean. Our Senior Drill Instructor's name was Gunnery Sgt. Cartwright. He was short like me and was soft-spoken as he addressed us, but I wasn't fooled. I could tell he was a badass. He was in charge, and that was evident from the get-go. Ryan was just, as I suspected, a mean SOB, and I didn't like him from the start, and it showed in my face when I grilled him hard. The first thing we're going to do is take you for a haircut. You're not hippies anymore, and those mops on your heads are coming off. Sgt. Ryan approached a recruit with long hair and asked him, "What are you, a hippy or a rock star?" As the tall white boy started to respond, Sgt. Ryan said, "Shut your pie hole; that was a rhetorical question; it doesn't need a response." Listen up, ladies, your former lives are over, you aren't in Kansas anymore, and your asses now belong to my beloved Marine Corps and me." As he continued giving us the drill, he approached me, and I immediately put a look on my face that said, don't mess with me. He noticed, got close to me, and started screaming at me like he would hit me or something. I did not like that very much, and I gave him a major attitude and told him to get the hell out of my face.

I had forgotten where I was; he immediately got close to my face and started hitting me on the forehead with the brim of his Smokey, which is what they call the brimmed hats the Drill Instructors wore. He asked me where I was from, and when I said the South Bronx, he said, "Well, I'm from Brooklyn, and I will kick your sorry ass if you ever fuck with me again, you got that maggot? Now give me a yes, sir!" I was almost reluctant, but I could tell he would probably kick my ass if I didn't, so out came, "Yes, Sir!" He said, I can't hear you since; apparently, I had not said it loud enough, and so I let out a loud "YES SIR!"

I knew right there and then that I had to get with the program, I had joined the Marine's which I knew was the most challenging branch of the military services, and for me, they were the best. We trained hard every day for the next three months, and I got into the best shape of my young life. I also proved that I would be a good Marine when I won the obstacle training course with the fastest time in my Platoon.

I also qualified as an expert marksman on the Rifle Range, which I was pleased about because I got props from my Drill Instructors. The Senior Drill instructor held a meeting one day, and he made us all sit on the floor of our Barracks and started telling us about Vietnam and the possibility of us going there. Now, by 1974, they had stopped sending Marines over there to fight, but they were preparing us for war nonetheless. He then asked who wanted to go home to see who didn't want to be there. A few hands went up, which made him angry, and he called them all a bunch of cowards.

It's true when they say, we never promised you a rose garden, the training was hard, and we were not allowed to watch TV or listen to the radio either.

There was no co-ed, only a bunch of hicks from the sticks mostly, but a few of us from big cities as well. Some recruits couldn't take it, and they would try to escape from Parris Island; many of them would later be found dead, killed by snakes or crocs. One guy even jumped off the roof of the Barracks and killed himself. There was another guy who wanted me to break his back so he could go home. He showed me a picture of his girlfriend, who was very beautiful, by the way, and said he wanted to go back to her. One Sunday afternoon, after we came back from Church, which was a Sunday ritual, we started cleaning the Barracks, and he insisted that I break his back. I told him if I broke his back, I would get in trouble, and he would not be able to walk again.

One guy even told him, "If you break your back, you won't be able to screw your girlfriend anymore, but if you like, I can do that for you; she's hot."

We all started laughing but tried to keep the noise down; our D.I. was in his room, and we were at the end of the Barracks, but if he heard us, he would come out and scream at us for sure. Anyway, even after trying to convince him not to do it, he said he didn't care. I told him OK, bend over, and when he did, I walloped him on his back with the heel of my boot, which I had taken off. He started crying and fell to the floor. I had not broken his back, nor was I trying to; I only wanted him to see what would happen. After that, he changed his mind, and the Drill Instructors never found out.

After almost three months of training, we were nearly finished, and the worse was behind us, or so I thought. One night one of our Drill Instructions came in drunk at 2 am and woke us all up but kept the lights off. He started making us do sit-ups and pushups while still in our racks, and after that, he started doing rifle checks. As he went down the row, making sure the padlocks securing our M16s were all locked, he found one open on the rack next to where I was. He got furious, started screaming bloody hell, but when he got to my bunk and found my bunkie's M16's lock open as well, he went ballistic. Sgt. Cartwright started hitting other recruits with the stock of the M16, and everyone started running from him. When he went after me, I tried getting away from him by jumping from one side of my bunk to the other.

What a mistake that was. Before I got to the other side of the bunk, and my right leg was still on the bunk, Sarge cracked me across my right knee cap with the stock of the M16 and dislocated it. I started screaming from the pain, and I couldn't run from him. Right about the time he was going to hit me again, one of my friends named Muncie, who was from Alabama, jumped him from behind, and a few others helped wrestle him to the ground. They held him there while others called for help. The MP's came, handcuffed him, and took him away, and the ambulance came to take me to the hospital. I was in a lot of pain, so they did an X-Ray on me, and as it turns out, he had knocked my Knee Cap out of its socket. I was in the hospital for a few days, and in the end, they told me I would need an operation to fix my injury. The only problem was that they said I would never walk properly again if I had the surgery.

I asked them what my other option was, and they told me it would probably get better on its own, so long as I didn't do any strenuous exercise. The Doctor wrapped up my knee and gave me a pair of crutches to get around, and then I was taken to Casualty Platoon. After a week or so, I was told I would be held on Parris Island on legal hold until Sgt. Cartwright's court-martial, and then I would be going home with an Honorable Discharge under medical conditions. After I had gone through all that hard training, and I knew I would have made an exemplary Marine, I was now injured and incapable of executing my duties as a Marine on the battlefield.

The Marines no longer wanted me, and I was distraught. After all the hard work I had put in, my dream of being a Marine was now over. They made arraignments for me to go home to visit my family for two weeks and told me when I came back, I would have to testify against Sgt. Cartwright. I was very angry with him for injuring me and killing my dream because it meant I would be returning home to a different type of war.

Home on leave

When I got home on leave, what should have been a happy homecoming after graduation was instead just coming back to the same old ugly, and violent world from which I tried to escape. The surrounding neighborhoods were still burning, and all you heard all day and night were Fire Trucks & Police Sirens, not to mention the sirens from Ambulance trucks, taking victims to the hospital or the morgue.

I had lost a few friends to gang violence in the past, and I was sick of hearing, "Guess who got shot, stabbed, or bludgeoned to death?"

I was only 17 years old, but I had seen enough death and violence to last me ten lifetimes by that age. To be honest, before I left for the Marines, I had not even given that much thought, as it had become a way of life for my friends and me.

For some reason, I felt different now, I had a new sense of pride, and I was also tired of the old ways. I knew I had to go back to Parris Island one last time, but I wanted to establish something new when I came back. I went to see Henry, the Supreme President of the Imperial Bachelors, and let everyone know I was home on leave. I wore my uniform the first day I got back, as I was proud of my Rifle Expert's Badge and my National Defense Medal. I wanted everyone to see me in uniform so they would know that I was proud to be a Marine, even though I knew I would not be one for much longer. As I started walking down the street on my way to St. Mary's, people I knew started greeting me and telling me how good I looked in uniform. When I got to St. Mary's, I was greeted like a returning hero and got an extra big hug from Rita Pasquelagua. She told me how proud she was of me. It brought a big smile to my face because I cared about her. She had been one of the best mentors I had ever had. When Dorka, the President of the Bachelorettes, saw me, she said, wow, you look like a real Marine Boy. That's what I'm going to call you from now on, and then she started laughing as she gave me a big bear hug.

Dorka and I were born on the same day, September 24th, and we were very close. She was probably one of the toughest females I've ever known. She was so crazy she would fight with guys with no fear in her heart. She was fearless with a twist of crazy, that's for sure.

Her brother JJ was always with her. He and I were good friends, and he was also a member of the Imperial Bachelors. Willie Marine Boy came out of JJ's mouth as he greeted me, and from that moment on, that was my new nickname. When I finally saw Henry, he was pleased to see me, and the greeting was, "Our War Lord has returned."

Dorka protested, "No, he's Marine Boy now, and he's in uniform, Henry, so don't suck him back in." Dorka was a year younger than me, but she was like a big sister. Henry told her I would always be a Bachelor, but not to worry, he had bigger plans for our future. Before I left for the Marines, even though I was involved with gangs, dancing was another way of escaping for us. We frequented many house parties, and in 1973 we were already cultivating the first six-step Hustle, which we had added a lot more turns and spins to the dance. The first Hustle before the six-step version was simple and intended to bring male and female partners together through social dancing, which was more acceptable to parents in terms of house parties and how their young teenage girls danced with the guys. In the early stages, the dance lacked turns and intricate steps. It was sensual and sexy when dancing very closely with a partner.

That first version was short-lived, as the dance morphed into what was known as the Push and Pull Hustle, which utilized the 5 step approach in 1973. Later that same year, the first 6-step hustle was created, better known as the Rope Hustle, implementing simple turns and spins. In 1974, the Latin Hustle was born, and it spread quickly.

The new version was a 6-step dance combining turns and fancy spins and exciting. A new era of dance was born in New York City, spearheaded by Puerto Rican teenagers within our community. Some of the most famous artists were capitalizing on the disco explosion using all the buzz words in their lyrics like "Latin Hustle, Spanish Hustle, Do the Hustle".....

As the music caught up with this dance craze, the competition became a lot more intense, and inevitably, the Hustle gained global prominence on the pages of History. A few of the 1st generation Hustle dancers led the way, such as Billy Fajardo. They started adding lifts and tricks to the Hustle, taking it to a whole new level. The Latin Hustle remains the last original partners' dance created in New York City.

Billy Fajardo and Sandra Rivera of the Dance Dimensions – Circa late 1970s

Willie Estrada and Millie Silva (The Latin Symbolics Dance Company) performing the Latin Hustle.

Circa 1976

Imperial Bachelors in 1973 Gus Martinez and Willie Rivera with President of the Bachelorettes Dorca Laguer.

Above, Cabeza (RIP), Odalys, Moe, Nestor, Apache (RIP), Tarzan (RIP), Guz, and me. Gone but never forgotten!

CHAPTER TEN: THE PLAN FOR PEACE

Henry had been doing small jams for us since before I had left to the Marines, and now that I was back home, he wanted to do these jams regularly on Tuesdays and Thursdays at St. Mary's Center. I told him I would be coming home for good soon, and he wanted me to help him build it up because he knew I had already been hanging out at the clubs with Moses and Willie Whip, and we were very popular. The 310½ was the club we frequented the most in the early 70s, but I suddenly recalled the first time I went to my first downtown club.

It was called the Fresh, and supposedly that is where all the best dancers went to a party. Moses Martinez had started teaching me how to Rock in 1972 when we moved into the same building. The first time he took me to go dance Rock with him was at the Fresh. It was a lot bigger than 310½, and I was initially scared to dance because many good dancers were there. I was standing with my back against the wall when Moses found me, and he asked me what the hell I was doing standing there by myself. He grabbed my arm and said, "Come on, we're going to Rock." I was hesitant, but he insisted, and before I knew it, we were standing on the dance floor, and he started Rocking in front of me, so I just followed his lead. The song playing was "Who is He" by Creative Source, which I liked to Rock to. We started doing some of the same steps together, and before long, a few girls were watching us Rock.

It was like an addiction after that. I was no longer afraid to Rock. We ended up meeting a couple of cute girls and hung out with them for the rest of the night.

Anyway, as Henry told me about his plans, I started getting excited and sharing my ideas with him. After our meeting was over, many more of my friends were there now, and they were all pleased to see me when I went back outside. We made plans to hang out that night, and I went home to change into my civilian clothes. When I got back, I changed and put on a pair of jeans and a Maine Corps T-Shirt but right as I was about to go down to get my best friend Tony, the phone rang. I was home now, and as excited as I was, I picked up the phone and said hello. The voice on the other end asked me if this was the Estrada residence, and I said, "Yes." He wondered if it was the Eduardo Estrada residence. Again I said, "Yes," who's this, but he asked who I was, so I told him I am his son. Then I asked him again who was calling, to my surprise, he said, "This is your oldest brother Eduardo Estrada Jr." I was a bit surprised because even though I knew I had three older brothers, I had never met the eldest son from my father's first wife. I asked him where he's been, and he told me he had not seen my father since he was a young boy. He then told me he was on a layover at Kennedy Airport on his way to Germany. He was in the Army and was going there with his family, wife, and daughter, and wanted to see our father before he left. I told him we had just come from the airport earlier that day and that I was in the Marines.

I was happy to be speaking to my eldest brother, but I knew he wanted to talk to my father, so I put him on the phone.

My father got a bit emotional because he had not seen or spoken to his eldest son since he divorced his mother. When my father got off the phone, he asked me if I wanted to go with him to the airport and of course, I said "Yes," and mom came with us as well. He told my father he would be at the International Flights Terminal, and when we showed up, I went inside first. It wasn't long before I saw someone who looked just like my dad, and I went up to him as he was standing there with his wife and young daughter. He looked at me and said, "You're my brother Willie aren't you?" I started laughing and told him I knew he was since he looked so much like dad. My father and mother got there soon after, and it was a happy reunion. We stayed with Eddie, which he called himself, and I was glad to finally get to meet my eldest brother, whom I had heard about since I was a young boy.

It was an emotional meeting for my father, but he was thrilled to have seen his eldest son all grown up and in the Army, married and doing well. He asked him to write and stay in touch before we left. Eddie agreed and told us he would never lose contact with us again. As he walked away towards the gates, he turned around one last time, waved at Dad, and told him he loved him and would never forget him.

My father told me how he had missed him growing up because his mother moved to Chicago when they got divorced, and he was not allowed to have the address or phone number and never got to know his eldest son. I could tell those events saddened him, but he was equally happy that my brother found him after all those years, and they would build a relationship again in the near future. Dad was teary but had a pleasant smile on his face as he waved goodbye, and then he was gone. I wondered if we would ever see him again. He seemed like a good man, and I felt sad that he had not known my father, who was also a good man and a great father.

It had been a bittersweet meeting, and I could tell my mom was glad my dad got to see his son.

When we got back to the neighborhood, a building was on fire right up the block from where we lived. Not something out of the ordinary considering where we lived, but as it turns out, an older woman named Mercedes, who had been taking care of her grandkids, couldn't get out in time and died from smoke inhalation that day. She was a lovely old lady who had a few kids of her own, but sadly, nobody was home to help them get out when the fire broke out that day.

This time it was more tragic because two young kids had died in that fire from smoke inhalation; even though it was contained, that building wouldn't survive for long. You see, the truth of the matter is, when gang members set fires, they knocked hard on apartment doors after they had lit the fire, so there would be no loss of life. Fires mainly were set at night, and some people did not wake from the knocking. They would perish in the flames of abandonment. So, in effect, landlords got away with murder during those days, but if they didn't pay the gangs for setting the fire, they would be killed. I recall the first time my family had to rush out of bed because of a fire in our building. I lived in Claremont Parkway between 3rd Ave and Fulton St. One night, at about 2 am, a neighbor coming home from work started banging on doors to wake people up so we could get out.

My father grabbed my two sisters, and my mother had me in her arms when I was only about five years old. As she went down the stairs, a fiery pile of debris fell from above right in front of us.

Mom jumped over it and landed on her feet without skipping a beat as she continued to run out of the building. I was scared, but my mother was brave, which gave me courage.

She had saved both our lives that day, and I have never forgotten how horrific it was to see our building burning down that day. It had been a long and eventful day in my neighborhood, and it wasn't over yet. As I think back on the day, I returned to my community, my meeting with Henry stands out the most. You see, it seems I had also started something big when we started protecting our neighborhood. More than anything, Henry wanted to improve conditions and make peace among the other gangs in our surrounding areas and throughout the South Bronx. And so did I.

He wanted my help, and I gave him no resistance since I wanted the same things as him. Now, I had something to look forward to when I returned for good from the Marines. I shared what Henry spoke to me about with my best friends, Moses, Tony, Willie Whip, and Tarzan. They were my closest friends, and we always had each other's backs. During my two weeks home, I had gone out several times with the guys, and the 310½ was still our favorite place to hang out. There were always a lot of pretty girls and the best dancers in the Bronx, without a doubt. When it was time for me to go back to Parris Island, my best friend Tony went to the airport with us.

I had to call Parris Island to let them know what flight I would be on to get picked up from the Airport and taken to Parris Island when I spoke with the duty Sgt. I didn't say "Yes sir" when responding to him, probably because Tony was standing there with me. After a couple of answers on my part without a Yes sir, the Sgt. screamed at me. He then asked me if I had forgotten my training already and asked for a "Yes, sir." I then snapped my heels together and responded with a loud "Yes, Sir." Tony jumped up and was startled. Suddenly, in my mind, I was in boot camp again, and that loud yes sir came out instinctively, but Tony did not know why until I told him. We both started laughing as he made fun of me and mimicked my quick and loud response after the Sgt. screamed at me.

It was goodbye for only a short while, and we both knew I would be back soon, so I just said, "See you later, Alligator." And he, of course, responded, "After a while, crocodile." As I reflected on my visit, I realized something was different. What I didn't know at the time was how other things would be upon my return because my thought process had changed considerably.

1974

Willie Estrada and Willie Martinez

From gang leader to U.S. Marine – Semper Fi...

CHAPTER ELEVEN:

THE COURT-MARTIAL OF SGT. CARTWRIGHT

When I got to Parris Island, I got there late at night, and as I got close to the Barracks where I had to report, I ran into a sentry. "Halt who goes there," said the recruit on guard duty. "Private Estrada," I replied. "Private Estrada advance to be recognized." As I approached, I could tell he was nervous; it was apparent he had never actually had to stop someone while on guard duty. I decided to have a little fun with him. When I was right in front of him, he asked me for my Military ID Card. So as I was about to hand it to him, I dropped it on purpose.

When he looked at me with a clueless look on his face, I said, "Well, pick it up, recruit" he was under the impression that I was already a staff Marine, so when he hesitated, I raised my voice, "I said pick it up Recruit!" He bent over and picked it up, and I let him have it; I said, "What are you stupid? Suppose I was someone trying to take advantage of you and take your M16?" If I had been out here to hurt you, you would have been injured. He got scared like I would report him or something, and then I laughed. I could tell he was from the sticks, so I told him I am Private Estrada and just got back from leave, but I have not finished Bootcamp, I was 3rd Phase, but I'm not going to tell anyone. He still had a confused look on his face, but I told him I wasn't kidding, so he could relax. He said, "Dam, you got me. Please don't tell anyone."

I just shook my head and walked away; as it turns out, he was a recruit and had no business being on guard duty as far as I was concerned.

I had done it myself several times, and I got approached only once, but I was also from New York, so my entire mentality was different from many guys in my unit. It takes a long time to become a good Marine, especially those from the sticks.

Once I was checked in, I was sent back to Casualty Platoon, and I was told I would soon be appearing at Sgt. Cartwright's Court Martial. At this point, I just wanted to get it over with, so I could go back home and get together with Henry and the rest of my guys. But, let's not forget the girls. The best thing about Casualty Platoon is that we had no training, so we would just hang out and talk shit, and at times we would dance. You see, in a regular Platoon, we couldn't have a radio or a TV, but in Casualty Platoon, we had both.

Sometimes, I would go to the back of the barracks and teach the guys how to dance rock, and many of them had no rhythm, but there was one guy there who learned pretty quickly. His name was Ruben Torres; he was a Puerto Rican from Brooklyn. He was due to get a Section 8, which meant he was crazy, but boy, could he dance. Funny how when he wasn't speaking to the D.I., he acted normal, but it's like I said, some guys just weren't cut out to be Marines. When he danced, he did crazy moves, but we all knew he was completely sane.

Don't get me wrong, he played his part well but told me once why he wanted to go back home to Brooklyn. First of all, he was young but a couple of years older than me. He told me the story of how he stabbed a guy because he got fresh with his girlfriend at school.

Ruben was a high school dropout and didn't attend school, but he always picked up his girl after school.

One day when he didn't pick her up, some guy from her school got fresh with her and grabbed her ass after rejecting his advances. She slapped him, and he punched her in the face causing a black eye.

She told Ruben about it when he went to see her, and he got furious when he saw her black eye. He got some of his boys together and went looking for the guy, grabbed her ass, and hit her. She told Ruben the guy's name and where he lived, not far from where they lived. When he got to the guy's block, he found him at the Basketball court and ran up to him without saying a word and stabbed him several times, then ran off. As it turns out, the kid didn't die, but now they were hunting for Ruben, so he joined the Marines to get away from his neighborhood. At least, that is what he told me. I asked him if the Police were after him, and he said, "No, we don't snitch in Brooklyn; we get even!" I could relate to that, so I left it alone, and we never spoke about it again. After that conversation, I could tell he was just a little crazy, so his section 8 was probably well deserved. Not that it's a good thing, because it meant his discharge from the Marines would be, an-other than Honorable Discharge, and that's not good.

On the other hand, I was getting an Honorable Discharge under medical conditions, and my discharge would say, Honorable Discharge USMC. Casualty Platoon was a big party, but we still had to take orders, even though we never had the same D.I's from week to week. No serious Drill instructor wanted to be a part of it, and they called us the "Lame Ducks of the Marines," or the Retards. It was a title I did not like because I was there through no fault of my own.

The morning I was going to court for Sgt. Cartwright's Court-martial, I was both excited and a bit nervous. I knew I would have to point my finger at Sgt. Cartwright, and while I didn't like what he did to me, I also knew he was a good Marine.

He had served our country well, done three tours in Vietnam, and had the scars and the medals to prove it. He was a bit crazy, considering he had done three tours and seen many violent deaths. I would say he was afflicted. Either way, I was not looking forward to testifying; however, I knew I would be going home after my testimony, so I wanted to be done with that. As I sat there waiting to give my statement, Sgt. Cartwright was brought in with shackles on his hands and feet. I felt sorry for him because I knew he would probably be convicted and sentenced to a Military Jail or prison. I guess that's what happens when you get drunk and do something stupid because you were not in your right frame of mind. I believe it's called dereliction of duty or conduct unbecoming.

Oh sure, you regret it later, but what's done is done, and now he would have to pay the piper. When I finally got called to the stand, they asked me to recount the events of that night. After I told my story, they asked me to point out the person responsible for my injury, and sadly I did. Sgt. Cartwright had a look of remorse on his face. They asked him why he had done what he did and said he had a flashback from Vietnam because he had been drinking that night. He told us that he thought he was back in the bush and how discipline needed to be kept, or people would die.

The judge told him there was no good excuse for his behavior and for hurting a couple of other recruits, with me getting the brunt of the blow, of course. In the end, they court-martialed him and busted him down to Corporal. I gave him a nod as I left, and I believe he knew I held no animosity towards him.

However, they could have given him time since he was the recipient of the Silver Star, a couple of Purple Hearts, and satiations for bravery, so they let him off lightly. I was glad they weren't too harsh on him, mainly because he had apologized for hurting me and ending my Military Career as a Marine before it got started. The following day, they sent me to a different part of Parris Island. I had never seen where they prepared my discharge papers and gave me a haircut. Since I had been in the 3rd Phase of Training, I got a 3rd Phase Haircut, while many others who were being sent home got a crew-cut. I was there for two days while all my paperwork was done, but I had to go home by bus, which was a long 22-hour ride, but I was happy.

I forgot to mention that the Vietnam conflict was not a popular war, so whenever I traveled in uniform, I was never greeted in a friendly way. They considered Vietnam vets to be baby killers and called us ugly names for the most part. I had not been to Vietnam, thank God, but that was enough for most men when in uniform. Goodbye, Parris Island; I will never forget my time there. My memories of Parris Island will always be bittersweet, but I am glad I went through the training. They instilled the meaning of teamwork, discipline, honor, and pride I still carry around with me to this day.

Fire watch duty - Parris Island 1974

Don't ask me how someone snuck a camera into the
barracks because I simply do not recall. All I know is,
had we been caught, I wouldn't have this great picture!

CHAPTER TWELVE: THE BIRTH OF ST. MARY'S JAMS

1974 Honorable Discharge from USMC "Honey I'm home" has always been my greeting when entering my mother's house, but it was extra special on this occasion. The first thing I wanted to eat was some of my mom's home cooking.

My homecoming was a promising one, but most importantly, my mother was proud of me, which gave me pride in myself. I was only 17 years old and had already experienced things that many others of my age could only imagine. The truth is, there was a new passion in my life that had been a long time coming, and yet, it was always there. It was a Saturday afternoon at about 1 pm, and everyone knew I was coming home that day because my mother had already told Tony about it.

I left Parris Island the day before by bus and arrived in New York the following day from South Carolina. I took the train from 42nd St. with my duffle bag full of momentums from my short time in the Marines, and I was happy to be home.

There were still fires being set by the gangs, which the Landlords paid off. Yet, there were also buildings being constructed in place of those which had gotten torched. When I got back, I found out that a landlord had been killed for not paying gang members who had burned down a couple of his buildings in our area. One of my friends showed me where he was dumped in St. Mary's Park down a water well in the park.

He also told me how a rival gang member had been hung from a tree in St. Mary's Park.

It seems I had come back to the same old shit, and I knew I had to do something about it; if not, I would fall to the streets. I was excited about Henry's ideas for throwing jams at St. Mary's Center, so I went to speak to him soon after I arrived home. As it turns out, Henry had been waiting for me to return so that we could talk to Rita, the Center Manager, Rita Pasquelagua, and get her permission to host the parties at the Center on Tuesday's and Thursday's.

Now that I was home, Henry involved me with all his plans. He knew I could help since I was already very popular and knew many people.

Don't get me wrong; Henry could have done it without me; however, we were very close, and he trusted me to carry out his orders and help him build up the jams.

When I got to St. Mary's, things were a bit quiet, and I was surprised that I didn't see any of my friends there. All except one, my best friend Tony, and when he saw me, he was pleased I was there. He told me the guys were in a meeting, and he had been waiting for me.

Tony and I went upstairs to attend the meeting, or so I thought. When he opened the door to the game room, there was a loud cheer and a banner that read, "Welcome Home Marine Boy."

I was surprised and had no idea my friends had gone through so much trouble to welcome me home. Everyone was there; all my closest friends and even Rita were there to greet me, as were many of the staff from St. Mary's. Henry had set up the speakers and the phonograph, and the first song he played was "Date with the Rain" by Eddie Kendricks. Henry knew that was one of my favorite songs to dance to because it was one of the songs I used to practice with Moses and Willie Whip, who had become my Rock Partner before I left for the Marines. It was a homecoming I would never forget. The gang was all there, I was happy to be home, and life was good. The Gang was all together again, only now it was more about dancing than gang banging with Henry leading the way.

After we partied for a while, Rita called Henry and all the gang leaders into her office to discuss hosting parties at St. Mary's on Tuesdays and Thursdays on a larger scale. The idea was to bring peace to our neighborhood and invite others throughout the surrounding areas to enjoy peace through dance.

She shared her conditions and terms with us, which were non-negotiable as she broke down the rules.

We agreed to everything she asked of us. One of her biggest concerns was making sure there were no fights. Peace was Henry's most significant reason for putting these parties together, and it was the reason Black Tony had left Henry in charge before going to prison. It was his last wish before going away for a long time.

A little-known fact is that Henry De Sosa, Supreme President of the Bachelors, was the person responsible for putting those Tuesday & Thursday night parties together. I was Henry's right-hand man, and so was the Vice President, who we called Sad Eyes. It was understood that the Bachelors would set an example and act as security to make sure everyone was safe, and we conducted ourselves respectfully at all times. We had to give Rita our word and promise her nothing terrible would happen, which we all agreed to. I gave Rita my word, as Warlord of the Imperial Bachelors, which I still was, even though I had been away for several months, and she was content.

Rita trusted Henry and me, and she believed in us most importantly. After we met with Rita, Henry called a meeting of our division of the Imperial Bachelors. We discussed the promotions of our jams and the rules of conduct. We initially made posters, but we only posted them at the Center. We had already decided to do most of the promotions by word of mouth and phone calls to family and friends. Our main gang rivals were welcome to come so long as they did not start any trouble, behaved themselves, and didn't wear gang colors.

There was the promise of peace, which Henry made clear from the very beginning, and he would speak to everyone about it, which included the other divisions of our gang. I mention the other divisions because some of them were just a bit crazier than most and would often start trouble with other rival gangs.

Henry, however, gave them a stern warning about starting trouble, and he was the Supreme President, so they had to show him respect, which he had earned, long before he became the Supreme President of the Bachelors. Once we picked our start date, which was the following week, Henry insisted on having tight security out in front of the Center. Our Division was allowed to wear our gang colors as a sign of force and intimidation. This was our home turf, and we would protect it at all costs. He told us he wanted to make sure everyone knew we were in charge and wouldn't tolerate violence by anyone.

Remember that St. Mary's Center was built right on 145th St. and St. Ann's Ave. It was a part of St. Mary's Park, which was a square mile, and we were in the middle of the St. Ann's street side of it. There were no lights in the park back in those days, so if some had the balls, they could shoot at us and escape into the darkness of the park. Henry thought of everything to ensure everyone would be safe in our neighborhood. He placed sentries on the backside of St. Mary's behind the big formation of rocks close to the entrance as scouts to make sure nobody snuck upon us. Now, some of you might find this a bit strange, but back in the early 1970s, the South Bronx was a war zone, and violence was a way of life for us.

The violence in our neck of the woods was terrible, which is why Rita asked a couple of our neighborhood police officers to stop by from time to time to check on things. Batman & Robin were already around, but there was also another cop whom we always respected, and he was a badass. His name was Chuck, which he allowed us to call him, but we always called him Big Chuck because he was a tall brother. All our plans were in motion, and I was so honored and excited to be coming home to this movement executed by Henry De Sosa and even happier that he had involved me as soon as I came home. That same night we all went to the 310½ because promotions for the jams at St. Mary's were left to my closest friends, which were Tony, Willie Whip, Moses, Tarzan, and me.

When we got to 310½, I saw lots of my party friends, whom I knew from 310½, as that was the club where all the best dancers went. Remember that this was in mid-1974, and we had been regulars at the 310½ before I went away, so I knew just about everyone who partied there. We put the word out about the St. Mary's Jams and invited everyone wherever we went, including the best dancers from Manhattan and the Bronx. Names like Eddie Ramundi, Rubberband, Mejico, Salsa, and Dee Dee, as well as every single pretty girl we met a clubs and on the street.

I first met Dee Dee at St. Mary's Center in 1972. I had not seen him dance at the time, but he was well respected throughout my neighborhood and had a reputation as the best Rocker from our community. The first time I saw him dance was at 310½, and I liked what I noticed right away.

He was an incredibly smooth and stylish dancer and did lots of really cool spins. That is where I first saw Rubberband and several others who were great Rock Dancers. I did not dance with them initially; I was just learning and did not dare get on the same floor with them at the time. When we got to the 310½ Tommy Cuevas, the owner was at the door, and he greeted us in a friendly manner as he always did. He asked me why he had not seen me in so long, and I told him I had just gotten back from the Marines. He let me in for free, so I saved $3 bucks on admission.

The 310½ was right off Prospect Ave under the elevated 2 & 5 trains on Westchester Ave, and Tommy owned the building. It was on the second floor, and the Salsa section was on the 3rd floor, where Tommy hung out the most since he was a great Salsa dancer. When we walked in, the old gang was all there, and I was home.

I was greeted left and right, and after a short while, I knew I was home. DJ Javier was also a classmate of mine from Morris High School, so the minute he saw me, he played one of my favorite songs, "Zing went the strings of my heart." I danced the Hustle with a girl named Arlene who came running to me when she saw me and grabbed me by the hand, and we went off to the dance floor. The great thing about dancing with the girls at 310½ was that they also danced Rock, so we sometimes switched from Hustle to Rock.

There was no alcohol served at the 310½, only soda, water, and juices, so we would go outside and buy beer, smoke a few joints, and come back in to dance the night away.

The guys and I told everybody that St. Mary's would be hosting Jam's starting that coming Tuesday and on Thursdays. By the time the night was over, everyone knew where to be on Tuesdays and Thursdays for sure, and they would invite their friends as well. During those days, we all communicated without cell phones, beepers, or the internet, and yet we always knew the spot we would meet on any given day or night.

We were young, always craving fun, and had a network of friends who spread the word about Hooky Parties and Jams primarily by word of mouth and phone. Rita wanted everyone coming into the building to be registered and have a Center Card, which cost only $1.00, so if there were a problem, she would have the member's name and address on record.

Our job was to make sure that they formed an orderly line when everyone got there and purchased a center card for the $1.00 fee, which was the price of a one-year membership before they could go into the building.

The first day was a Tuesday, and people got there early because we had told everyone they would have to get membership cards. Those who already had their cards could just walk in with no problem. The Imperial Bachelors were there in full force on the first Jam, and we were all wearing our colors; however, that would soon change. Rita was always out front with the Center's Assistant Manager Tally to ensure all was going well. Tally was a very short Jewish lady who wore thick glasses, but she commanded respect because she did not back down from anyone.

She was a brilliant woman with a major attitude, but she was polite and professional. The line was long on the first day because many new people signed up for membership cards. It was a warm and beautiful summer evening in 1974, and Rita was pleased about how smoothly things were going, as was Tally.

She told us what a great job we had done in promoting the gathering, as she called it, on such short notice. Henry was outside for a short while and left Sad Eyes and me in charge since we were also leaders of the gang, and he trusted us to make sure things went smoothly. Soon after Henry went upstairs and started the music, we could hear it clearly from downstairs. Everyone outside got excited as the music began to play, and one of the first songs we all heard was "Date with the Rain" by Eddie Kendricks. Everyone started dancing as the music blared from the open game room windows. And all of a sudden, the line was no longer straight, as the girls began to do the Hustle while most of the guys danced Rock. Rita and Tally had smiles from ear to ear, and in that instance, they knew our friends had come to dance and have fun.

It was a day I will never forget, and we all knew it was the start of something big, and the birth of a new era of music and dance in the South Bronx was born. After a while, some of the 7 Immortals showed up wearing their gang colors to the Center, and Rita told them they could not enter the building wearing gang colors. We were allies with them, but they started pointing at us and asking Rita about us wearing our colors and why they couldn't. Right then and there, Rita decided to suspend the wearing of colors for all gangs to prevent future confrontations with rival gangs.

Our allies had been able to wear their gang colors in the building before that day, which is why they made such a big stink about it, but Rita knew what she was doing, and we respected her wishes.

We all knew she was just trying to prevent future problems when she nipped it in the bud that day. She told them they could wear colors outside the building but not indoors. She asked me to let everyone know that gang colors would no longer be permitted in the building and that we had to take them all off. She said, "Starting today, colors will not be allowed in the building, even if you take them off and turn them inside out." I have to give credit to Rita. She had our best interest at heart, and everybody knew that, and we all respected her for it. Unlike Tally, Rita was tall and stocky with a deep voice that commanded respect. She was never afraid of us and was one tough cookie. But the main thing about Rita was that she genuinely cared about us, and it showed. When I finally went upstairs to let Henry know what was happening, the music smacked me in the face as soon as I walked through the door, and I fell in love with what I saw.

The crowd was festive and full of life; it was an incredible sight to behold. I had been going to the Center for many years, but I had never experienced anything like that before. Word of mouth worked like a charm. We had done well, and everyone was having a great time. Music and dance were like drugs for us, and we were all addicted. Once I got inside, I was mesmerized by the music, and it became apparent that the spirit of dance had consumed everyone.

At the front of the room, I saw guys dancing Rock, and as I made my way toward the middle. All of the best Latin Hustle dancers were there from those early days. Soon it would be my turn to show off. When I got to the back of the room, all eyes were on Henry as he played one great song after another. The music had captivated them all, even though I was on a mission to tell Henry about Rita's decision not to wear colors. I couldn't help but notice and feel all the positive energy emitted in that room. When I told Henry, he asked me to take over as DJ, which was pretty simple because we only had one phonograph at the time. I put a big smile on my face because it meant I could play whatever song I wanted to hear myself. Henry also had a great selection of 45 RPM records and two crates of LPs to choose my favorite songs to play.

The trick was changing the record quickly when one finished and making sure it was a song everyone would feel. Considering that mixers could not be purchased yet, and with only one photograph, you might think people wouldn't complain if you played a song that was off tempo from the previous song, but they always did. I chose carefully, but that was easy because I knew what I liked, and that was good enough for everyone else as well.

This scene was new to everyone and had never been done like this, or at least not in such a prominent place like St. Mary's Rec Center. When Henry played the slow jams, the lights would be dimmed, and if there were a girl there who you liked, you would hopefully get to her before someone else snatched her unless she wanted you to, then she would be the one doing the asking.

The dance floor was full of couples grinding and doing a move we called the 500, which is when you hold a girl tight and dip down while your legs are between each other's and grind tightly on the way down and on the way up. After the slow jams were over and the lights came back on, most of the guys walked around with boners and would try to hide their stiffies with their hands, while others paraded around prideful, with their manhood sticking out like a sore thumb. Some girls blushed, while others couldn't take their eyes off of the guys displaying their boners with amazement and lustful desires.

Don't get me wrong, we always danced slowly, but it was mainly at Hooky parties, gang parties, and small clubs like the 310½. We never had a place as big as St. Mary's, which was much larger than the 310½, or any of the basement clubs where we hung out. The other thing we got into doing was swimming with the girls and hosting cookouts in the back of St. Mary's Lifeguard Room. We pretty much ran St. Mary's and would even have pool parties after the center was closed and the managers left for the night. It was a fantastic time in my life. We were happy go lucky, and carefree for the most part.

But every once in a while, we still got into fights with rival gangs, none of which we would start, but we always tried to finish.

I must mention that even though the music and dance craze were getting a lot more attention during those days, the violence did continue for a short time longer.

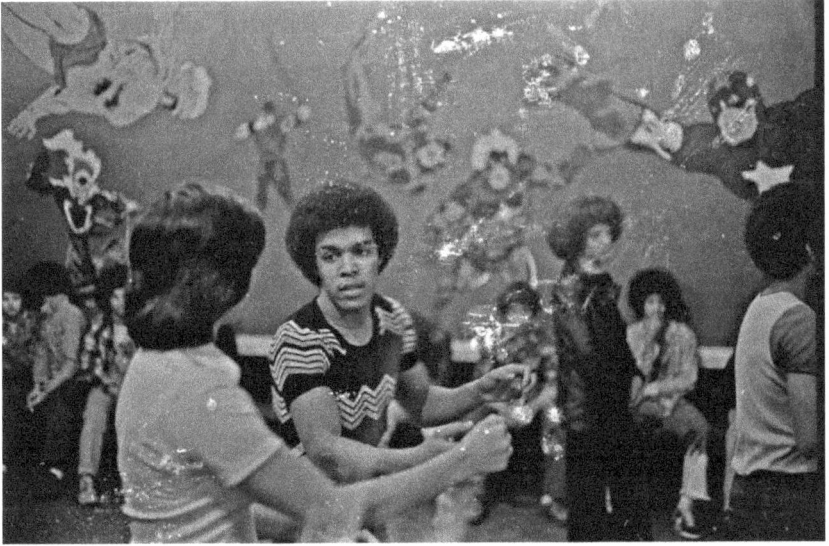

Willie Estrada and Debbie Benitez doing the Latin Hustle
at St. Mary's 1974

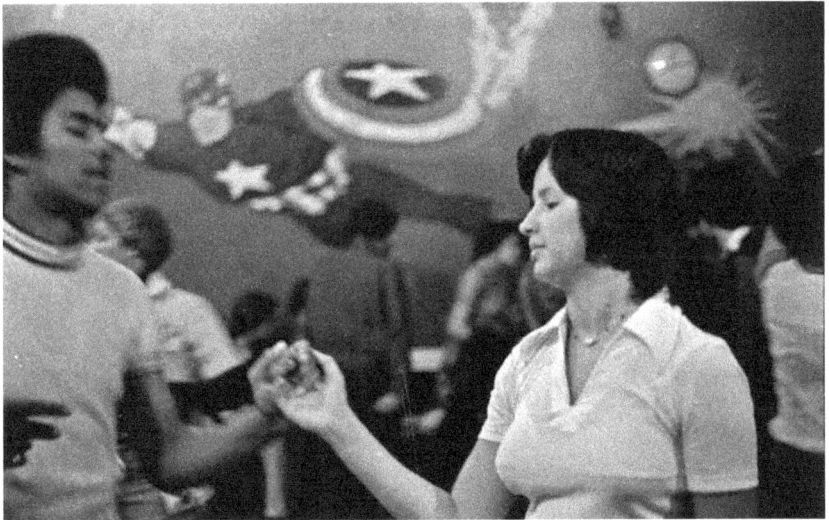

Pioneers of the Latin Hustle

Dante Wynn (RIP) & Debbie Benitez

Latin Hustle Pioneers Willie Whip and Norma at St. Mary's Recreation Center 1974

Willie and Norma doing the Latin Hustle

Sara Silva and Norma doing the Hustle above.

In a way, Rita became our savior as a result of not allowing us to wear gang colors after the first event when she made us take them off. She never let any other gang wear gang colors, whether they were allies or foes, from that day forward. The Imperial Bachelors became the first gang in the South Bronx to take off our gang colors in 1974, and we never wore them again after that day. We started dressing cooler, and the girls liked it.

After a couple of weeks being home and a few dances at St. Mary's, which were very successful, one of our guys managed to get into trouble with some guys from Courtland Ave. Naturally, we had to have his back, so there I was again, back in the middle of the bullshit I had tried to escape from. A group of about ten of us got together with Cowboy, who had a beef with his girlfriend's ex-boyfriend because he had slapped her in the face during an argument over her dating Cowboy, whom he didn't like. I didn't like the idea of getting into a fight over some girl I didn't even know, but we were brothers, and I had no choice. When we got to 153rd St. between Melrose and Courtland Avenue, Cowboy saw the guy he was looking for, and we started walking faster towards him and his boys with a chain in his hand.

When they saw us coming, one of them ran into a building, and a short while later, as we got closer, he came out with a gun and started shooting at us. Cowboy was a little crazy, and he stayed right in the middle of the street, swinging the chain over his head like a real Cowboy with a lasso.

I had to scream at him and tell him to run; she wasn't worth dying for. We weren't wearing our gang colors, so they didn't know who we were, not that it made a difference; we were on their turf. We got away without a scratch, but it was a good thing the guy couldn't shoot straight. When we got back to the block, Cowboy was not happy, and he wanted revenge at all costs. The following day we all went to Morris High School to wait for his girl to come out of summer school.

We were not in plain sight, but we waited at different parts of the school block. Cowboy waited alone by the entrance, where he knew she would exit the school, as the rest of us watched on.

We were over 20 strong and had weapons, not that I was looking to hurt anybody, but just in case.

We didn't have to wait long before Cowboy was approached by his girl's ex-boyfriend and a couple of his friends. Cowboy gave us the sign, and we all ran upon them seconds after they had gotten to him, and the ex-boyfriend started talking shit to Cowboy. He didn't know that Cowboy was packing his gun, but he never had to pull it out of his waistband. The guy had no weapon, and neither did his two friends, who were lucky since they were outnumbered 4 to 1.

As they were giving Cowboy a hard time, we surrounded them before they knew it. When they realized they were surrounded and outnumbered, they started bitching up. They had nowhere to run and knew they were at our mercy. One of our guys bent down behind the guy who had been talking the most shit, and Cowboy pushed him, and down hard he went. I never liked bullies, but neither did I want to be one, so I told them to stop and told everyone we would settle the problem with a fair fight. I knew Cowboy was a good fighter and knew he could hold his own.

I also knew how angry Cowboy was that the guy's friends had shot at us the day before. We told them we would allow a fair fight, but things would be different the next time he messed with Cowboy's girl.

Cowboy gave me his gun to hold, and the guy's eyes opened wide, and he quickly agreed that win, lose or draw, this would be the end of it. All I can say, without giving you a blow by blow, is, Cowboy kicked his ass, and when I saw he had enough, I stopped the fight. The guy was pretty banged up, but he would be all right, and we knew that would be the end of it. They found out we were part of a much bigger gang, so they also knew if they tried to retaliate, so would we. The bell rang a short while later, and summer school students came out. I thought that I had been attending Morris High and recalled being suspended because of a girl with a crush on me less than a year earlier. As we walked back to our block after Cowboys girl finally came out, he told her ex-boyfriend would not be bothering her again. She was thrilled to hear that and started kissing him wildly, so we told them to get a room, and we all laughed.

When we got back to the block, I called a meeting with all our guys. I told them I was tired of getting into fights over petty things and that we had a lot to lose if we continued with all the senseless violence. I emphasized pointing out the problem we had because of Cowboy's girlfriend.

I was tired of the stupid fights, my mentality had changed, and I wanted to do positive things going forward. I pointed out how Henry, who was also there, had established something positive that we could all be proud of, and I didn't want us to screw it up. I had already spoken to Henry about how I was feeling; he agreed with me and wanted to make a difference and bring peace through music and dance into our volatile community.

He said a few words and told us that things were going well with our jams, and he did not want to bring any problems which could jeopardize our weekly parties at St. Mary's. Everyone was ordered to be on their best behavior or else.

I spoke with Willie Whip that day, and I told him it was time for me to decide what I wanted to be going forward, like a gangster or a dancer.

It was a no-brainer for me, so I told him I wanted to start practicing with him again and enter dance contests. I always loved dancing Rock, but the Latin Hustle had gotten popular by then, and the girls were always asking Willie and me to dance with them. The first time I danced the Hustle was at a house party, but it wasn't called the Hustle yet. By late 1974 I and a few others who were also trendsetters added fancier spins, turns, and fancy footwork and developed it into a complete dance. We also added style and grace to our beloved Latin Hustle by watching the masters such as Fred Astaire and Ginger Rogers among a host of other dancers from the 30s and 40s. But we were also influenced by Salsa and Mambo dancers from the past. I danced with all the best female hustle dancers in those days, but we also danced to Rock with the girls. My friends Gladys, Debbie, Maggie, Maritza, and a couple of others used to walk from their neighborhood on Kingsbridge Road to St. Mary's. They were fanatical, and I know the spirit of dance lived within them as it did with most of us, with few exceptions. As I think back about those days, so many different things come to mind, and I feel as though I have to pick and choose what I want to convey. I share those things, which I believe will provide a vision or illustration of it.

To be honest, no other time in history were things so distinctive and unique than the era of the 1970s during my youth. There were a lot of girls who were good Rock dancers, and some were as good as the guys. Names like Candy, Anna, and Nerada, whom I also dated for a short while, but there were many others as well. As I spoke to Willie Whip about how I felt, he agreed, and we decided to practice more and eventually join a Rock Contest.

When Tuesday finally arrived, Willie and I were dying to show some of our new short routines, and that we did. During those days, Willie Whip and I created short routines, and we called them by numbers, like routines 1, 2 & 3. We would execute them during certain breakbeat parts of the song, and that night we shined. I will admit, the girls drove us crazy, always wanting to dance the Hustle with us, but we never said no. We would cut in on each other, and others would cut in as well.

A big crew of us were the best dancers, and we were all friends. The best male Hustle Dancers were Dante, Jose (Sabu), Floyd, Willie Whip, Eddie Ramundi, Click, and myself in the early days. The Best female Hustle dancers were Sara Silva, Debbie Benitez, Denise Florencio, Norma, Liz, Raleska, Gladys, and Maggie. There were many hustle dancers, but we were the best throughout the city and everywhere we went, and the girls always wanted to dance with us.

The best thing about being a good hustle dancer; the girls flocked to us like rabbits in heat. Those were the days of free love, and by that, I mean we were having sex all the time and in the strangest places.

We had a few hidden places at St. Mary's Recreation Center, but one of our favorites was a small room right after the girls' locker room entrance. We didn't always go in there to have sex; mostly, we went in there to smoke pot and drink beer because we could lock the door from the inside as well. The one thing I can say I miss the most is that we danced to slow songs with girls we had just met, and it was very sexy. Girls liked to feel the stiffness of our loins rubbing against their lower extremities, so we did that as often as we could to make them happy. Well, OK, it made us happy too, and we were like dogs always sniffing the girl's butts. We often grabbed a handful of asses as we grinded against their tender young bodies. Some of us got into it on the dance floor when dancing to slow songs, and after the song was over, you'd see a bunch of guys walking around with a stiffy. And yes, the girls also loved seeing that, and you would see them giggling when the lights came on and see some guys trying to hide the stiffy in embarrassment. We danced to songs like "The Touch of You" by Brenda and the Tabulations, "In the Rain" by the Dramatics, and a ton of other great slow jams.

I will just say that dancing slowly with the ladies was a ritual for us; there was just something intoxicating about dancing slowly with a perfect stranger and getting aroused on the dance floor. If you did it right, that girl was yours, at least for that night. As popular as we were, we didn't have regular girlfriends, but only because they all knew we were players, and all we wanted was to have fun, and as much sex as we could get, which was quite often. However, the Hustle was our passion, and we always practiced and created new moves in the hallway of the building I lived in.

As the weeks went on, I found myself captivated by my love for music and dance. I started to see significant changes, and it was notable to everyone throughout my neighborhood when we traded in our gang colors for dancing shoes. It was a gradual change, but for me, it was a cultural movement, unlike anything I had ever seen or experienced, notably when the gang violence and killings decreased by a considerable margin. The South Bronx lost the title of being the murder capital of the United States.

Perhaps it was something I saw in others, but probably because the most significant change was in me. I was always looking to create new steps and dance moves, so I started watching as many movies about dance as I could. I was fortunate that most of the TV movies at night were with Fred Astaire and Ginger Rogers, who became my favorite dancers. I loved their style and grace when they danced together and even when they danced apart. I would get up from bed during a commercial and try to do some of the moves Fred did, and since I couldn't do it like him, I would create my own rendition, which was a good thing as far as I was concerned.

I loved to watch Gene Kelly, and from time to time, I got to see the Nicholas Brothers, who were amazing to watch as well. I had the dancing bug in a big way, and it was during that time that I decided I no longer cared to be a gang member, I was in love with Dance, and that's all I wanted to do. I admit that I was impressed and influenced by dancers from my neighborhood, particularly a Rocker named Dee Dee. He was also the President of the Brothers of Satan.

I watched Dee Dee dance and battle against Rubberband regularly and improved my Rocking skills from watching them go at it. I later emulated a few of Dee Dee's steps and style, but by watching Fred Astaire tap dance, I developed my own style, steps, and moves.

During the early 1970s, and before I left for boot camp at Parris Island, we always hung out at the 310½, but thanks to Moses, we also hung out at clubs in the city. Everywhere we went, we would invite other dancers to St. Mary's, and after a short while, it was the place to be every Tuesday and Thursday. We got a lot more popular as dancers after the Hustle came out, notably by 1974 when we developed more turns and moves to the dance.

Before the Latin Hustle was born, Rock dancing had been more popular, especially at the 310½ where we danced Rock before we did the Hustle. Willie Whip & I had been practicing Rock ever since before my return from the Marines, and now we were getting ready to dance in our first Rock Contest, which was coming up. We were always together in those days, and we became the best of friends after a while.

Willie Whip was also called Willie Jackson because he resembled Michael Jackson. He and I hung out at clubs all over the city, and we dated girls from different boroughs so that we wouldn't get caught. But let's face it, most girls didn't take us seriously anyway during those days. We were players, and they all knew it. The day of the Rock Contest came, and Willie Whip and I were going against some of the best Rock Dancers from the Bronx. The one I was worried about most was Dee Dee and his partner shorty.

He was always the one I looked up to regarding Rock Dancing, along with Moses. We're still great friends more than 40 years later.

Unlike some other gangs, we always treated our girls with respect, and they loved us for it!

Ever since I was a little boy, Mom always taught me to respect my elders and treat girls the way I want others to treat my sisters.

Grandma used to say: "He who doesn't take advice will never reach old age!" RIP Grandma

Initially, many of the girls danced together because there were not that many good male Hustle dancers, and you also have to keep in mind that guys still had that gangster mentality. The Latin Hustle was not initially considered to be a Macho thing. However, there were some exceptions, and the best male Hustle dancers during the early days mainly were my friends and I, who were considered the best, and people came from all over the city to watch us do the Latin Hustle. We were a considerable influence during those early days, but guys grew out of their shy shells a short time later and started following our lead.

RIP Peaches, pictured above on the front left side.

Latin Hustle Jams at St. Mary's Recreation Center 1974

Rubberband was already an icon, even though to me, he did the coolest and the craziest drops and tricks on the dance floor. The thing is, he stayed on the ground doing floor moves.

I firmly believe, to this day, he should have been considered the first B-boy. A few others could also be called B-boys during those early days. They all did floor moves and many of the things B-boys do today. However, Rubberband was the best of those who did those floor moves. I guess it was because he could do elastic moves that nobody else could do, which is why we called him Rubberband. Other Rockers there that night were Boca and his partner Ralph, Rubberneck Ritchie, and a few others, most of which were from my neighborhood. I was very nervous because we were going up against the guys I considered the best. My partner Willie Whip was a really good Rocker, and I had come a long way since I started Rocking with Moses Martinez. Many of the girls who knew us, and hung out with us, not only at 310½ but at the clubs and St. Mary's, were all there that night.

The 310½ was packed that night, and the music was always excellent. As always, Javier kept us on the dance floor all night long. My good friends, Gladys Rodriguez & Maggie Solis, with whom I also danced the Hustle regularly, were also there. They always danced Rock with us, even when they wore heels.

Jose Sabu doing the Latin Hustle with Abby (1974)

Willie Wip & Me

My best friends Willie (Whip) above. Below are Tony, Papo, Chico, and his mom Pepa (RIP).

A Puerto Rican Band of Brothers!

Maggie Solis, my Latin Hustle partner and member of the Latin Symbolics Dance Company

Maggie was an outstanding Hustle Dancer, and she was shorter than Gladys, so she made an ideal Hustle partner for me. I was already leaning towards Hustle more than dancing Rock, but Willie Whip and I had been preparing for this contest for some time.

Willie Whip and I danced together since 1973 and were now prepared to enter our 1st contest. The 310½ was not a big place, and on a night like this, where many Rockers competed, it was a packed house. I don't remember who we beat to get into the finals, but I do remember that Dee Dee and his partner were the Rockers we were going up against. They had gone head to head with Rubberband and his partner and beaten them, and now we were the last ones standing. I was not scared anymore because I knew that, win or lose, we had made a statement already by getting to the finals. Willie and I saved a couple of our best moves for this moment, and we knew we had to execute them flawlessly to pull this off. When the music started, we faced off, and the song DJ Javier played was, It's Just Begun, and I would have to say, that was the perfect song to get us going primarily because we had danced to that song so many times. We also knew when to execute our skids, which were burning moves. Dee Dee's partner that night was a guy we called Shorty. You will hear more about him later, but that night he messed up, and we didn't, our friends went crazy as Willie Whip and I executed our short skid routines with perfect timing, style, and flavor.

When the Judges announced us as the winners, everybody went crazy, including us. I could not believe it; we had won our first Rock Contest against the Rocker I admired the most.

Not to mention that Rubberband had also been in that contest, and even though we didn't face off with him, we were the victors. Dee Dee came over and shook our hands and told us we deserved it and that we were better than them that night. Dee Dee was a class act and still is to this day.

We are still good friends after more than 40 years. Willie and I did not make a big deal about it, we knew we had danced well that night, but we also knew the guys we beat would be coming back for revenge sooner or later. As far as dancing was concerned, Willie Whip & I preferred dancing the Hustle, but then again, we couldn't help it because the girls would ask us to dance with them everywhere we went. We often danced with 2 or 3 girls at a time, or we would switch partners in the middle of the dance floor. I guess you could say that the Hustle was our drug of choice, and it was not only because it was a beautiful dance, but because we met a lot of beautiful girls. That night I met a girl I had never seen before. Her name was Debbie. She was pretty, but she was too much like me, a player. All the guys were constantly flirting with her, and she would flirt back.

I only spoke to her for a short time because I was being interrupted by my friends or other girls who wanted to dance, and I never said no; unless, of course, she couldn't dance. There are always exceptions to the rules, such as if she was pretty, I didn't mind getting my feet stepped on.

You could say we were conceited, but we were also spoiled because many girls loved dancing with us. The thing is, if we went somewhere new where the girls didn't know us, once they saw us dance, they would want to dance with us as well. That was the beauty of doing the Latin Hustle with style and finesse. I can honestly say that girls were a bit aggressive in those days, and many of them slept around so that you could be with one today, and the next day she was sleeping with one of your friends.

We didn't care about it that much because we were all single, and that's all we wanted anyway. We called it. Wham bam, thank you, mam, and we kept it moving. The girl who always would grab me to dance wasn't even a love interest; however, she was one of the girls I could do the Hustle with the best. Her name was Maggie. She was a short, pretty girl and could spin like a top. She always asked me to be her Hustle partner everywhere I went there. I said no for a while because I was having too much fun, and being partners meant rehearsing just about every day. I kept telling her I was not ready to have a partner, but it would be her when I was. We would always dance together at St. Mary's and were part of the crowd of the best dancers everywhere we went. I wouldn't call it a crew, but in a way, we were because we always went to the same clubs, hooky parties, and of course, St. Mary's. Those of us who were the best Hustle Dancers always danced in the middle of the dance floor. Or towards the end of the room, which was close to the DJ booth.

The front of the room was where we would dance Rock for the most part. However, there would be rock battles in the middle of the floor every once in a while. That was where Dee Dee, Rubberband, Mejico, and Salsa would do battle. I liked to watch them battle, but I was never into floor moves, especially against those guys; they didn't rock like the rest of us. They mixed their rocking with floor moves, which was a part of who they were as Rockers. Yes, Willie and I had won a Rock Contest against most of these guys, but the rules were different in a contest. On the streets, the code was different. If you battled someone doing floor moves, you had to have floor moves in your arsenal as well as burns.

I never really liked disrespectful gestures, and I stayed away from those types of battles. Willie Whip and I were more into showing off our style and spins and doing the same move simultaneously. However, when we danced the Hustle with a girl who could also Rock, we would break away and dance Rock with them as well. The worst thing was when a girl burned you, so I tried to stay away from getting into those types of battles with girls. I mean, I couldn't see myself throwing my privates at the girls, and to be honest, I never liked that style to begin with. After our win, Willie Whip and I entered and won a few more Rock Contests; however, my most memorable was at a club called The Bon Sua, which was in lower Manhattan. I will get back to that in a minute. First, I want to tell you why, in my eyes, it became my most memorable.

We continued doing our Tuesday and Thursday Jams at St. Mary's Recreation Center; we also started going downtown to other clubs. At a lower Manhattan Club, I met a beautiful Puerto Rican girl named Elba, who everybody called Kitty. She had a beautiful face and a nice body. But it was her charismatic demeanor and amazing smile that captivated me from the moment I saw her. She was not easy to approach because she was surrounded by a small army of guys and girls, most of whom I did not know. I had been practicing the Hustle with Maggie regularly by then. She and Maggie were also there. I couldn't take my eyes off Kitty, but since there was no way of getting to her, I danced with Maggie and made sure she saw me.

There was a girl with Kitty named Joyce, and I knew her, so I asked her what her story was. She told me she had a crazy boyfriend named Leo from Alphabet City in the Lower East Side and that I should just forget about her. I asked Joyce to introduce us anyway. She was highly reluctant, so I told her I only wanted to have one dance with her, and I promised I would not hit on her. Joyce liked me, so she agreed to do it, provided I kept my word. She told me she didn't want to see anything bad happen. I shook my head, rolled my eyes, and just smiled at her. Kitty had already been watching us, and as we walked towards her, she smiled. Joyce introduced her to me, and I kissed her hand, which she seemed to like, and she smiled once more. God, she had a killer smile to go with her beautiful face, and I was truly captivated.

I told her that I knew she had a boyfriend, and all I wanted was one dance with her if she didn't mind. She had already seen me dance, but I was unsure if she could do the Hustle, so I asked her. She said, "Yes," so I smiled and said, "Let's dance the next song that comes on," and she agreed. I never forgot the song we danced to, "Date with the Rain" by Eddie Kendricks. I didn't know what to expect when we got on the dance floor, but to my surprise, she could follow me as though we had been dancing together for years. Her turns and spins were flawless, but when I held her close, it was like magic. I could tell she was a bit nervous as she danced with me, but it was because she knew some of her boyfriend's friends were there, and they were watching us. I can honestly say I fell for Elba from the moment I laid eyes on her, but when we danced together, I knew I had to make her mine. I also knew it would not be easy, but the butterflies in my stomach told me I had to try.

Once we were finished with our dance, which was very elegant and passionate, I asked her if I could buy her a drink so we could talk for a while. She told me she couldn't because her boyfriend's friends were there and that she did not want to cause me any problems. It was apparent that she was attracted to me, but I said, "Perhaps some other time," she smiled and walked away, and my heart went with her. I couldn't help but watch her as she walked away, and I couldn't help noticing the dirty looks I got from the guys with her.

Not sure why her boyfriend wasn't there, but I was glad he wasn't; if not, I would never have had the opportunity to meet her and have that beautiful dance with her. I did not want to cause her any problems, so I left shortly after that, but not before making a good impression. I left a message with Joyce and hoped to see her again soon.

Elba (Kitty) Santiago RIP

Priceless memories of a time long gone, but forever in my heart!

St. Mary's Recreation Center Circa 1974

Many gang members convened at St. Mary's that summer, and we never had any gang violence, in part because of our newfound love for the Latin Hustle, Rocking, and dancing with the girls.

Long before Hip Hop was born, the Latin Hustle and Rock Cultures held the way.

CHAPTER THIRTEEN: THE DEATH OF RUBBERBAND

Things had been going great at our St. Mary's Jam's for a few months, but our efforts in keeping the peace at the center during these dances came to a grinding halt on Tuesday, October 1st, 1974. As I was on my way up the ramp to the game room, I encountered Rubberband, whose real name is Jaime Rosendo, and a 14-year-old kid arguing over a dollar RB owed the kid for a loose joint he had taken on credit the week before. I asked them to stop arguing or leave the center because we had a strict policy about fights in the Center. They stopped arguing for a short while. However, when they got inside, the kid got in RBs face again in front of everyone. Rubberband became angry because he felt disrespected since the kid wouldn't let it go. The kid approached and got disrespectful with him again, and RB slapped him in the face hard. I was up on the DJ Table with Henry, and I saw that they were at it again, but now it had gotten physical.

The kid was scared now, but then I saw a guy hand a 007 knife to him, and now he was brave and threatened RB with the knife. When I saw the kid had a knife, I jumped off the elevated DJ Booth and ran over to them to stop it. By the time I got to them, it had happened too fast for me to do anything, and I saw Rubberband trying to get away from the kid, but RBs bumped into his girlfriend Blondie and her friends, as he backed up, as my friend Evelyn, and Dante dance nearby, and he had nowhere to go. The kid lunged at him and stabbed him once in the upper right chest. After that, he and his friends ran out of the dance room. Rubberband went down, and all the girls started screaming as people gathered around to see what happened.

Dee Dee and I immediately told everyone to back away and give him air, but I could see he was mortally wounded as blood started coming out of his mouth. We began to panic and decided to carry him downstairs to call an ambulance and save his life. As we were taking him down the ramp, I looked at RB, and he looked up at me with a scared yet sad look on his face, and then he closed his eyes for the last time. What I didn't realize at the time was that we should not have moved him because he began to choke on his blood by lifting him and carrying him. We were young and didn't know better, and Dee Dee and I only wanted to save his life by bringing him downstairs so that when the ambulance got there, they could care for him quickly. When the ambulance finally got there, they worked on him right away. After a short while, they put him on a gurney, put him into the ambulance, and took him to the hospital. Everybody was downstairs now since everyone came down behind us as we were carrying him, and Henry had turned the music off. Rita was freaking out, and so was Tally, and I knew it wouldn't be long before we would hear it from them both. Henry was not happy, and we all knew that this killing would mean the end of St. Mary's Jams.

In the weeks before Rubberband died, several gangs from the worst area of the South Bronx were already at peace. Thanks to the outstanding efforts of Henry De Sosa and the leaders of the Imperial Bachelors. Members of a few rival gangs would hang out at St. Mary's, and we never had a problem until the day Rubberband was killed in a dispute over one dollar, which was not gang-related.

I consider the three months when we hosted those Hustle Parties at St. Mary's among my fondest memories from my youth. Although we never got news media coverage for the positive things we did, those who attended those jams will never forget what we accomplished in such a short time. The ironic part is that although we did those things many years before Hip Hop was born, we never got the recognition, and neither did Rita Pasguelagua or Tally.

I can say the same for all of the other staff members who had a part in making those events as successful as they were meaningful and memorable for our community.

Hosted by the Imperial Bachelors, the Latin Hustle Jams at St. Mary's created peace among several rival Puerto Rican gangs in and around our territory during the summer of 1974. A fact that has never been made public for over 40 years, until now.

Willie Estrada and Debbie Barcene (Photo Bomb - Peace)

The Hustle Revolution swept throughout New York by
the end of 1974, and in 1977, when Saturday Night Fever
hit the big screen, it went Global.

But don't get it twisted; it was Latino teenagers from the
South Bronx who developed and nurtured it long before
the birth of Hip Hop, and it was our gift to the world!

When the cops got there, everybody scattered, as nobody was willing to come forward to testify. I went home after a short while because I was so sad about what happened to RB, but we already knew that Rubberband was dead by the time I went home. Rita spoke with one of the cops who frequented St. Mary's, and he found out that RB had indeed died of his wound. It was a sad day for us. We lost a good friend, and the parties at St. Mary's were now officially over. The following week we all found out the kid had been arrested for stabbing RB, and soon after that, he was sent to a Juvenile Detention Center called Spotford in the South Bronx.

I am not sure who gave the cops the kid's name, but everyone had to have a Center Card with their names and address on record when attending St. Mary's, so I guess that is how they found him. It was the end of an era; St. Mary's was like a beacon of light for us. It kept us off the streets, and for the most part, out of trouble. Henry was distraught but not as upset as Rita & Tally, who the Parks Department crucified for not having proper security. Still, we all knew it was something nobody could have prevented. I had tried my best to get RB and the kid to stop arguing, but the kid, even at the young age of 14, was tough, and he wouldn't back down from RB, although RB was older than him. RB should never have slapped him, considering he was a minor, but then again, the other guy should never have passed the kid the 007 he used to kill Rubberband.

Either way, he is immortalized to the world now that his story is being told by those of us who were there and knew him.

During the weeks that ensued, I couldn't get the sight of RB dying in my arms out of my head. To keep my mind occupied, I rehearsed with Maggie regularly as we prepared ourselves for the show we would be doing soon. I guess I was just too sad about RB's death, and I needed time. I found myself doing the Hustle a lot more than Rock because they played mostly Hustle music, and besides that, Willie Whip and I always managed to pick up more girls dancing Hustle than Rock. One day, we met two girls from El Barrio, Spanish Harlem, and we visited them and hung out. They lived between Lexington and Park Ave in the Projects, somewhere in Spanish Harlem. When we went out to the store and were on our way back, a group of about ten guys approached us and began some trouble. They knew we were not from the area, and since there were only two of us, we had to back down when they made threats towards us, Whip caught the eye of the primary troublemaker, and they almost got into it, but the girls started screaming at them, and they backed off. However, they told us they would be waiting for us to come out and jump us. When we got upstairs, I asked to use the phone, calling St. Mary's. To my pleasant surprise JJ picked up the phone, and I told him I wanted him to get the guys and get us, that we were in trouble with some guys from Spanish Harlem in El Barrio.

I gave him the address, and he told me all the guys were upstairs and that they would be there soon. El Barrio was only a few train stops away from the South Bronx, so I knew they would be there within half an hour. I told Willie help was on the way, and the girls told us not to go outside until our guys got there.

Whip and I were in no hurry to go outside until reinforcement arrived anyway. After about a half-hour or so, I heard a familiar whistle, and when we looked out the window, the guys who were waiting for us were still there. They did not realize that all the guys rolling up 40 deep were from our gang, the Imperial Bachelors. As we got downstairs, they started surrounding the guys waiting for us, and they knew they were in a world of trouble. They looked scared when we approached them and started trying to back down and talk their way out of an ass whipping. Willie Whip approached the guy talking the most crap and said: "How about now, you still want a piece of me?" I could tell he was scared, so I said, "Whip, give him a fair fight, and whop his ass!" Whip was a good fighter, and I knew he would beat the big mouth because fear has a way of making a man weak. After I made my offer for a fair fight, there was a sign of relief on all their faces, and the guy's friends started egging him on to fight. Whip squared off on him and took his fighting stance, and the guy put up his hands, and the fight got underway but ended pretty quickly. Whip hit him with a couple of one-two shots to the face, followed by a hard punch to the stomach, which was the blow that ended the fight.

Just so everyone knows, had the other guy beaten Whip, I was next to fight, and it would not be over for them so quickly. Once the guy was out for the count, we told them if you ever messed with any of our boys when they visit here, we will be back, and the next time they will not get off so easy. I do not believe in kicking a man when he is down, and I have instilled a strong sense of fairness since I was a young boy.

The punishment always needed to fit the offense. The bigger the offense, the bigger the response has always been my mentality, and it still is.

As time went on, I found myself getting further away from the gang scene; however, we still carried guns on many occasions when we went dancing. It wasn't because we were looking for trouble, but at the end of the day, we were still volatile teenagers, and as a result, having a gun was a deterrent. By early 1975, the Latin Hustle reigned supreme as the dominant dance of our era; however, very few people nowadays know the true origins of our beloved dance, so I'm going to share that story with you.

In the early 1970s, and before the Latin Hustle was born, the most prominent social dance among the Latino Culture was a slow dance, we called the 500. One of the reasons it is thought the Hustle had to emerge was because, at house parties, all you would see were young teenagers dancing to slow jams and grinding or dry humping their young bodies.

It was done in a fashion almost like making love on the dance floor to romantic and intoxicating music. When some parents would see what was going on, they would abruptly end those parties on many occasions as a direct result, and because some parents did not want to see such a perverse sexual dance at house parties. A new social dance started being nurtured, which would not replace the slow jams initially; however, it did make some parents more comfortable when they saw it.

It was an elementary 5 step dance that resembled Bachata; however, it had no turns. The slow dancing continued at hooky parties and basement clubs all over the South Bronx; however, it was evident that the first Hustle was born in the Bronx because that is where all the best Hustle dancers came from in the very beginning.

The first Hustle was simple and intended to bring male and female partners together through a social dance, which was more acceptable to parents in house parties and how their young teenage girls danced with the boys. In the early stages, the dance lacked turns and intricate steps. The first rendition was sensual and sexy, dancing very close with the partner. That first version was short-lived, as the dance morphed into what was known as the Push and Pull Hustle, which utilized the 5 step approach of 1973.

Later that same year, the first 6-step hustle was created, better known as the Rope Hustle, implementing simple turns and spins. Then, in 1974, the Latin Hustle was born. The new derivative was a 6-step dance combining turns, fancy spins, and amalgamations. A new era of dance was born in New York City, spearheaded by the Latino Community.

Had it not been for the killing of Rubberband, who was both iconic and legendary, the story of St. Mary's would probably be a lot more mainstream and acknowledged throughout the Hip Hop community today. After all, it was where many gang members started taking off their Gang Colors and came in peace to dance with the girls and with each other. The Latin Hustle and Rock were dominant before Hip Hop was born, and Bboys, contrary to popular opinion, did not yet exist.

After the death of Rubberband, St. Mary's center was not the same; it became a ghost town in comparisons to what it had become, as well as what it meant to those of us who used that platform to advocate for peace, in one of the most violent neighborhoods in all of the South Bronx.

The Bachelors created a peace that had not been seen in these parts of the Bronx for many years. Although RB died, our efforts were not in vain, and our hopes were still alive!

Rita was not a quitter, and she came up with a great idea to bring people back to St. Mary's, even if only for one day, where the greatness of one man would help heal the heartbreak of a senseless killing. She reached out to the people's Champion, his name was Muhammad Ali, and he responded like the true Champion and Hero that he was to us all.

While we weren't allowed to continue our weekly parties, Ali's visit immensely helped us heal. The best part was that we all got to meet the Champ, and he made us all laugh so much we cried with laughter as he clowned around with everyone, including myself.

Pucho's hands were so fast, they were invisible to the naked eye, but Ali's reaction was priceless!

St. Mary's, Bronx, NY — Dec. 9, 1974

THE DAY I MET THE GREATEST!

That is me on the bottom left-hand corner of the picture, looking up at the Greatest as he refereed an exhibition match between two of my friends. I still have that picture framed on my wall, and it remains one of my most cherished memories from that era.

I am The Greatest! Muhammad Ali

I whopped Foreman because they said I couldn't do it, and now they know I am THE GREATEST OF ALL TIME!

The Nation of Islam was present alongside Ali, and the rest of us there. It was a day of spiritual healing, made possible by the people's Champion.

RIP Ali – The People's Champion forever!

CHAPTER FOURTEEN: THE 310½ STUCK ON STUPID

By late 1974 peace among many of the gangs from the South Bronx had been established. It was facilitated in part by the power of music and dance, as well as those of us who were tired of all the violence and killings that came with it. Those who knew her gave Rita credit for making us take off our gang colors as a condition for allowing us to produce the dance jams at St. Mary's.

The death of Rubberband weighed heavily on all our minds, and his loss was monumental and sad because it had also put a stop to the amazing jams at St. Mary's, which RB was so fond of. Dee Dee and I were holding him in our arms, and as he looked up at us, there was a look of sadness in his eyes that said to me he knew he was about to die. As we started carrying him downstairs, he looked at me one last time, rolled his eyes back, and never opened them again. By the time we got him downstairs, Rita was waiting, and I saw the look of panic and concern in her eyes; she knew this would be the end, but she also felt responsible because it happened on her watch. The sorrow of watching him die stays with me even today. I had seen many deaths by the time RB was killed in my presence. However, his death had the most profound impact on me; I believe in part because I had seen him take his last breath after he closed his eyes for the last time. Another senseless killing is all that came to mind, as I asked myself, what if he had lived? Who would he be today, and what could we learn from him? Most people don't think about those types of things, but I have to wonder if his death didn't cause a ripple in time, and what could have been never was as a direct result of his death. We will never know, but I have to wonder.

Although we didn't know about it yet, Hip Hop was on the Horizon, but I can't help but think what might have been had RB not died on that fateful day.

Those jams at St. Mary's had been hugely influential in helping with the gang peace process in our neighborhood, and that for us, that was huge.

We had only been doing those jams for a few short months, but the impact we made was huge. That was evident by the number of people from the Tri-State area to either participate or learn by watching us dance. Rubberband, Salsa, and Mejico were pioneers in doing floor moves, which B-boys would later adapt, and I can't help but think how far they would have taken this form of dance had Rubberband lived?

There were some gangs who, I will say, were still stuck on stupid and wouldn't make peace for one reason or another. One night, as we waited for Tommy Cuevas to open the doors to 310½, about 40 of us were waiting at the front door. Right before Tommy opened the door, a group of Savage Skulls wearing their gang colors and hell-bent on making trouble showed up and started talking trash and making a nuisance of themselves.

We were a much bigger group, but we weren't there to cause problems for Tommy, a gracious host and an all-around nice guy. He was also a Salsa dancer who had a lot of love for our generation, and most of us had much respect for him. He had, after all, given us a haven with an atmosphere of peace, filled with those of us whose only interest was music and dance.

That mindset was rudely interrupted when he opened the door when the Savage Skulls started cutting off everyone at the front of the line trying to get in. Tommy didn't have it, and he stopped them dead in their tracks and told them they could not enter wearing gang colors.

This infuriated the pack leader, whom I recognized as one of the guys who jumped me a few months before when I was alone in their neighborhood visiting my grandmother. Cowards that they were! The only reason I survived was because of an old lady who was screaming at them out her second-floor window, but not before they stomped on my face pretty good with their MC Boots. We retaliated a short time later. It would have been the perfect opportunity to strike them again, but revenge had already been taken, and attacking them would only make matters worse. Especially for Tommy, who had his hands full as it was, and provoking retaliation on the 310½ by the Skulls, would mean not being able to go there anymore. A metamorphosis within us had already transformed our mindset, and irrational behavior was no longer a part of our thought process. We just wanted to dance!

I wish I could say the same for those damn Skulls who messed with our Chi. We spoke amongst ourselves as Tommy laid down the law and decided to go to another club. That's when we heard their leader saying, "If we can't come in, nobody else is going in either!" Tommy looked at him and said, "I'm not opening the club tonight. You can all go somewhere else; you happy now that you screwed it up for everybody else?" He then turned and closed the door, and everyone walked away in disgust.

As we walked down the street and away from the idiots who had seemingly just ruined our night, we decided to invade Brooklyn and go to a club called "The Orange Peel." By that time, our dress style was changing as dress styles did in rapid succession during the early to late-70s. We were dressing more elegantly, and a touch of class was ever-present.

We weren't into wearing suits and ties yet, but with more of a stylish look with slacks and shirts instead of sneakers and jeans. The influence of the Latin Hustle helped us make that transformation and the best yet to come. When we got to the train station, a cop was waiting for us. He had seen us walking down the street in significant numbers, making our way towards the station, and wanted to make sure we would not enter without paying. There were about thirty of us when we entered the station. There he was, just standing with a smirk on his face and baton in hand. He had no idea what was about to happen. We stood in front of the turnstile, waiting for the train to pull into the station, and when it did, someone screamed out, "Let's Go!"

Abby Latin Hustle Pioneer - St. Mary's 1974.

St. Mary's Center Tuesday & Thursday Dances

Ralph, Andre, Cabeza, Moe, Willie MB, Julio, Willie Whip & Afro, South Bronx Rockers.

1974 with Julio and Guz (Imperial Bachelors)

You could take the boy out of the Ghetto in those days, but you couldn't take the Ghetto out of the boy.

We weren't brainwashed, but we were conditioned to act and speak a certain way because our violent environment dictated our behavior for the most part. It's almost as though there was a particular pride in knowing we had a reputation for being Bad Asses and that the South Bronx was known as the murder capital of the United States in those days. Of course, that sounds stupid, and trust me when I say it was. Nevertheless, it was the mentality of that era if you were a gang member who lived in the South Bronx.

The power and beauty of music and dance brought us all together in peace, and the Latin Hustle and Rock cultures became mainstream throughout all the boroughs of New York City, long before the birth of Hip Hop.

Our Legacy is not only that we brought peace when all we knew was war. Our legacy is the dances we developed and gifted to the world, known as the Latin Hustle and Rock Dance Cultures.

I will never forget the look on that Cops face as we all started jumping the turnstile as he panicked and didn't know who to grab first. He tried holding one guy who pulled away, so he went after another, and that went on for a short while; in the end, he was able to grab one of the girls, as the rest of us looked on from inside the train laughing. We knew he couldn't catch us all, if any at all; there were just too many of us for him to handle by himself. We didn't like cops much in those days; they were primarily prejudiced bullies who often beat and arrested us for the slightest infraction. It was like they were above the law, and more times than not, they would get away with crimes against us, as police brutality was the norm. Brooklyn was a long way to go to a party, but we had heard of the Orange Peel and that they supposedly had good Hustle dancers. So our mentality was to show them who the best hustle dancers were by taking over their dance floor, and we were going through great lengths to represent the South Bronx.

We all made our way towards the last car, so we could all be together, and since we didn't know what to expect, we had pledged to each other to make sure we would all be safe. As we occupied the entire last car of the train, we started our party as we banged on the seats and windows, making our music to dance to. When we got to 86th Street, the train filled with rowdy Puerto Ricans, and the White people who wanted to get on took a pass and waited for the next train for the most part. Those who did come on board would soon move to another car or get off at the following stop. That is what happens when you get a big group of teenagers together on a train, or the streets, they act up, but for us, it was more like a party and a celebration of life.

By the time we had to change trains to head to Brooklyn, the train system was packed with party-goers, and we had to spit up into different cars. We all knew which stop we would be getting off at in Brooklyn, but at every stop, we would yell out, "Don't' get off yet; this is not our stop." We annoyed the hell out of everyone on board but could care less; we were the Kings and Queens of our dominion and came in peace, even if everyone else was annoyed. After over an hour in transit, we had finally reached our destination, and everyone was festive as we vacated the train headed to a new adventure. We had very little money to spend, so we purchased a few quarts of beer and drank them before we walked into the club with a nice buzz. I had never been to that club before, so I didn't know what to expect, but from the looks of things, it was going to be a fun night. There were pretty girls all over the streets, and even though there were many girls from the Bronx with us, they were just the girls we danced with, and we were all just friends. The looks we got from the regulars were promising regarding the girls, whom we started flirting with right away. However, the guys were a different story, and we did get some stern looks from a few of them.

We were a big group, so the looks and stares didn't last long, especially because some of the guys with us were a bit unruly and quick-tempered, and it showed by their behavior. Once inside, we immediately made our way towards the dance floor to check out the competition and see just how good they were, if any good at all. The Orange Peel was pretty full by the time we got there, so we couldn't all get on the dance floor at the same time. I was more focused on all the pretty girls there, so was Willie Whip, who was just as big a Casanova as I was.

We approached two lovelies and introduced ourselves as Hustle dancers from the Bronx, and they were very receptive to our flirtation. We asked them to dance with us, and as we were holding their hands walking towards the dance floor, all of a sudden, the lights went off, and it got pitch black. Girls started screaming when guys started grabbing asses all over the place. Our friend Johnny began walking around with his lighter and lighting up girl's faces, and if he bumped into a girl whom he didn't find attractive, he would blow the light out and say, "OMG, you're a boot!" He had us all cracking up because he was doing that to pretty girls as well, and they responded with a big "Screw, you pendejo!" and he would run away laughing. Johnny was a good-looking guy, but he was very immature yet playful and funny at the same time. The lights came back on after about 10 minutes, and you could see the relief on the faces of the girls who had someone grab a handful of ass.

We were just all laughing as we heard some of the guys saying they had nothing to do with grabbing any girl's ass. But as we say in the Bronx, whoever smelled it dealt it! The same guys who said they didn't grab any girl's ass were probably the culprits. I wanted to call that night "Ass Fest," but after the lights came back on, the dance floor was empty, so our crew took to the dance floor when the music came back on. We lit up the dance floor with the girls who came with us as the regulars looked on in amazement.

After our demonstration, it became apparent to everyone there that we were from the Bronx, but we had come in peace to partake with Brooklyn, and we all had a great time.

We left our mark before leaving, and there was no resentment whatsoever. We came and went in peace, and I'd like to think we made a very positive impression on all the Hustle dancers from Brooklyn who were not as advanced as we were. After all, the Hustle was a dance created in the South Bronx, so naturally, we were the best at it during the mid-1970s, and everyone knew it. Don't get me wrong, great Hustle dancers came out of Brooklyn in years to come, but they had obtained it from us, and nobody could ever deny that historical fact.

The fact of the matter is, we partied at many Disco clubs during the mid to late 70s, and we shined at places like the Boombamacaoo, the Ipanema, Roseland, The Starship Discovery, The Copacabana, the Red and White, Studio 54, as well as many other clubs/discos. We were always the best dancers at all the places we frequented, and when we invited people or told others where we would be, that's where everyone ended up going that night.

To say we were the trendsetters would be an understatement. We were the best of the best in those days, and we always proved it on the dance floor, regularly. The Latin Symbolics Reigned Supreme during the mid to late 70s, and many of the best dancers from throughout New York City were members of our dance team. Long before there was Hip Hop, there was the Latin Hustle. During the later 70s, I became a promoter after being recruited by David Maldonado, and I helped him promote all his events, but more about that later.

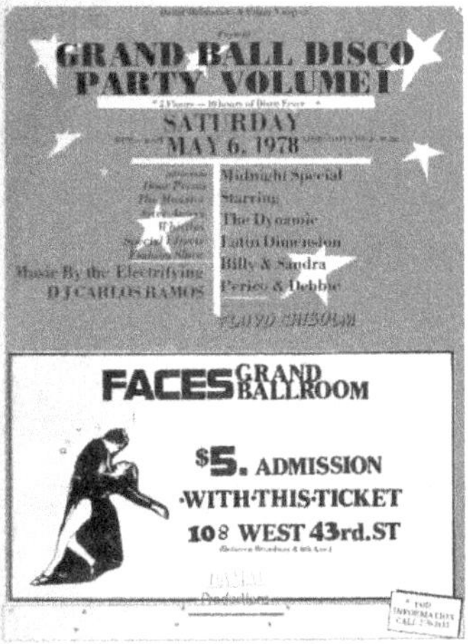

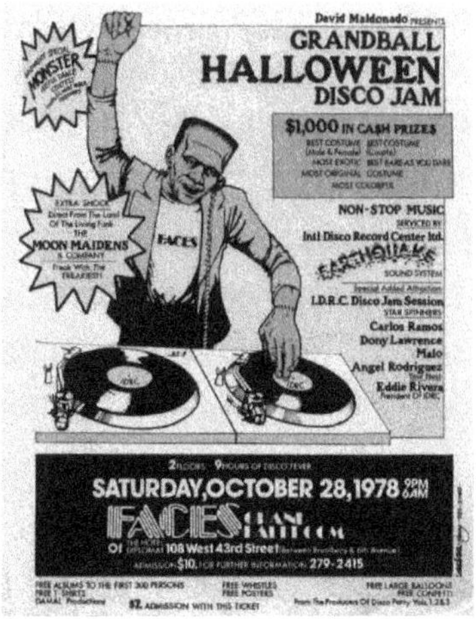

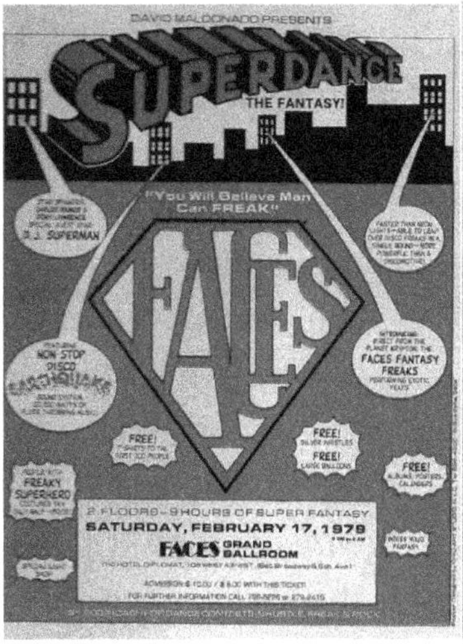

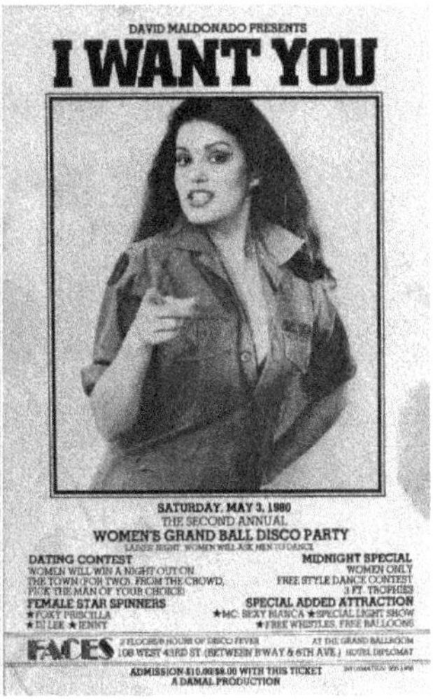

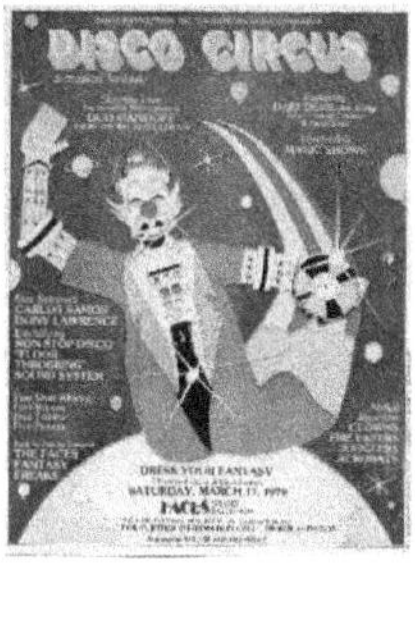

Theme Dance Parties Became the Thing

CHAPTER FIFTEEN: ROCKING THE LOWER EAST SIDE

Time went by, and I had not seen Elba for a while, but I thought about her often, and I wondered if I would ever see her again. I hoped I would, and I always searched for her pretty face in all the clubs I went to. She was all I could think of, and I knew I had it bad for her, but I started to think it was an impossible dream. I was going dancing seven days a week in those days, and we continued to do Jams at St. Mary's every Tuesday and Thursday. Our Jams had gotten very popular with more people coming from all over the Tri-State area who would come to learn the Hustle. I started practicing and creating more moves with Maggie, and we would show off at the St. Mary's Jams and everywhere we went. Willie Whip and I were also practicing and rocking at St. Mary's and the 310½ as well. After a while, Maggie and I were noticed by George Vascones, President of the Latin Symbolics Dance Company, and he invited us to join the team. He also wanted Willie Whip, but Willie was far too busy sleeping with as many girls as possible and having too much fun to join a Dance Team. We started rehearsing at St. Mary's for a while on Mondays, Wednesdays, and Fridays. St. Mary's was our home away from home without a doubt. We kept in mind that I lived right up the block; from there, Rita recruited me to volunteer there regularly. It was how Rita kept us out of trouble, but I also enjoyed setting a good example.

On the following Tuesday night, out of the blue, when I got to St. Mary's, the front desk told me that two pretty girls were looking for me and that they were upstairs.

The other person at the front desk said, "There is always a pretty girl looking for him." They made me laugh, but as I was going upstairs, one of my boys told me, "Willie, there are two beautiful girls upstairs asking about you, they are both fine, but I've never seen them before." I asked him what they looked like, and all that came out of his mouth was, "Pretty faces, one has green eyes, and the other one has light brown eyes, but they are both fine as hell." I was inquisitive, but I didn't know who it might be because I knew many girls that fit that description.

I had gotten there late that day because I had been helping my father with a project. My Dad was a Master Carpenter and built custom-made furniture for a living. He was the best carpenter I ever knew, and he created works of art as far as I was concerned. When I got upstairs, the game room where we did the Jams was packed as always. I walked in, and everyone started greeting me as usual. You could say I was popular, and there were always girls grabbing my hand and pulling me to the dance floor. When it came to the Hustle, I was one of the best, and I hung out with the best from the Bronx, and we were family. However, this time someone tapped me on the back of my shoulder, and when I turned to see who it was, I couldn't believe my eyes. It was Elba, and while I didn't know who the other girl was at the time, it was her sister Nilda. I was delighted to see her, and I was sure she could tell by the look on my face. I had a lot of female admirers, so there were a lot of them looking at us, trying to figure out who she was. The music was loud, so I asked her to come outside with me. She said OK, but first, she wanted to dance with me, so her sister Nilda whom she introduced me to, could see us dance.

I couldn't say no, so I went to the DJ Booth and asked Henry to play the song we had first danced to the day I met her. I then introduced Elba, who preferred the name Kitty to Henry. He reached down to shake her hand, but instead, he did what I did when we first met; he kissed her hand. That brought a big smile to her face and Nilda's as well. I told Kitty Henry was going to play a particular song for us, and she just smiled. Now, remember, we ran St. Mary's, and since I told him how much I liked Kitty before he ever met her, he didn't hesitate to play my request.

I took Kitty out to dance in front of the DJ booth, so Henry could see us dancing together. I knew the rookie dancers who always danced in that area would give us room to dance, and they did. Kitty did not know which song was about to play, but when she heard Date with the Rain come on, it brought a great big smile to her face. She had told her sister Nilda about our dance at the Charisma, so she just blurted out, "How romantic," which brought a big smile to our faces. Our second dance was even better than the first because now I knew she liked me as much as I liked her, and this time there was no denying it. As we started to dance, everyone in that area formed a circle around us to watch me dance with the most beautiful girl in the room. Kitty was an amazing girl, and she looked and danced like an Angel. I think she was just as good as the other girls from the Latin Symbolics who were also there. Her elegance on the dance floor, coupled with her beauty, captivated everyone who watched us dance, and I was in heaven. It had a lot to do with how I felt about her, which was evident in how we danced together, touching everyone there. After our dance, everyone clapped and cheered.

Kitty just smiled while I was walking on air. Nilda told us that we would make great partners and consider dancing together.

Kitty said that wasn't a good idea and that Leo would probably kill her. Nilda reminded her that he would also kill her if he found out she had come to the Bronx to see me. I didn't like what I heard, and I could see she was afraid of him, so it was time to speak about leaving him. Elba and I went outside to talk. Nilda entertained two of my friends who were hitting on her. What they didn't know was that Nilda preferred girls over guys. When Kitty and I got downstairs, Rita was there, and when she saw me, she said, I would ask you why you're not upstairs dancing, but this pretty girl by your side and the smile on your faces says it all.

Kitty and I laughed, and I introduced Kitty as a friend from the Lower East Side or Alphabet City, which most New Yorkers called that area.

Rita was happy that people were coming to the Center from all over the city. She was always delighted to meet our friends. She had noticed the changes transpiring right before her eyes, as we kept the peace with rival gangs, and attendance at the Center had never been higher. I took Kitty to a bench at the edge of the park where nobody would bother us so that we could speak in private. I told her how I felt about her, but I was uncomfortable with her boyfriend. That's when she laid the bomb on me and told me her boyfriend was not a good person and how most people were afraid of him because he was the leader of a crazy crew who was known to kill people for money.

I asked her why she stayed with someone like that, and she told me she knew how to keep him under control so that he wouldn't hurt people. In other words, she thought if she left him, he would get worse. I told her that she was not responsible for his behavior, and that's when she said to me that most guys who try to talk to her were always scared away or intimidated by Leo and his crew of killers. I wasn't afraid of anybody in those days because my friends and I were also a bit crazy, even though we were becoming a lot more subtle because of our love for music and dance. Not all my friends were into the dance portion even though they enjoyed the music; many were still gang members with short fuses.

Kitty made it clear that she liked me but didn't want me to get into any problems with Leo. I asked her why she came to see me if she didn't want me to have problems. She told me she had gotten messages from me from Joyce, and she wanted to see me and explain her situation. I told her I didn't care about Leo. I wasn't afraid of him or his friends, and I also knew he would never come into my neighborhood to start trouble. She told me he wasn't into going to the clubs and stayed local most of the time. She invited me to a club downtown which he's known for going to and asked me to meet her and her cousin Rosa there on Saturday. I was happy that she wanted to hang out with me, but I also knew that sooner or later, I would have problems with Leo. After we spoke for a while, Kitty and I went back into the Center. We found Nilda on her way down, escorted by my friends. When she saw us, her eyes opened wide as in to say thank God. As I stated earlier, Nilda was not into guys, but guys couldn't help themselves when they saw those beautiful green eyes and fabulous body.

Kitty smiled because she knew why Nilda was so happy to see us. I walked them to the train with my friends because we didn't want them walking through our tough neighborhood alone, especially at night. Kitty and I walked behind and continued talking and getting to know more about each other, but it was evident that we were attracted to each other. After waiting to make sure they got on the train safely, I went back to St. Mary's, and I told Willie I wanted him to come downtown with me on Saturday. He told me he had a date and couldn't go with me.

All my friends stayed local when Saturday came, so I went downtown alone. It felt a bit strange being at a club I had never been to on my own, but only because I didn't know what to expect. When I got there, I was happy to see Kitty and Rosa out front, and I guess they had been waiting for me. Kitty was delighted to see me, but I could tell she was also a bit scared. As it turned out, a couple of Leo's boys were there, keeping in mind that we were downtown at a club not far from Alphabet City, where they were from.

I was not particularly comfortable, but I played the role like I was there with Rosa, Kitty's idea. They both started introducing me to their friends as a friend from the Bronx, and while they seemed calm, I was not convinced. I asked Kitty why she invited me to a place where her boyfriend's crew hung out. She told me they never go there, and she wasn't sure why they were there. I asked them if they wanted to smoke a joint, and they both said yes, so we went outside to find a place to smoke.

They took me into a building down the street from the club, and we started smoking, when all of a sudden, the door flew open, and a guy started screaming at Kitty and asking her what the hell she was doing with me in the building. He was angry as hell and started telling her I was going to get hurt. However, the minute I heard him making threats, I went after them and told him to come and kick my ass.

I wasn't afraid of him, and when I was angry, I could care less who was talking shit; let's fight not talk shit. Kitty started screaming at him, telling him we were smoking a joint and that I was Rosa's friend from the Bronx. Leo's boys were all outside when we got out there, and I was outnumbered 10 to 1, but I didn't care.

I wasn't going to allow him or anyone else to treat me like a punk, especially in front of Kitty. She took notice when I came after them, showing him I wasn't afraid of him or his boys. She finally calmed him down, and I was right behind her with Rosa, who was asking me to chill out. I was pretty angry that he had spoken the way he did to me, putting on a show calling me all types of names like he was going to kick my ass. After he calmed down and saw I was not backing down, he and his boys left, but I was not feeling comfortable because I was alone and on their turf. We went back into the building and finished smoking the joint. Kitty told me she had never seen anybody stand up to Leo, and she was kind of happy about that. I guess she figured I was not the type of guy who cowered even when I was outnumbered, and she liked that. I would say she had a newfound respect for me and knew I was not a punk, which excited her.

We spoke about it as we smoked the joint, and then she told me she would not invite me again because she knew he might come with a gun the next time.

I told her that I would bring one myself, and next time I would be with my boys. She did not want me to get into trouble over her, so she told me she would meet me somewhere else the next time. I told her she should break up with him and end her misery. Rosa agreed with me, but we left it at that for the time being.

I left a strong impression on Kitty that day, but I didn't want to push my luck because I knew I had no backup, so I told her I was not staying and asked them if we could go somewhere else. We did not see them when we came out of the building, so we took a cab to Times Sq., which was a bit grimy in those days, but all that mattered to me was that Kitty was with me. We hung out for a while, and then I sent them home in a cab, and I took the train back to the Bronx. A couple of days later, Kitty called me and told me she was breaking up with Leo, but she didn't want him to think it was for me, so she wasn't going to see me for a short while. I was OK with that and told her, "So you must like me, huh" She started laughing and said, "Yes, but don't let it go to your head!" "Never mind, I'm just making sure!" Even though I wasn't seeing her, I talked to her every day.

One night when she called, she told me about a Rock Contest at another club in the East Village she knew Leo would be competing at with his right-hand man, who was a guy they called Cool-Breeze. She asked me to invite my boys so I wouldn't be alone this time.

I loved how she was trying to protect me, but she was right in doing so because I knew it would not be pretty if we won on their turf.

The next day, I told Willie Whip about it, and we started practicing our short rocking routine skids. We used short routines to battle when rocking against other rockers, intended to burn them. I told a few of my other boys that Willie and I would enter a contest at the Bon Sua and invited them to join us.

They were about 10 of us going that night, just in case we got into a beef with Leo and his boys. I didn't know what to expect, and I had butterflies in my stomach because I knew Kitty would be there, as would Leo. The club was packed that night, and many contestants participated in the contest.

Little did I know that the contest would soon turn into a battle against the guys from the lower eastside. Three judges watched everyone Rock that night, and after the first round, they started eliminating dancers. There were mostly pairs, and we were competing for a $500 1st Prize and no second or third place that night. It was winner take all. After the 3rd song, Willie and I noticed more room to dance because most contestants had been eliminated. We only executed a couple of our short routines because we saved the best for last. With only four couples left on the floor, it became a free for, and Willie and I found ourselves battling with guys using disrespectful hand gestures.

Willie looked at me and said, "Let's give them what they want," as we danced against two guys from the lower east side, and Leo & Cool Breeze danced against two other guys.

Willie and I had prepared for this moment, knowing we would probably have to use tactics we did not really like, but we're good at, and those types of moves are met to be disrespectful. The trick is doing them to the beat of the music without missing a beat, which makes them look better. Before long, there were only four rockers left on the floor, Leo and his partner Cool-Breeze, against Willie Whip and me. How ironic that it had come down to us battling against the very guys who hated me with a passion. They were now in front of us, ready to do battle. Before we did battle, the primary judge announced that the winner of this final round would win $500 and be the Bon Sua Rock Champions. Willie and I faced each other initially, but Leo and Cool Breeze were out to battle and started doing burns in our faces. Leo was facing Willie Whip, and Cool Breeze was in front of me when we began to do battle.

But Whip and I had a surprise for their asses. Routine 5 was a burn we had put together with this type of battle in mind. We executed it with pure passion and conviction and a look on our faces that said, "Fuck you motherfuckers!" After that, we split up again, and since Leo was hell-bent on burning me, I jumped in the air, grabbed his head, and put my privates in his face.

The crowd erupted with "Ohhhh's and Oh Shits," which Leo did not like very much, but I had a look on my face that said it all, and that look was "SCREW YOU!" Whip did his thing against Cool-Breeze, and it was apparent to everyone there that we were not only the better dancers, but we had beaten them at their own game. When the music stopped, the crowd was still going crazy, and our boys were cheering us on, then the announcement came.

The announcer had taken the ruling from the judges and simply said, "The Winners and Bon Sua Rock Champions are the guys under the Red Light." Whip & I looked up, and there we were, standing under the Red Light. We raised our hands in Victory, and as customary, we went over and shook hands with our opponents, not that they wanted to, but were obligated to. They didn't want to look like sore losers, and they had, after all, made it to the final round. Not that it made a difference to Leo, whom I could tell was heated about the move I did on him. They all knew we were from the South Bronx, and my boys were no punks, something they all noticed.

We were a little older than them by at least two years, not that it made a difference if they decided they wanted to shoot it out with us. That type of battle had now become prominent, as opposed to fighting in those days; they had to take their lumps like men. We purchased a few bags of weed for smoking with our winnings and celebrated our victory. When we went outside to roll up, Leo was sulking with his boys and looking at us.

We felt bad for them, so we went over to them and told them they did a great job and put up a great battle. Then Whip gave Cool-Breeze a bag of weed and said, "No hard feelings, guys," and we just crossed the street with our crowd, which now consisted of several of our boys who came to the club with us and some new acquaintances. Kitty was at the club, but we didn't speak that night as we had agreed; however, she did wink at me after Whip, and I won. We didn't want to make waves, especially since we had just humiliated Leo on his home turf, so that was the extent of our communication.

Leo and his boys did not like us, but I know that they at least respected us and knew we had our crew and were no punks. Kitty and I continued talking, but we kept things cool for a while, making no waves. Maggie and I were practicing for a televised show called "Night Life" George was putting us in a Hustle show coming up soon. Whip & I hung out almost every day and always had adventures with different girls. Our dancing made us very popular, and even though I was talking to Kitty a lot, we had not gotten together yet, so Whip and I did our thing with girls from other parts of town. We were still hanging out at St. Mary's every Tuesday and Thursday and dancing seven days a week.

It was a busy time in my life, but I found myself wanting to be with Kitty more than ever, especially now that Leo was out of the picture.

One day she called me and told me she wanted to be my dance partner, but I had to tell her I was working on a routine with Maggie. I told her George was putting us on a TV show and that I could not get together with her to practice yet because I was too busy getting ready for that show.

I could tell she was disappointed, so I told her that I wanted nothing more than to dance with her, and perhaps we could even do shows soon. I told her how much I missed her and wanted to take her out. She came to terms with what I had to do because of my commitment to Maggie and George, the Latin Symbolics Dance Company president. Then, Kitty told me she wanted to see me and was tired of waiting.

She wanted me to meet her family and invited me to dinner to meet her mom and her brother Hector.

I had already met Nilda, who would also be there, and we made a date. I was happy she wanted me to meet her mother, but I was also curious. I asked her why she wanted me to meet her mom, and she told me because her mom wanted to meet me. I was inquisitive now and asked her why? She told me, "Because my mother does not like Leo, and she wanted to meet the guy who stood up to him." I started laughing, but I completely understood her reasoning. Leo did not have a future because sooner or later, he would be either dead or in jail; it was just a matter of time. The day I went for dinner, I told her I was not comfortable going to her neighborhood because I didn't want to run into Leo by myself, where he would have the advantage.

She told me her brother Hector had already spoken to him about not starting any shit with me because he would start a war with the guys from the Bronx.

Leo had to get it in his head that Kitty was my girl now, but that didn't mean he would go away quietly. Kitty lived on 8th St. and Avenue D, a bad neighborhood in the heart of Alphabet City. When I got to her neighborhood, I walked with confidence, like I belonged there. The rule on the streets is simple; if you look like a victim, you will be. Especially in that neighborhood which was very much like my own, only I wasn't in my hood; I was in Alphabet City, Leo's home turf in every sense of the word.

When I got to Kitty's block, there she was, waiting for me with her brother Hector.

She was concerned about my wellbeing, and as we were testing the water's so to speak, she wanted to be sure nobody would mess with me. When I got upstairs, her mom invited me in and gave me a big hug, which I didn't understand until Hector told me about the people Leo had killed. It turned out he was a contract killer for a drug gang from Alphabet City, with two killings he was known for having committed. Kitty's mom did not like him at all, and he was not allowed to come to her house. On the other hand, I was a welcomed guest and Hector, and I also hit it off as I shared stories from my neighborhood with him. Nilda finally came out to greet me and was happy to see me, and she told me she was glad that Kitty and I had gotten together.

I had an enjoyable visit, and her mom told me I was always welcome to come and visit her any time I wanted. Well, it looked like I was in good with her mom, brother, and sister, and I was happy that I went to visit them. Her family treated me like family, and I understood just how bad Leo was and why Kitty wanted to get away from him. I got out of her neighborhood without incident, but I knew I would someday have a confrontation with Leo, and I had to remain on my guard going forward. The following week, Kitty invited me to the Bon Sua again, only I would be going alone this time. I knew Leo might show up, so I prepared and took my gun with me.

I wanted to show Kitty I was not afraid of him, so I didn't even invite my friends because this was a date, not a reunion. Back in those days, they did not have metal detectors, and nobody got searched; all they cared about was paying at the door and buying liquor.

The drinking age was 18, and many of us did not know about coating our stomachs with food, milk, or olive oil before going out drinking. You would naturally see many drunken teens getting into fights for the dumbest of reasons by the end of the night. Most of the time, it was because they couldn't hold their liquor and couldn't help but act stupid. I didn't mind it so much when I was with my boys, and we didn't even drink a lot; for us, it was all about dancing. Leo and his boys did show up that night, but all they did was stare me down and not move towards us.

I always had my eyes on them, as did Kitty, but we still managed to have a great time that night. I went to the bathroom at one point, and I bumped into a guy named Tony, and he started talking to me about Leo and how he had it in for me. I told him I was not alone and opened my jacket to reveal a 38 Special on my waistband. I told him that if he started something, I would finish it! I knew he was friends with Leo, and I also knew he would say to him what I said, that's not to say I was looking for trouble, but Leo needed to know. I would not be taking any shit from him or his crew. The truth is, I had become a different type of gangster, and it was not by choice, but because of the environment I lived in, as well as the City of New York, which was full of outlaws and stick-up kids. I was no longer wearing gang colors; I wore sports jackets and looked dapper to the clubs. The other reason I carried a gun was that I wore a big Cuban link chain, which was worth a lot of money, and I wasn't about to let anyone rob me. In those days, there were many robbers, which we called the stickup kids, who would go out to rob people for their valuables.

When we were going home, I decided to put Kitty in a cab, so I wouldn't have to go to her hood, which was not too far away. I didn't believe in tempting the hands of fate, and I knew Leo would sooner or later make his move. After she drove off, I started walking towards the train, and I noticed Leo and his boys were walking about a block behind me. When I got to the train station, I purchased a token from the clerk and went downstairs on the uptown side to get the train back to the Bronx. Usually, we would not pay to get on the train; we would sneak in. However, I didn't want to take the chance since I had a gun on me. After I was at the station for a few minutes waiting for my train, I heard a loud commotion, and when I looked down at the station, I saw several cops on the other side. They were arresting all the young people on that platform, including Leo and his boys.

I didn't panic because I knew I had done nothing wrong, but I had to get rid of my gun, so I threw it in a trash bin behind the stairs and walked away. Good thing I did because a few seconds later, some cops came down the stairs on my side as well. I was the only young person on that platform, so they grabbed me as well. I asked them what this was all about, and they just said, you and your friends were harassing the token booth clerk. I told them, "What, friends? I am by myself!" But they didn't want to hear it, and I could tell they were biased.

They took me upstairs to the token booth, where I saw Leo and his boys. They asked the token booth clerk if I was with them, and she said: "Yes, he was there too." I got so upset because I was not with them, nor was I dressed like them. I was wearing a nice sports jacket and shoes, while they had jeans and sneakers.

When I told them that, all they said was, "You heard what she said," then the worst thing they could have done happened.

They handcuffed me with Leo on one side and Cool Breeze with me in the middle and no free hands. I thought they would kick my ass since they both had one hand free, and I didn't, so I was at their mercy. I started cursing out the token booth clerk and the cops for arresting me when I had done nothing wrong, but I did that to show Leo and his boys that I was street too, and didn't want them to let the fact that I dressed nicely fool them. We got thrown into a police van, and when we were in the back together, I told them I had to ditch my gun, and I was hoping it would still be there when we got released. I was furious, and to my surprise, they didn't talk shit to me. I said my piece and remained quiet for the rest of the ride as they all spoke about what they would say in their defense. I was just hoping they would tell them I was not with them but didn't mention it because I knew they didn't give a shit about me.

I am sure they were happy that I got arrested because they were evident to me. When we got to the precinct, we were taken upstairs, and we got searched before being put into the holding cell. The precinct had a bigger cell, but it was full of others who had committed more serious crimes. The officer who put us in didn't even lock the cell bar doors but was sitting at a desk right in front of the cell, writing up our desk appearance tickets. Now I was in a small cell, surrounded by my enemies, but contrary to what I thought, they all seemed pretty cool, with Leo and Cool Breeze being the only exceptions.

They just kept giving me looks like they wanted to beat the shit out of me. I stood my ground and never put my guards down. After a short while, there was a big commotion. Suddenly, the cop who was working on our papers ran over to help the cops who were fighting with two drunk guys. Then all hell broke loose when the guys being arrested grabbed a baton from one of the cops and started swinging wildly at the others after he hit the first cop. It was chaos, but it was also my opportunity to take the key from the cell, which I had seen hanging on the wall when they put us in the cell. I didn't say anything, I just stepped out of the open call, and I took the key quickly and went back into the cell. Leo and his boys saw that I had taken the key, and they told me that when the cops find that key on me, they will beat the shit out of me. I told him I didn't give a shit; I was not supposed to be there since I had not done anything wrong. I told them I was going to take a small token to remember this event. They just stood there and shook their heads and told me I was crazy. That is precisely what I wanted them to think; this way, they were less likely to mess with me in the future.

I looked at Leo, and I told him he owed me a gun since I had to ditch mine, and it was his fault. He just looked at me and started laughing. The fight with the two guys ended badly for them. They were beaten and bloodied to a pulp and thrown into the smallest cell adjacent to ours. Once things calmed down, we were given desk appearance tickets and released shortly after. When we got outside, the Sun was out, and it was Sunday morning. It had been a long and eventful night. I started walking towards the train station with Leo and his boys following behind me.

I thought there would be more aggression, but instead, they asked me if I still had the cell key. I reached into my pants and pulled it out, and showed it to them. They all started laughing and telling me I was crazy again, but at least they weren't trying to start any shit with me. As it turns out, it appears I had gained their respect for acting just as crazy as they were; what they didn't know is that I was. Leo asked me what I was planning to do with the key. I didn't answer him, but instead, I told him, "Don't forget, you owe me a gun." He started laughing, and his boys laughed as well, so I laughed with them, and then we went our separate ways with smiles on our faces.

It was kind of weird for me to be laughing with these guys, mainly because a few hours earlier, we were ready to kill each other. I figured everything happens for a reason, and at least something good had come from my close encounter with the Alphabet City Boys. The following week, I had to go for my court appearance, and as soon as I walked in, I saw Leo and his boys sitting in the back row. I went to the other side because I wasn't friends with them and wanted to represent myself as not having been part of that crowd. However, the minute they saw me, they called me over and wanted me to sit with them. I reluctantly went over, and as soon as I sat down next to Leo, he asked me, "What did you do with the key?"

I started laughing and told him it was hanging on my wall as a souvenir and in memory of getting busted with the Alphabet City Boys. He began to laugh, and it was right there where I noticed all hostilities were gone from his face. He then started asking me how it was in the South Bronx and that he had never been there.

I told him it was like the lower east side, but the streets were wider, and more Puerto Ricans lived there.

I told him we had a lot of gangs and that there were a lot of violent crimes. He asked me if I belonged to a gang, and I told him, "Yes, I am the warlord from one of the South Bronx's biggest gangs." I also told him I had gone to the Marines and tried to escape the gang scene. I told him how we all got into dancing to bring peace into our hood. Then I shared stories about all the killings and building burning in my neighborhood and how we were trying to put a stop to it. Keeping in mind that gangs were getting paid for setting the fires for the landlords. As we continued to talk, I realized that Leo was having a hard time liking me because of Kitty and that she was with me now. I noticed that he had accepted that nothing he could do about it. That became more evident a short time later when a friend of his, whom I remembered from the night I first met Kitty. His name was Scorpio; he had long black hair and a long scar that ran down the side of his left cheek.

You could tell he had been to Rikers Island, which is where gang members would cut your face with a razor blade if you gave them any shit. Some people seem to think that someone with a scar like that is badass; I would tell them, "The badass is the one who cut him!" Anyway, he came over, took a seat in front of us, and turned to greet all his other friends. He also greeted me; he asked Leo how Elba was doing. Leo looked at him then pointed at me as he said, "I am not with her anymore; she is with Willie now." Scorpio lifted his eyebrows, looked at me, then looked at Leo and said, "And you're OK with that?"

Leo shrugged his shoulders and simply said, "What do you want me to do; she doesn't want to be with me; she wants to be with him." Scorpio had a look of surprise on his face and just said: "Alright, well, if you're not saying anything, I won't either." Leo just looked at him and said, "Will's cool, people. We got locked up together last week, and he did some crazy shit." For a minute, I thought he was going to yell out that I had taken the key, but I guess he knew better. A short while later, and after that uncomfortable feeling of thinking, what if this guy incites Leo's wrath, and they jump me when we were done with court. I thought when the court officer called all our names one by one and asked us to step in front of the judge. As we were all standing in front of the judge and thinking about saying I was not with them, I changed my mind and just remained quiet.

As it turned out, it was just a small offense, so the judge let us off with a warning and told us if we got in trouble again and came before him, we would regret it! I was content with his decision, glad I had not said anything about not being with them. We were told we could leave, and he dismissed the case against us. It was apparent that the jails were full enough, and they had to leave room for more serious crimes. We all went, and as I was walking down the streets with them, Leo told me he would not bother Kitty again and that we had nothing to fight about anymore. I told him I was glad we were not going to have any more problems and wished him well. He did the same, and we walked in separate directions. Getting arrested with them was the best thing that could have happened to me regarding not getting into any beef with Leo and his boys from the Lower East Side.

When I finally got home, I called Elba, and I told her what had happened, and she couldn't believe it, but she got thrilled. She was so happy she told me she'd call me later because she wanted to tell her mother. After that day, I never had a problem going to Elba's neighborhood again and visiting her Mom, who loved me for obvious reasons. I didn't dance with Elba (Kitty) until late 75, but more about that later.

Lifelong friends who also attended the jams at St. Mary's in 1974 - Wilma, Mercedes, Mara, Mayra, Ivett, the Latin Hustle was our drug of choice during those days!

CHAPTER SIXTEEN: THE DISCO BANDITS

In 1975, I met a guy I will just call Papo. He was a straight-up stickup artist and older than my boys and me. (Stick up artist, means he likes to rob people) He lured us into doing stickups with him into getting money to go out dancing, or so he said at the time. Papo convinced us by telling us we would only rob people who could not report the crime, such as prostitutes and their Johns, while in the act of having sex in John's car at the Hunts Point area of the South Bronx. We would always go there at night and watch from a distance for a John to pick up a prostitute, then park his car and sneak up on them from both sides and rob them both. They didn't give us a hard time most of the time since we had 38 Caliber guns with long barrels, a scary proposition when looking at a canon pointed at your head. After we robbed a couple of John's, we would cop some drugs and head downtown to party. Papo was a crazy driver and sometimes would drive on the FDR Drive in Manhattan without looking at the road, but ducking his head down and asking us to tell him which way to turn the car's wheel. We had a few close calls, but he never hit anyone, and we all thought he was just out of his mind or had a death wish. That went on for a while, and we always got money for going clubbing. On Easter Sunday, we had broken night and spent all the money we had stolen the night before, and as it was too early to hit the Prostitutes, Papo drove us to the Projects on 137th St. and St. Ann's Avenue.

He asked Willie Whip and me to rob whoever went into the building and gave me his 38 long to do the robbery.

We went in and waited for a short while before a Black couple walked into the stairwell. As the couple walked in, they both looked at us and said, "Happy Easter, Guys." What else could I respond, but say Happy Easter to them both.

A switch went off in my head, and I knew right then and there that I could not rob these good people, and I was ashamed for even having contemplated the idea of robbing hard-working people, especially on Easter Sunday. Willie felt the same way I did, and once they were gone, I told Whip I didn't want to do this; he responded in kind and told me he didn't want to do it either. We walked back to the car where Papo was waiting, and he asked if we had robbed the two people who walked in. Whip and I looked at him and said no, and told him we weren't going to do it anymore. I gave Papo back his 38, and he asked us why. I told him because it's Easter Sunday, and I didn't like robbing people anyway. It was one thing to rob the prostitutes and their Johns because they wouldn't report it, but it was quite another to rob innocent, hard-working people. (Not the prostitute was not hard-working, mind you.) He got mad at us and told us we were just scared, so I told him I wasn't like him, and he should know it was not about being scared since we had done so many robberies with him at Hunts Point.

I got pissed off with him and told him to do it himself; then, I told him that we would walk home, which was the last time we saw him. A short time later, I got a call from his wife, Nancy, and she told me Papo got locked up for robbing and shooting someone in the City.

Russel Stern – Recreation Specialist at St. Mary's, during the early to late 1970s. We called him the watcher because he saw everything our gang did, good and bad, and never said a word. He was also a teacher at a local JHS and a hell of a Ping Pong player. RIP, my friend! One of my favorite things about St. Mary's was the boxing gym, and I also studied Martial Arts there.

Sparring with Enrigue El Gallo at St. Mary's

That did not surprise me, and while I felt terrible for her, I told her there was nothing I could do for Papo; he would have to do his time and hopefully change his way of thinking while he was away. She agreed with me and asked me to check up on her and her son from time to time, and I promised her I would, and I did for a while. Willie and I started hanging out with a couple of new friends, one called Junbug and the other called Blue. Not sure why we called him Blue since he had green eyes, but that name stuck. The girls called him greed-eyed Joe. We also hung out with my other best friend Tony, who lived in my building, and we called ourselves the Jive Five. We were always together, and we always hooked up with the ladies wherever we went. We were players, and they all knew it, but most did not care. Many females would play the field and mess with one guy after another in those days.

Debbie Benitez, and Gladys Rodriguez, with Willie Estrada at the Red and White, in early 1975.

I was not into sharing my women with my friends, though, and we respected each other that way throughout our time together. It wasn't long before we started hanging out at the Red and White club, one of the most popular clubs for Hustle Dancers, in 1975. You have to keep in mind that during those days, all the best dancers from the Bronx hung out at the 310½, and we would all hang out at the same clubs in the City whenever we ventured into Manhattan. While my first club in the City was the Fresh, that new club caught our attention; it was called the Rouge Blanc, in French, translation, The Red & White.

One night while we were all there, the DJ announced a Hustle contest, which would start the following weekend. It was their way of packing the club because lord knows everybody and their mothers were doing the Latin Hustle by 1975. The competition was stiff, as all the best Hustler dancers were there that following weekend. The crème de la crème as I called it. Some of the names participating were Floyd Chisolm, Jose Sabu, Dante, Billy Fajardo, and most of the Latin Symbolics Dance Team. I was no longer dancing with Maggie because she had gotten spinal meningitis and was very sick by that time. She almost died on us, so we all went to the hospital to see her and wish her well. I believe our visit gave her the strength to live, and she soon after recovered. Maggie was missed, and while I no longer had a regular dance partner, there were so many girls to choose from who were outstanding dancers. I asked one girl named Liz to dance with me, but she said she wasn't going to dance because every guy had asked her to be their partner, and she didn't want anybody feeling bad.

The same went for her best friend, who was also an amazing Hustle dancer by the name of Releska. I was approached by a girl I had never danced with named Arlene, so I decided to give her a spin on the dance floor to see if we were good together. To my surprise, she was excellent and easy to maneuver on the dance floor, and her spinning was superb. I asked Liz to dance with me because she could spin like a top, was short, and looked good together. Arlene was a bit taller, but she could follow just as good, and she was my complexion, so we also looked good together. She was from my neighborhood, so we knew each other, but I had never really seen her dance until I danced with her. When the contest was about to start, I saw Floyd dancing with Jose leading, and I knew I was in trouble because Floyd could follow better than most girls and was always really fancy with his steps. By now, you must have guessed that Floyd was gay, and you would be right. But he was a good friend and a part of our dance crew, but I knew we would all do our best to win.

I saw the two girls I had asked to dance with me, Liz and Releska, dancing with two other guys. I shook my head, but I was determined to win, and I already knew Arlene was a good choice in partners because we danced exceptionally well together. The rules were simple when the contest started; you had to get off the dance floor if you got tapped on the shoulder. Three judges were walking around watching us all; however, they allowed everyone to finish the 1st song without being tapped out. Once the second song started, the judges went around tapping couples on the shoulder and eliminating them. After about the 4th song, I noticed that there were only 4 of us left, Floyd, Jose, Dante, and myself with our respective partners.

Out of about 25 couples of the best Hustle Dancers the City had to offer, all the guys and girls from the South Bronx were the only dancers left on the floor. After the 5th song came on, only two couples were left on the dance floor: Jose Sabu and Floyd Chisolm, and Arlene and myself. They allowed the last song to come close to the end, and Arlene and I were tapped out. Floyd and Jose won 1st place, but the fact that Arlene and I had never danced together and came in 2nd was huge in my eyes, and I was thrilled to be there until the end, with two of the best dancers from our crew winning 1st place. Arlene and I congratulated Floyd and Jose, and we all hugged. We all enjoyed that the finalists were from our close group of friends.

We were, without a doubt, the best in the City, and all from the South Bronx. That contest piqued the interest of many others, and the following week the club was more packed than I had ever seen it.

Here we go again; I found myself ready to dance against the best in the City, but this time Floyd and Jose could not dance together because they had already won 1st place the week before. Arlene and I had gotten together a few times during the week and were even better now that we had the opportunity to practice. We were ready to take on the best in the City and even happier to find out Floyd and Jose could not dance together.

Arlene and I knew we would do well, and we didn't want to use some of the moves we had been practicing right away; we were saving the best for last. When the contest started, we were both nervous but confident.

For some reason, I felt like my time had come, and it was time to take my place among the best and prove I was as good, if not better than all the rest. One by one, our competition had to leave the floor. As a result, we had a lot of room to travel the dance floor, and that is precisely what we did. You could say we were showing off, and in a way, I guess we were, but it was our style and grace that was most outstanding, as we also won over the crowd. Our turns and spins were flawless, and the new turns we had practiced all week were executed with style, confidence, and grace, and we never missed a beat. The dancers who had been on the dance floor the week before at the end were with us. However, in the end, I found my partner and I were the only couples left on the dance floor one by one; our biggest competition had all been tapped out and eliminated. The judges allowed Arlene and me to finish the last song, and we took over the entire dance floor with big smiles on our faces and pride in our hearts. It was a feeling of euphoria for us both.

Once it was all over, everyone came over to us and congratulated us, and we knew it was genuine because we were like one big happy family for the most part. After all the congratulations were done, I got approached by the club manager, and he told me the owner wanted to discuss something with me. I didn't know what to expect other than the fact they owed me and my partner, Arlene, the money for 1st place. His name was Joey Swartz, and to my surprise, he offered me a job at the club. I asked him what I would be doing at the club. He told me he would start me off in the coat check because it would soon get cold. I had never worked at a club before, so I told him I would think about it.

I, however, did speak with a guy who was working there, and he told me I would make a lot of money working the coatroom. I asked him how, and he said, "Simple, you put several coats on one hanger and keep the rest for yourself."

So you mean if a few friends come together, I can put all their coats together and keep whatever extra I made besides the regular price of checking their coats? "Yes" was his response, and it brought a big smile to my face, especially after he told me after the crowd was all there, I could dance. I took the job and was told I could start the following Saturday. When I started working the next weekend, I started doing precisely what the other guy told me to do. Many of my friends were surprised I was working in the coatroom, but they didn't know my secret. I was putting up to 5 coats on one hanger, and by the end of the night, I had a few hundred dollars in my pocket.

I also had the opportunity to dance after the coatroom was full. I met a lovely girl named Lisa on my first day, and I had a chance to dance with her. She had pretty light green eyes and was a pretty good hustle dancer. I started dating her after that day and liked her. However, one day she called me and told me she had a big fight with her mom and asked me to pick her up at Grand Central Station on 42nd St. When I got there, I looked all over the place for her, but I could not find her and give up after an hour of searching. As some of you may or may not know, Grand Central Station is a huge place with many trains that run through there, so trying to find her was a real mission for me. In the end, I never saw her, so I went home. After a couple of days, I got a call from her, and she was angry with me because she thought I did not go pick her up.

I told her I did and looked for her for over an hour, but she didn't believe me and told me she didn't want to see me again. I told her it would have helped if she had told me exactly where she was, but as it turned out, many people had let her down in the past, and she was under the impression I did the same.

What could I do but wish her well, as it seemed she had made up her mind, all because I couldn't locate her? I never did see her again, and she never went back to the club either. As the weeks passed, I found myself being hit on by the club owner, Joey, and it turned out he was gay.

One weekend, as I was ordering a Tequila Sunrise, Joey approached me at the bar and started talking to me. HE GRABBED MY PRIVATES before I knew it, and I systematically punched him in the face.

Joey was in shock that I had struck him and told me I was fired, so I made believe I was going to hit him again, and he cringed. I told him I didn't want to work for anyone who would disrespect me that way and that he shouldn't have done that. I told him if he ever did that again, I would break his face, and I walked away. One of my friends, Flaco, saw what happened, he started laughing, then told me that they were all like that. I asked him what he was talking about, and he said the people who own and run this club. He said they were paying young guys to have oral sex with them, and I was disgusted by that. But we both started laughing when he said, "Did you see the look on his face when you punched him in the face?" I had not hit him hard, but I'm sure he felt it and was pissed that I didn't let him get away with touching me that way.

After that, my boys were making fun of me, which infuriated me even more, but eventually, I laughed at what they were saying. The strange thing is that things like that were happening regularly. Not so much at clubs, but on the streets of the South Bronx and urban areas in general. I'm not saying that gay men were going around grabbing genitals, but they were soliciting oral sex from young boys. I know because I got approached many times, and it would just piss me off.

At any rate, I continued going to the Red & White for a short while longer, but the last time I went was very eventful. Willie Whip and I started dating two sisters with blond hair and bright blue eyes. They were Dominican, but you couldn't tell by looking at them; they looked more like white girls. My girl's name was Becky, her sister Lisa was Whip's girl. We decided to take them dancing to the Red & White one night, and we had a great time.

However, after we had a great time with them at the end of the night, Becky went into the lady's room after almost everyone had left. The club manager, who we called Yummy because he was short and round, started rushing us to leave, and all of a sudden, we heard a scream come out of the ladies' room. Her sister came running out, asking us to help that a demon from Hell had possessed her sister. Whip and I looked at each other, and we started laughing, but Yummy was not amused. He went inside the ladies' room to get her out. The funniest thing happened a few moments after he walked into the ladies' room. He came running out, screaming, "Get the crazy bitch out of here"...

The funny part was not only that he came out of the ladies' room, screaming like a little girl, but his glasses were missing. It turned out she had slapped them right off his face and then began trying to beat him up. Her sister told us that she sometimes gets possessed by evil spirits or demons, as she put it. We didn't believe her, but we didn't know them that well, so we proceeded with caution.

Whip and I went into the ladies' room with her sister to get her out as Yummy continued having a hissy fit over getting bitch slapped. When we went into the bathroom, the look on Becky's face was much different than when she went in. She had a crazy look in her eyes, and when she looked at me, I could tell she was not herself. To be honest, it was kind of scary to look at her because she seemed to be possessed by something evil, and even her voice was different. She let out a scream when she saw us walking in, or when it saw us walking in, better said. Her sister Lisa started talking to her and telling her we had to leave, but she said she wanted the beer. I grabbed her on one side, and Whip grabbed her on the other, and we walked out.

Her sister told her we were going to get a beer, and she came pretty calmly at first. When we got to where Yummy was, you could tell he was scared, and he stayed away from us as we walked out the door. Once we were outside, we started walking towards the train, but they lived on the Westside, and I decided to get my father's car so Whip and I would have a ride back home afterward. Becky was saying all types of crazy things about the Devil and how she was his daughter, and although we were all scared, we did not show any fear.

However, when we got to the hallway of my building, I held her around the shoulders tightly, and she turned to me and asked me why I was holding her. I told her I was holding her because she was beautiful. I didn't expect the response I got from her when she said, "If you saw what I really looked like, you would die of fright."

The way she said it made my skin crawl and sent shivers up my spine. Yes, what she said scared me, but I proceeded to the elevator and took everyone upstairs to my house to get my father's car keys. Thinking about it now, I realize it was a dumb thing to do, but I was young and naïve at the time, so up I went. When I told my father what happened and asked him to lend me the car, he insisted on taking us, so I said OK. Pops had a funny look on his face, but he was amused. When we got in his car, Becky told us again that she wanted a beer, so Dad drove us to the 24-hour store, and we got her some. Once she had the beer, she seemed to calm down, so we drove her home. Her sister asked us to come up and not leave them alone. Dad was intrigued by what was going on, and he didn't believe it, but he enjoyed her antics, and when we were on the road, he tried to converse with her, to no avail.

When we finally got to the Upper West Side where she lived, my Dad asked us if we wanted him to wait, but we told him we didn't know how long we would be there, so we thanked him, and he told us to be careful, and off he went. When we got to Becky's house, her mother opened the door, and her sister told her what had happened. It was daylight by then, but her mother was worried about them, so she was up early and waiting for them to return home.

Her mother was gratified that Whip and I had stayed with them through this ordeal and asked us to wait until Becky was herself again, and reluctantly, we did.

Becky passed out a short time later, after threatening to jump out the window, which I had to stop her from doing. We went into the girl's room with their mother's blessings because she knew we were good guys, or at least she thought we were. Whip got into bed with his girlfriend, and I got into the bed right across from hers, which is where Becky slept. As I lay next to her while she was passed out, I admit that there was nothing sexy about it. To be honest, I was scared and couldn't close my eyes as she slept.

The room was pretty well lit since it was daylight already, which was a blessing in disguise. I would probably not be lying next to her if it had been dark. All types of crazy ideas went through my head, such as, what if she woke up and bit my face off, or cut my throat or something crazy like that, I thought to myself as I laid next to her.

It's crazy how fear of the unknown can scare you more than anything else, especially when it is supernatural. As I lay there thinking all these crazy thoughts, Becky opened her eyes quickly and scared the shit out of me. I jumped off the bed, looked at her, and said, "Becky?" She looked at me and sighed, "Yes" "Oh my God, you scared the shit out of me."

I said to her as I got back in the bed with her. She was herself again, but I still was not entirely convinced. What if the crazy Demon came back, I asked myself. OK, I am not usually that easily scared, but we're talking Demon's here, and that's not something I take lightly.

I asked her if she was OK and if she remembered anything, but she just shook her head and asked me what had happened. Whip was under the covers, doing, I guess you know what, but when they heard us talking, it all stopped, and I could tell Whip was not happy about Becky waking up at such an inopportune time. We all got up and started telling her what happened but told her the funniest parts first so it wouldn't be that hard on her. We managed to make her laugh for a short while, but just as we all thought she was OK, she started crying. As it turned out, Becky had been afflicted with what she called a curse for some time and didn't want it to happen anymore.

It was sad seeing her cry, but as I started thinking about our relationship, I realized I was not cut out or prepared for this type of paranormal activity in my life, besides that fact, that it scared the shit out of me. Her mother came into the room when she heard her crying and tried her best to comfort her, but Becky was now really bawling, and it was all a bit too much for me. I told everyone I was exhausted and was going home once Becky calmed down, and even though her mother offered breakfast, I couldn't get out of there fast enough. It was like something from the "Outer Limits" to me, and I wanted no part of it. It was a long way back home because it was Sunday, and we had to take the train downtown before traveling back into the Bronx. I thought about taking a cab and then running out, but I was too damn tired to run, so we took the long way home.

Whip and I laughed at specific parts of our unfortunate encounter with an evil spirit. Still, we both knew we didn't want to go through that again, so we decided we would find adventures with new girls, which would hopefully not be as scary.

St. Mary's 1974

Willie Whip and Jose Sabu (Latin Hustle Pioneers)

We saw the girls in our neighborhood sometime later, but we didn't speak about what happened, and while it was good to see them, we didn't speak for very long. Somehow I knew they both understood that ordeal had affected all involved, but there were no hard feelings, and we went our separate ways, never to see them again.

Willie, Diana, Lilly, and Richie at the Boombamakaoo 1975

CHAPTER SEVENTEEN: THE JIVE FIVE

By 1975 I had made a name for myself as a dancer. As I think about it now, my friends helped define me as a person and a dancer.

I was only 19 years old, but within that short period, I had been a part of the gang world for nine years, and I had seen a lot of death at a very early age. I took part in things I am not very proud of to survive, but I would not be here had I not. Many of my friends fell to street violence and drugs. My four best friends at the time were Willie Whip, Tony, Blue, and Junbug, and even though we came from the gang world, we were also good dancers who loved to seduce the females on the dance floor. We also started hanging out with Chino, a martial artist and a pretty good dancer himself.

One day I went to pick him up at his house, which was a few blocks from where I lived on 145th St. between Brook and St. Ann's Avenues, and when I got there, his father killed a goat right there in front of his two-story house on Beach Terrace. I was shocked when I saw what was going on right in front of many kids. They were all yelling at him not to kill the poor goat. That did not stop him. He had two weapons, a bat and a big butcher knife, but apparently, he had already hit the poor goat over the head a couple of times, and still, the goat wouldn't die. Whip and I tried talking some sense into his head to no avail; he was determined to kill that poor goat to make a stew.

When the blows to the goat's head failed, even though it was lying down on the cement floor, he grabbed his big butcher knife and started stabbing the goat in the throat.

As the goat continued to move and cry, he started jumping on the goat's head to make sure it died. Needless to say, all the kids in the neighborhood were a bit disturbed by how Chino's dad killed the goat, but so were we.

The following day, I was hanging out at Blue's house with Willie Whip, and we got a call from Chino, who was in a panic and seemed scared. It turned out several men were banging on his door who wanted to hurt him and his father for reasons unknown to him. I put two and two together and imagined it was about what his father did the day before in killing that poor goat in front of the kids. But I wasn't sure, so we got our guns and jumped in a cab. When we got to Chino's block, I was the first to run out of the cab and started running down the street to get to Chino. When I got into the hallway of Chino's house, it was dark and dingy, but I saw several men banging on his door still and screaming for him to come out. Now it had taken us at least 12 to 15 minutes to get there, and these guys were still at it, so I knew they were serious, but so were we. I took out my gun and screamed at them to stop banging on the door, and when they turned and saw me standing there by myself with a small-caliber weapon, they stopped but started walking towards me anyway.

I pointed my gun at the ring leader's head and told him I would put a hole in his head if he didn't stop walking towards me. The doors behind me swung open hard at that moment, and in came Blue and Whip with their guns drawn. The older guys we were pointing our weapons at were terrified now. They all put their hands in the air. We called Chino to come out, and the minute we saw him, his face was filled with rage.

The first apartment to our right was empty, so Chino told the five guys who had been banging on his door to go inside after he punched one of them in the face. I had never seen Chino that angry, but I understood that those men came after him and his father, which is why we had his back. Chino grabbed my gun and pointed it at the ring leader's head when we got them all inside. Chino was ready to shoot the guy, so I stepped in and stopped him by pulling the gun up and away from the guy. He was so angry he wasn't thinking straight; that is when he decided to put a hole in the wall instead, but the gun misfired and did not shoot, or so I thought. I immediately grabbed the gun from him, one of Blue's weapons, and checked it. The damn thing did not have any bullets in the clip, so I told Blue, "You gave me a gun with no freaking bullets." It was no laughing matter at the time. What if they had attacked me and I tried to shoot? Chino was so crazy he grabbed Blue's big gun, a 38 Caliber with a long barrel, but when he aimed it at the wall, Blue grabbed it and told him to stop. He said, what if a kid next door gets killed when the bullet goes through the wall.

Chino got mad, but he knew Blue was right, so he punched the guy in the face again, only this time he kept hitting him. We had to pull him off the guy because he was hurting him, while Whip held the others at bay by pointing the gun he was holding, which was also Blue's gun. But he had a look on his face, as though he was saying to himself, I wonder if this gun has bullets in it? We let the other guys go with a stern warning and told them if they ever messed with Chino or his father again, we would be back, and it would be much worse next time.

We could all tell they were scared and knew we meant business. After allowing those men to leave, we all went back to Blue's house, just in case they called the Cops, even though we knew they wouldn't. I got into it with Blue and asked him how the hell he could give me a gun with no bullets in it. He told me he had been practicing with that gun a few days before and forgot to reload it. I told him he might as well have given me a weapon that would shoot a little flag that said "Bang," and we all started laughing about it. Whip joined in and confirmed that he started thinking his gun didn't have any bullets either, so he was getting ready to pistol-whip them. Well, your name is Willie Whip anyway, but your weapon does have bullets, "Did you check it?" asked Blue. "Dam, I hadn't thought about it since we left so fast," so he checked it in front of us, and as it turns out, his gun had bullets in it, so we all started to laugh again. The following day I saw a couple of the guys who messed with Chino walking right towards me as I was crossing St. Mary's Park to get to Chino's house.

They looked at me hard, so I reached into my jacket as if I had a gun on me, and I asked them what the hell they were looking at. They both raised their eyebrows with a scared look on their faces and said, "Nada Nada, no ay problema," and they hurried away like the cowards they were.

It was easy for them to intimidate Chino when there were five against one, however now that they knew Chino was not alone, they showed their real colors. In those days, you were either a hunter or the prey, and we were no man's prey; we held our own and feared nobody.

But we weren't bullies either, we just didn't let anyone mess with us, but we also had a significant number of gang members who were our brothers, so if things got a little too much for us, we would call in backup all hell usually ensued.

From left to right: Willie MB, Tony, Blue, Junbug, and Willie Whip AKA the Jive Five.

Sensi George Vascones (RIP) during the late 1970s.

CHAPTER EIGHTEEN: 1977 AFTER THE BLACKOUT

By early 1977 the Latin Hustle was also being done in Puerto Rico, but not with the same proficiency level as we did here in New York, and there were many opportunities for me to go there and make some money doing shows. My partner Millie and I had broken up because I danced with my former partner Maggie at a contest we had rehearsed for. Still, a female I once dated named Diana told me she would be in Puerto Rico, and she had some connections for getting us a few shows. I knew she still had some feelings for me, but I was not looking to rekindle anything. However, she was a pretty good Hustle dancer, so I jumped at the chance of doing the Hustle in Puerto Rico with her, and I also wanted to visit my family there. We got there on July 9th, and true to her word, Diana got us a show at a High-End hotel in San Juan on July 13th. We did pretty well, considering we had only rehearsed a couple of times before we performed, and it was no surprise that people knew we were from New York by the way we danced together.

Willie Estrada and Diana Santiago - 1975

The following day, we saw on the News that there was a Blackout in NYC, and they showed the aftermath, and people were still breaking into the stores and looting in shopping areas, especially electronics stores.

I was glad I was not in New York when that happened, especially after hearing all the horror stories about how many people got hurt, including a few people I knew from my neighborhood. Diana and I did a few more shows, but I missed my friends, and although Diana wanted me to stay, I went home just a few days after the blackout. Once I got there, I saw some of the aftermaths of what I knew had been chaos. I spoke with a guy I knew named Bozo, who had almost severed his right leg when he kicked a jewelry store window, and a large shard of glass came down on his leg. What the hell were you thinking, I asked him? "Bro, I was so high, I didn't even feel it, and I managed to get a few pieces before I passed out!" He went on to describe the chaos, and all I could do was shake my head and laugh at his bungled attempt to get rich quickly.

I soon noticed many more teens DJing at community parties in the parks, in community rooms, and centers all over the South Bronx, and I am sure in other boroughs. The birth of Hip Hop was looming in the years ahead, but Disco still ruled supreme during the summer of 1977 despite exaggerations about Hip Hop being born in 1973. I always ask people one thing when they make such a ridiculous statement. What other culture in the history of humanity do you know of that has an exact starting place, date, and time with one creator? Of course, nobody I know ever heard of such a thing. Not even in those days had any of us ever heard the term Hip Hop spoken or that it started at one party invented by one individual!

After the Blackout of 1977, Jams in the park became commonplace throughout the South Bronx, and the biggest DJ name in my hood was Grand Master Flash.

My 21st birthday was coming up, so I decided to ask Elba to be my date, and we would be celebrating it at Latin Times, where all the best dancers hung out in those days. David Maldonado was the promoter for that club, located on 43rd St. between 6th and 7th Ave. at the Diplomat Hotel. The night of my birthday, there was a series of Contests beginning; however, I decided not to enter but celebrate my birthday instead. All my friends came to help me celebrate, and David Maldonado was always happy to see us because he knew we were very popular, and the place would get packed with our crew there. The truth of the matter is whatever club we frequented always got packed because our group consisted of the best dancers in New York City, and needless to say, we had a following. The week after my birthday, Lucky and I entered the Rock Contest, and we faced stiff competition but came in 2nd place.

I don't remember ever winning 1st place with Lucky as I think about it now. However, when dancing with Willie Whip as my partner, we always took 1st place, so I would have to say he was my best Rock partner during the early to mid- '70s. There were five more Rock Contests held there, and every week they picked 1st, 2nd, 3rd, and 4th place winners to compete in the finals. The best Rock dancers from throughout New York came each weekend to compete, but most of the winners were from the Bronx and Manhattan for the most part. The winners in the finals were: 1st place, Papo 184 and Calvin from the Bronx; 2nd place, Cucuso and his partner (whose name I don't remember) also from the Bronx, Lucky and I came in 3rd place and my boys Mike Latuf and Eddie Pinero from Manhattan and came in 4th place.

After the Finals, David Maldonado approached me and told me he wanted to show me something upstairs. I didn't know what he was trying to show me but said he knew I was very popular, and he wanted to make me a part of something he was looking to do. He asked me to bring a couple of my friends and that he would buy us drinks when we came back, so I invited Chino and Tony with me, along with a couple of girls who were hanging out with us that night. When we got upstairs, and David opened the doors to the Grand Ballroom, we all were amazed at how big the place was. It also had a stage, a balcony with seating, and a Bar. It was a much bigger venue, which held over 2,500 people. I asked David why he wanted us to see this place, and he told me he wanted us to help him promote dance jams there regularly. I told him I didn't know anything about promotions, but again he said to me that I was very popular and that he would teach me and pay me to work for him to promote dances there.

We all looked at him like he was crazy, but then he told us he was asking us because he knew we would help make his jams the biggest and best in the City. I asked him what we would have to do, and he said he would give us a dollar for every flier that came into the Box Office with our stamp on it, and whoever brought him the most people over 500 would also get round trip tickets to Cancun Mejico, or take the money which was $800. He offered to pay us by the hour to help him put up posters all over the city, but we would have to use our cars to do it, and he would also take care of the gas. In the end, he was talking about making money and becoming Club promoters, and he offered us a piece of the pie. We started talking about the possibilities right away, and in his presence, he liked what he heard and asked me to join him in a meeting with Carlos Ramos, who would be the main DJ for the events, which he would call "Faces Grand Ballroom." It made sense since Carlos Ramos was also the DJ at Latin Times, and he had a loyal following, namely us and all the best dancers in the city, and Carlos was from our neighborhood.

Chino and Willie at Latin Times 1977

Willie Estrada & Faces DJ Carlos Ramos 1978

Still brothers 44 years later, John Garcia, Carlos, and myself. Dancing Hustle with Veronica Castilla

David Maldonado and Willie Estrada planning Faces Grand Ballroom in late 1977

It was now early November 1977, and David invited Carlos Ramos and me to an initial meeting to discuss our strategy and develop themes for the events. He told us he wanted to continue doing Latin Times until we had everything set, and we would be proceeding with promoting the first event in early 1978. After the upcoming holidays, we would sit down again and go over everything. I told David we were preparing for an Award Show with the Latin Symbolics at the Diplomat Hotel, where he held his events at Latin Times and was also planning to do bigger events soon. I was pressed for time because we had to rehearse every day to prepare for the first-ever Latin Symbolics Awards Show.

I had to put David on hold because this show was significant to us and Lucky and I would be performing along with many of my fellow dance team members for the awards show on November 25th.

I was heartbroken to have missed the Award Show but was happy to hear that my fellow Latin Symbolics paid a special tribute to me, and my parents were proud to be there and watch with great delight.

Yamil Borges is a former professional dancer and actress who lives in Berlin, Germany. She is also a singer of many genres, including Jazz, Chansons, and an accomplished Actress and Performer.

She was born in San Lorenzo, Puerto Rico, but grew up in the South Bronx. She is known for A Chorus Line (1985), Miami Vice (1984), The Luckiest Man in the World (1989), and the Cosby Show (1990).

I have not seen her since the early 1980s, but we're still in touch and still friends since the day we met in 1977.

CHAPTER NINETEEN: THE BEAT DOWN

By late 1977, I had been with the Latin Symbolics for several years, and I had performed in both the Latin Hustle and the Rock Categories in many shows as a Golden Member of the Latin Symbolics Dance Company. On November 22nd, 1977, we were preparing for Latin Symbolics Awards Show, televised live from the Diplomat Hotel on 43rd between 6th & 7th Avenues on Thanksgiving Day, November 25th. On the day of dress rehearsals, we had a beautiful young woman named Yamil Borges trying out for our team, which was unheard of since we had a show to put on in two days. The rehearsal was in the Grand Ballroom of the Diplomat Hotel; however, the actual performance would be in a smaller venue of the hotel, where David Maldonado hosted events every Saturday Night.

We all sat around to watch Yamil dance. George Vascones asked us to check her out and wanted our input since she was trying out at the last minute for an important show that would reflect on us all as a team, which was his reason for asking us all to decide if she was good enough to be one of us. Yamil was a beautiful petite young woman in her early 20's. Right before she was to perform for us, the lights dimmed, and a spotlight focused on her as she stood gracefully with her head down and her eyes closed, in the middle of the dance floor. When the music started to play, it began with a beautiful melody that filled the ballroom with magic. In a slow, methodical manner, Yamil came to life as she lifted her head and opened her eyes. Suddenly, the music got louder with a faster tempo, complemented by the beauty of her elegant and spiritual dance routine.

I was in awe of her; she was the most beautiful dancer I had ever seen; her every move enchanted me so much I thought I was watching an angel dance just for me. I could see nothing else but her, as her dance captivated me as she took my breath away and made my heart smile. After only 30 seconds of her dancing, I knew she would be a member of our team, and as a matter of fact, she stole all our hearts, which was evident once she finished her beautiful dance in the graceful position in which she started her dance routine. We all gave her a standing ovation and yelled Bravo, Bravo, much to her delight. We all gathered around her and welcomed her to the team with open arms and big smiles.

We finished out the night of rehearsals by each doing the dance routines we would be doing on National TV in two days. I performed with my four-man Rock routine, with the Rock Masters, Robert Feliciano, Hector Berrios, and Pete Martinez. Debbie Benitez was doing a routine with her girls, Sugar & Spice, Yamil would be doing a solo, and George Vascones would be dancing with his partner Denise. Yamil got to see the rest of us dance, and while she was impressed, we all knew she was on a higher level than us. It was apparent that she had been training since she was a little girl by executing her moves and the beauty of her dance solo.

After we were done for the night, we all walked out together, and the guys huddled around Yamil.

While she gave us her attention, all the girls from our dance team saw what was happening. One girl in particular, who I had been dating for a short while, also noticed. It was evident Yamil had all our attention.

After seeing her dance, she mesmerized us all with her beauty and grace, as well as her good looks. I finally got Yamil's attention and the opportunity to speak with her as we walked to the train station down Broadway. We laughed along the way, and Yamil was extraordinarily charismatic and sweet, and I am sure she was happy to be getting all the attention we were giving her. I will never forget the words she spoke right before something terrible happened. When we got to 42nd St. and Broadway, she said, "New York, New York, there is no other place like it in the World!" as she looked up at the billboards. Suddenly and out of nowhere, I was attacked by an extremely tall black guy who hit me with an elbow shot right to the chest and knocked me to the side. He then started beating up Yamil, like she had done something terrible to him, and it looked personal. We had just met her, so we were in shock that this was happening, but we couldn't just stand by and watch this take place. I screamed at the maniac hitting Yamil, and he turned, looked at me with a crazy look in his eyes, and when Pete started yelling at him as well, he bolted and started running across 42nd St. The traffic was against him, and he almost got hit by a car as he ran like a crazy person across four lanes of traffic.

I was angry as we picked Yamil up from the floor. We could tell she was hurting, and I showed my concern. Once we knew she was OK. I turned to Pete and told him, "Let's get him, Pete" He looked at me and said, "Wanna get him?" I said hell yeah, and we both started running after him. Lucky and Hector stayed with Yamil, and off we went in hot pursuit of this maniac. We caught up to him on the following block, the corner of 41st St. and 7th Ave, and as we reached him, he turned and looked at us both with a terrifying and crazy look on his face.

Pete distracted him, and I kicked him in the ribs when he bent over; we knocked him to the ground with my knees on his shoulders, and I did like a pile driver on his face. I was so enraged; I didn't even hear when Pete told me to run when he saw the cops running towards us, with what looked like bats.

All of a sudden, as I was beating the shit out of this dude for what he did to Yamil, one of the cops struck me right on the upper left side of my head and cracked my head open. As I tried to look up to see who hit me, as I held my head, he hit me again hard on my left cheekbone and smashed it into a million pieces. After that blow, I was out of my senses, but they kept hitting me. By that time, Yamil had gotten there with Hector, and she jumped onto me in an attempt to protect me while screaming at the cops to stop hitting me. She finally got their attention and told them we were dancers coming out of dress rehearsals and that the other guy had attacked us for no reason.

She had a bruised face from getting a beat down from the guy who attacked us, but she was brave in her effort to protect me. After gaining my senses back, I was placed into a Police van, and Yamil was sitting next to me, with the guy who attacked us, handcuffed sitting behind us, with an officer next to him. Once I was lucid, I asked who the hell hit me, and the officer who was sitting up front on the passenger side turned around and said: "I hit you, and if you don't shut the hell up, I'm going to hit you again." I got so angry when he spoke to me like that; I said to him, "Come and try it now that I am facing you, asshole!"

He tried grabbing me, and I fended his attack, and Yamil started screaming at him, so the Sergeant told him to calm down and stop it. He did, and Yamil told him, "What the hell is wrong with you? He was fighting in self-defense, we are dancers, and we were coming from a dress rehearsal for an upcoming show on Thanksgiving Day." The cop who beat the shit out of me with his partner was sitting behind us, as was the guy who attacked us. The officer driving was a Sergeant. Leonard Torney was the name of the cop who beat me with the handle of an ax, he was an Irish Cop, who did not like Latinos or Blacks, and it showed. When we got to the station and I got out of the van, I was handcuffed by Officer Torney, despite Yamil's protest. When I asked him why he was handcuffing me, he told me for resisting arrest. "Resisting arrest, how the hell did I resist arrest? You didn't even identify yourselves. You just started beating the shit out of me."

Torney didn't like what I said very much and made the handcuffs tighter on my wrists. Apparently, this Cop was trying to cover his ass by arresting me because he and his partner had beaten me pretty severely. Once inside the Police Station, they put me in front of the Desk Sergeant, and he looked at both the tall black guy who attacked us and me. He asked Torney, "What happened to the big guy's face?" Since it was all lumped up from the beating I had given him. Torney pointed at me and said, "This guy happened to him." I told the Desk Sergeant, "Why don't you ask him what happened to me?" Torney got pissed again, grabbed me by the neck, and said, come on, wiseguy, I have to book you now.

I was covered in blood from the gash in my head, and my face was unrecognizable. My left cheekbone was shattered into a million pieces, and I was in severe pain.

When we got into the Detectives, Room Torney took off the handcuff from one hand and handcuffed me to a wooden chair. I found it hard to hold my head to stop the bleeding, so I started complaining, asking him to call an ambulance.

I was in a lot of pain, and I was still bleeding, which should have been evident to him. He told me to shut up, and he had to make a report first. I told him I wanted to make a phone call to let my parents know where I was. He allowed me to make the call, so I called Mom and told her what had happened.

She got distraught and told me she would call my cousin David, an NYPD Detective, and that she was coming to get me with my father. After about 30 minutes of my sitting there bleeding all over the place, the phone rang. When Torney picked it up, after a few seconds, he said, "Yes, Detective Estrada." I looked at him and said, "You're in for it now!" David was a highly decorated NYPD Detective from the South Bronx PSA 7 street crime unit. After a couple of minutes on the phone with David, he hung up and asked me why I had not told him I had family on the Police Force. I looked at him with a dumbfounded look on my face and said. I asked, "When before or after you beat the shit out of me?" It was then that he got up from behind his desk and started choking me, as I tried my best to defend myself while still handcuffed to the wooden chair. Suddenly, the door swung open, and I saw my mother walking through the door; when she saw what was happening, she started screaming at Torney to stop.

Mom spoke perfect English as she had educated herself in New York when she came here as a young girl from Puerto Rico. She said to him, "Are you crazy? Can't you see he is hurt and bleeding?" Torney stopped and told her I was disrespectful, and she replied, "That doesn't give you the right to try to hurt him again. Now you take those handcuffs off and let me take him to a hospital!"

Torney protested and told Mom he had to fingerprint me before going anywhere. He un-cuffed me, and we started walking towards another room down the hall. As we walked, mom started speaking Spanish and told me she had already contacted our attorney. Suddenly, Torney began raising his voice and telling my mother to speak English; she was in America now. The look on his face as he said that to her infuriated me. I pushed him and told him not to speak to my mother like that. He immediately attacked me, and my mother started screaming for help. As it happens, the Captain of the Precinct was coming to see us with a Lieutenant by his side; he started yelling at Torney to cease and desist. Torney was blinded by his hatred and did not listen right away. The Lieutenant grabbed him by the arm and screamed at him again, "Let him go right now, Officer Torney!" Torney stopped and looked at the Captain while my mother pulled me away from him and called him an animal.

The Captain was pissed at Torney, and you could see it in his face, but he apologized to my mother for Torney's lousy behavior. When Torney started to try and defend himself, the Captain told him to be quiet.

He then said to Torney, "Did you know that the other guy you arrested escaped from a mental institution for the criminally insane? While this young man has family on the Police force, no criminal record, and an Honorable Discharge from the United States Marine Corps?" Torney's expression changed, and as he started to speak again, the Captain told him to get out of his sight. Torney protested again and told the Captain he had not finished processing me or fingerprinting me. The Captain repeated his orders for him to leave as he gave him a stern look, and reluctantly, Torney turned and left, pouting like a child who had been told to go to bed without dinner.

The Captain turned to us, and after watching Torney sulk away, he apologized again and told my Mom to get me to a hospital and that he would take care of everything for us. He could see I was still bleeding and was not in good shape, as I was suffering from a shattered cheekbone and a concussion from the blow which cracked my skull. When we came out front, Yamil and my father were waiting for us. As she saw me walking towards them, she came to me and hugged me gently, and she asked if I was OK. Of course, I wasn't, but I could see the concern not only in her eyes but in the eyes of my father as well. As we walked out, I looked at the Desk Sergeant, and all he could do was look at me and shake his head. It seems Yamil had told him what really happened and everyone else who would listen as she waited for me to be processed. Once my parents showed up, she approached them and told them that I had saved her and that I was her hero. I didn't come to know that until later, but it was gratifying for me. We got into my father's car, and I don't remember the ride to Lincoln Hospital. However, I do remember once I got to the hospital, they attended to me right away.

Yamil and my mother made sure of that. After the Doctor had my head X-Rayed, he gave me the bad news in front of Mom, Dad, and Yamil. He told us he would have to operate and perform reconstructive surgery on my face right away.

I looked at him and told him there was no way I would allow that. He looked at me very seriously and told me, "Do you know what will happen to your face if you don't get this surgery right away?" I looked at him and said, "What will happen to my face?" He told me if I did not get the operation, my face would be deformed when the swelling went down, and I would look like a monster. I opened my eyes wide and said, "OK, you can operate on my face." I looked at Yamil, and she said, "good choice, I like your face," and I tried to laugh, but it hurt too much.

I was scared, but Yamil told me she would be waiting for me, and she wasn't going anywhere, and for some reason, that gave me courage. After hours of surgery, everything came out okay, but I was not lucid and in pain, so the Doctors told my family that I needed to rest. My mom took Yamil home with her, and she stayed in my room the entire time I was in the hospital, which was about a week. When I finally woke up, the first thing I saw was Yamil's, smiling face, looking down at me, and then kissing my hand, which she was holding. My head was all bandaged up, and I had a protective piece of aluminum on the side of my head. It looked like I had a phone on the side of my face. They had placed it there to ensure I did not lie down on the side of my face that they had surgically reconstructed and repaired so I would not disturb the afflicted area.

As I started gathering my senses, I realized that Yamil had never really left my side for long, and every time I opened my eyes, there she was. There was always a look of concern on her face, but there was also one of appreciation. She started telling me that I was her hero and that she was angry with the cops for what they did to me.

I didn't remember everything or how she came to my rescue when they were beating me with the handle of an ax wrapped in black electrical tape, but I did see them when I got into the Police Van. As we started talking about things, the Nurse came in and told me I had company but that there were too many to visit me, so they could not stay for long. It was the Latin Symbolics Dance Company she was referring to. It seemed all my friends had snuck upstairs to see me, and the Nurses did not have the heart to stop them once they found out what happened to me. I had a roommate in my room named Jose. When he heard the commotion, he woke up and asked me if I was some sort of celebrity, and everyone started laughing. It was then that George Vascones, President of the Latin Symbolics, asked me if I could laugh; I shrugged my shoulders and told him I didn't know. So he said, "Oh, because I was going to ask you if I could use the phone on the side of your head." Everyone started laughing. It was excruciating for me to laugh, and I let out a loud moan instead. I told George I could not laugh as much as I wanted to and asked him not to try and make me laugh again. Everyone was thrilled to see I was in good spirits. Everyone except the girl I was dating who was also there and had noticed just how close Yamil and I had gotten that is. We both knew it was over without saying a word, but we were both OK with that.

After about a half-hour, the Nurse came back in and told everyone they had to leave, or she would get in trouble since there were only supposed to be two visitors at a time in my room. As everyone started to go, the girl I had been dating looked at me with a bit of sadness in her eyes told me to get better soon. I nodded and smiled at her. I knew right then and there that it was over between us, and so did she. Yamil, on the other hand, never left my side. Not even the Nurse could get her to leave. The following day, Lucky, Pete & Hector came to see me with Mike Fonzy, and they asked me if I would allow Mike to take my place at the show the next day. They wanted to borrow my costume so Mike could do the four-man routine in my place. I told them I would, but only if he had learned the routine. We went into the visitor's lounge, and Lucky had brought a Boom box with him, so they played the music and started the routine.

Mike had most of it down but made too many mistakes for my comfort, so I told them no, they would not do the four-man routine. The routine was complicated, and while I was impressed that he had gotten most of it, it was not perfect, and I didn't want them looking like amateurs.

I told them that while I thought he could do the routine with a week of practice, it was not ready, and our name alone, "The Rock Masters," would dictate that we were professionals, and a sloppy routine would not do.

Instead, we let Hector and Pete do the routine as a two-man. While they were disappointed, Mike & Lucky, in particular, understood my reasoning and respected my decision.

On the day of the show, my parents went with Yamil and much to their content. Everyone who performed dedicated their dance routine to me. However, when Yamil got on stage, she wanted to say a few words before her performance, and what she said made my parents very proud. She paid homage to her hero and dedicated her dance routine to me as well. Her routine was a thing of beauty, and the standing ovation she got was well deserved and made my parents proud. When I finally saw the show's video, it made me cry and sad that I was not there, but I was also happy that they all paid tribute to me, and my parents were there to witness it.

The week after the show, I was released from the hospital, and Yamil picked me up with my Mom & Dad. She had been staying in my room while I was in the hospital. However, my parents didn't want her to leave; they asked her to stay if she liked. She looked at me and said, "Well, if Willie doesn't mind the company, I will stay." Needless to say, a big smile came across my face, and I didn't have to respond. Yamil and I hung out in my room, and I could tell she liked me, and I suppose it was apparent to her that the feeling was mutual. She was a beautiful young woman, with a great body, what's not to like. My parents, particularly my mom, would typically not allow a sleepover by a love interest. I usually sneaked girls into my bedroom while they were sleeping. Yamil was a different story, they looked at her in a different light altogether, and I was OK with that. She was an extraordinary and gifted young woman, but the best part was that she never left my side while I was in the hospital, and that, for me, was in itself very special.

We made love that night, and while I was not at my best, especially with a fractured left cheekbone, which made it hard to open my mouth or even kiss her, for that matter, we had an excellent time together. But we both knew it would not last, and she was missing many auditions for Broadway shows. I encouraged her to start doing it again because I did not want to hold her back. I knew she had a great future in dance, and I did not want to stand in her way, and I didn't. We went our separate ways soon after that, and a few years later, I heard she had gotten a significant part in a new Broadway play called "A Chorus Line," and I was very happy for her and even visited her once.

Yamil Borges

CHAPTER TWENTY

SATURDAY NIGHT FEVER – THE SHAM

By 1977 the Latin Hustle had morphed into the most beautiful and prominent dance in New York City, and everybody and their mothers were doing it. The only thing we didn't notice during that period was that others were taking credit for creating it just because they were teaching it in dance studios. They had dropped the Latin portion of the Latin Hustle and started calling it "the New York Hustle" initially, and after that shortened it to just "The Hustle." Even Hollywood got into the act and capitalized on its popularity, only they created fictional characters instead of using real characters. I have always been under the impression that nothing can replace authenticity. However, our Puerto Rican culture and story have never been truthfully told. We are always portrayed as drug dealers, criminals, and worse. God forbid Hollywood should give us credit for any of our significant contributions, creations, or influence in music, dance, or other positive things we have done. While the story from the famous movie **"Saturday Night Fever"** is based on a real character named Tony Manero. The story of him being a great dancer is fictional but leave it to Hollywood to hire the best dancers from the Latin Symbolics Dance Company to fill in as extras without letting them shine on the dance floor. In late 1977 someone who claimed to be the real Tony Manero wanted to capitalize on having his story told on the big screen, so he came to the Latin Symbolics Dance Studio located at 333 E. 149th St. in the South Bronx to learn how to do the real Latin Hustle.

When I first met Tony, I noticed that he was a handsome Italian guy with a beautiful Italian partner whose name I don't remember. He was well built and even better looking than John Travolta himself. However, he was a very stiff dancer with no natural rhythm to speak of. It seems he had been made an offer by a Las Vegas Hotel to do a Showcase, so he decided to learn from those whom he knew to be the best Hustle Dancers in New York City, "The Latin Symbolics Dance Company." George chose me as one of the Hustle instructors who would help train Tony and his partner and let me just point out; it was a challenging job. It didn't help that he had no training in the real Hustle whatsoever, and we had very little time to get him ready. He also wanted to do some lifts, but I was not into lifts, so someone else took over, but it wasn't long before he bruised his partners' ribs from doing the lifts wrong.

Eddie Vega and Lisa Nunziella - Starsearch Champions

The Latin Symbolics Dance Team

RIP ANGEL (INDIO) DEJESUS TOP RIGHT

Enter Alma, a Latin Symbolics Hustle Team member, who was chosen to go to Las Vegas with Tony Manero to replace his partner, who was now battered and bruised from being lifted and dropped several times. But don't get me wrong, she wasn't dropped from a lack of strength, but rather from a lack of skills. Nonetheless, Hollywood made him a celebrity by using his name and creating a bogus story about his dance skills. God forbid they should give credit to the Puerto Rican teens who had the best Hustle dance skills and made such a beautiful dance that eventually went global.

To be completely honest with you all, we didn't give a damn about that sort of thing during those days.

We were addicted to music and dance, which were the tools to escape from our volatile and disenfranchised environment— keeping in mind that mentalities were much different for Puerto Ricans during that era as well as the period before us.

The actions of our oppressors were not s blatant as they are today back in those days.

RIP George Vascones left and Charlie Torres middle far right.

Also pictured, Billy Fajardo, Pat, Floyd Chisholm, and Joseph, who were among the first to take the Hustle into the Gay community.

CHAPTER TWENTY ONE:

ROCK MASTERS, THE LAST HURRAH

In the coming weeks, all I could think about was dancing again as I continued to heal, but I also thought about David Maldonado and his offer and knew he was waiting for me to get better. I went back to the Latin Symbolics Studio, where I was received with open arms by all. My partner Lucky had been practicing with Mike Fonzy, who had learned the routine by that time, and Hector and Pete had made some changes to the routine I had created and added some cool moves. There was a big Rock contest coming up, and it seemed everyone was getting ready for it, everyone except me, that is. The competition would be held at the Hoe Avenue Bronx Boys Club on 173rd St., expecting all the best Rockers from throughout the City. I asked Lucky to dance with me, and Hector and Pete would also be dancing in that contest, but we were like brothers, only there was no rivalry between us. Fonzy would have to wait to dance with Lucky, I was back now, and he would have to wait his turn for a while longer. As we all prepared for the biggest Rock contest since the earlier 1970s, I knew there would be a lot of competition, so Lucky and I worked hard to perfect our routine. We were at the studio every day for hours practicing like crazy. After a while, I started noticing that I was not the same, the injuries to my head and the broken cheekbone were affecting me, and I couldn't spin as much anymore without getting dizzy. Even when I did a handstand, I felt dizzy at times.

Nevertheless, I continued to practice with Lucky as we got ready to compete at the Boys Club.

Hector Berrios and Pete Martinez were also practicing for this contest, and they had added a few Hustle moves into their Rock Routine, like a Death Sweep and a Lindy Sweep, which were Hustle moves. It seems they had been practicing every day while I was in the Hospital and had changed the routine I taught them and made it better. The day of the contest came, and Lucky was complaining about feeling sick to his stomach. When we got to the Boys Club, he ran to the bathroom and started throwing up. I was upset because all of the best Rockers from the City were there that day, and more than anything, I wanted to win. After he finished in the bathroom, he told me he wasn't feeling well enough to dance and would try. When the contest started, it ended for us very quickly. We were one of the first taken out because lucky could not do the routine, and even though I tried to encourage him, he was just not well enough to dance, out of all the days to get sick, why this day, I asked myself. We were sidelined early, so we watched the contest instead of still being on the dance floor dancing our asses off. I had never been taken out of a Rock Contest before, so I could barely hold a thought in my head. Instead, I judged the contest as it progressed, rooted for Hector and Pete. Everyone was dressed pretty cool; some had costumes the way we did, others just dressed similarly, but the ones who stood out the most were my boys Hector Berrios and Pete Martinez. When they did the Death Sweep, all you heard was "Ohhhhh's" and "Ahhhhh's" as they executed the move with great precision and style. They were up against the best the City had to offer but brought the house down on everyone with their new routine, which also had many moves I had taught them.

I felt terrific about it because my boys were shining bright, and nobody could stand in the way of their victory that night.

At the end of the night, Hector Berrios and Pete Martinez danced their way into the history books by beating the best of the best that night and making their mark. I have always been very proud of their accomplishments, and for some strange reason, I felt like I won that night as well. After it was all over, we celebrated Hector and Pete's win with a demonstration with the four-man routine I had choreographed, but after that day, we never performed that four-man routine again as a team. Hector and Pete had found their niche in the world of Rock, and the Rock Masters four-man Team was no more. I danced with Lucky one last time in a show on January 14, 1978, and shortly after that, he became partners with Mike Fonzy, and a short time after that, I started dancing with a new partner. We did a few shows and won 2nd place at a Rock Contest at the Starship Discovery and a show we did in Brooklyn for some rich folks. After we finished our routine, they gave us a standing ovation and asked for an encore performance.

However, by the time we were done with our routine, my right knee blew up like a melon so that I couldn't go on again. Nevertheless, we went out and took a couple of bows and showed our gratitude.

Many years later, I was told by the only two guys from Brooklyn who were also members of the Latin Symbolics Rock Team, by name names of Vinnie and Noel, that they taught my style of Rocking and my routine in particular others from Brooklyn as well.

It seemed my style of Rock had been passed down to the next generation, and I never knew about it until I was in my 50's.

JAN. 14, 1978

9 PM-9 AM

DISCO NITE! EXTRAVAGANZA

Featuring LIVE! THE LATIN SYMBOLICS DANCE COMPANY

Enchanted Castle
558 MELROSE AVE. BRONX, N.Y.
149 ST. & 3RD AVE.

TICKETS $3.00 IN ADVANCE

MR. PUPI UNISEX BOUTIQUE - 720 W. 181 ST.
STEP INTO MY WORLD 538 E. 138 ST.
CAMPUS CYCLES 120 AMSTERDAM AVE.

12 - HOURS OF CONTINUOS DANCING - 12

This was the very last show I did with the Latin Symbolics Dance Company and the end of an era I will never forget.

The RockMasters 1975
Willie Estrada & Lucky Feliciano

Hector Berrios and Pete Martinez below joined the Rock Masters in 1977, and we created the 1st four-man Rock Routine in NYC, for which I did all the choreography.

THE ROCK MASTERS
1977

CHAPTER TWENTY-TWO: 1978

The Birth of Faces Grand Ballroom

After my injuries had completely healed, I realized I was not the same as a dancer, and some of the things I used to be able to do with no problem, became difficult to execute, especially when I did spins. There was a time I could spin like a top, but after my head injury, I realized I would get dizzy when I did more than a couple of spins. As it turned out, the beating the cops gave me was worse than I initially thought. I couldn't help but curse them for their prejudice and beating me to within an inch of my life. It's a good thing somebody up there likes me, or I wouldn't be here today to tell my story.

I decided to contact David Maldonado again, and when I did, he invited me to come to his house with Carlos Ramos and another guy named Frank, who was also a DJ and good friends with Carlos. David wanted to bring in acts who had a following, and since the money to bring in big acts wasn't there yet. He decided to hire the best Hustle Dancers from New York: Billy and Sandra, Perico and Debbie, Floyd Chisolm, and Nelly Cotto. He added a fashion show and did a lot of giveaways. We promoted a Floor Throbbing Sound System with DJ Carlos Ramos as the Star Spinner. He made it easy for us to make money by offering a discount of only $5 if you came to the door with the flier.

Those fliers would have our stamp on the back, so he could know who brought in the most people to win the prize of 2 round trip tickets with the hotel to Cancun Mejico, or take the $800.

During the meeting, I told David I had friends with cars who would be helping us disseminate the fliers and help me put the posters up all over the City. The best part was that all my friends had CB Radios in their cars, including Carlos Ramos, which we communicated with each other. Keep in mind that we did not have Cell phones or beepers in those days, but we did utilize the latest technology as simple to today's standards as they were.   David was smart. He knew that I was very popular, and I had many friends who would follow me in whatever I did or wherever I went. I wasn't only popular because I was a good dancer. I was also charismatic and known as a Ladies' man, and because I hated injustice, I defended my friends with passion and resolve. I grew up during a time of blatant prejudice, and it was always in your face in one form or another.

I truly believe it helped me become a better person as I grew, and I knew precisely what I didn't like. I was a natural-born leader, and I knew that from an early age because I didn't' easily follow anyone. When I saw injustice, even from a friend, I would speak out, and I often took action to defend people I didn't even know. I guess David saw those qualities in me right from the first time he saw me and how I interacted with people in general, but I think most importantly, the way people responded to me.

My career as a dancer was winding down now, and I was in the process of becoming a promoter. David had chosen the date for our first Faces Grand Ballroom Dance, and it would be on May 6th, 1978. The planning stages had gone well, and we were now ready for the task at hand.

David was very excited to be working with us, and we were just as happy to have this opportunity to make money and be responsible for promoting the events ourselves. We would be doing one every other month. He had a partner named Edgar Vasquez, who was also putting up money for the promotions and the venue rental, but he never really attended the meetings David held weekly. The strategy was simple, David had 2,000 posters and 25,000 fliers made up for the event, and he chose other guys we knew to give out flyers, and very quickly, they became our rivals.

In the early days, I went out with David to put posters up and down the Grand Concourse and the Fordham Road area of the Bronx, and Edgar Vasquez sometimes went with us. We used staple guns and glue to put the posters up at night, and during the day, we left fliers by the hundreds in every single clothing store in all the shopping areas throughout the City. I initially had to rely on my friends who had cars to help us as I did not have a vehicle yet, and neither did David. We used shopping carts to put the posters in, and we walked a lot throughout the Bronx initially.

I had many friends who were still in high school, helping me give fliers out, and friends throughout New York helping as well. I took fliers with me everywhere I went, and so did my friends. We promoted every day, and by the time the week of the dance came, I was pretty confident that I would win the prize money David had offered to the person who brought in the most people.

After six weeks of promoting, the dance day was finally here, and we all showed up dressed to impress.

To David and Edgar's dismay, the turnout was not as good as we had all anticipated.

We had fewer than 600 people show up, but I still won the $800 for bringing in the most people. I had done my part, and so had my friends. David took it all in stride and said we'd do better with the next one, but Edgar, who had also put up the money, was not as enthusiastic and said he would only give it one more chance. It was all about the money for him, and I guess David was looking to build something unique that would pay higher dividends in the coming years. David called a meeting for the following Monday to discuss and plan the next event, and we all told him we would be there. David was an accountant by day and promoter by night. He was a good man who served as my mentor. He was very ambitious, and there was no quitting, which also inspired me.

During our meeting, I told him I purchased a car and a CB Radio so that I could go into the other boroughs with my boys to saturate the City regularly. I bought a 1972 White Pontiac Grand Prix, which had a 400 cubic inch engine from one of my friends named Zoilo for $500, which was a steal back in those days. He started crying and hugging the car's hood before he handed me the keys and asked me to take care of it. I was 21 years old and got my first car; it was so fast I named it Lightening.

Our next event was planned for July 1st, 1978, and we had the King and Queen of the Hustle Floyd Chisolm and Nelly Cotto, as well as Billy and Sandra from the Dance Dimensions putting on a Hustle Show. We had over 800 people, and once again, I won the $800 for bringing in the most people.

However, Edgar was not satisfied with the results and told David he would not continue as his partner. David knew we were building momentum and decided to continue doing the jams, and it was music to my ears since I was making good money now.

We had rivals who competed with us to see who would bring in the most people and win the $800, but they would also cheat to try and win. I mean that they would wait until the day of the event and give fliers out to people who came without a flier. They made the mistake that even when the person had one of my fliers with my stamp on the back, they would ask them to use their flier instead. I sat at my dining room table for hours with my sisters as they helped me put my stamp on the back of the fliers so David would know it was me bringing in whoever came to the door the day of the event. Once I found out that some guys were cutting my throat, I had my guys do the same to them, and I had more guys on my side, so they would still lose.

David's partner Edgar Vasquez had decided to give up since we were not getting the numbers he had hoped for.

What a big mistake that was, because, after our fourth dance, we always packed the place to capacity. However, when Edgar left, David became more dependent on our crew to blitz the city with posters and fliers. By that time, we had a bigger street team, and the best part was that we all had CB Radios in our cars so we could communicate with each other all over the city. When we were too far from each other, we had a girl whose handle was "Disco Queen," who had a big antenna on the roof of her building and would relay our messages when we needed to reach one another. The first time we met her in person, we dropped by her house, and when I stuck my head out the window of my car.

She saw I was wearing a cap lit up and said "Disco" on it in different colored lights. She started laughing and told me she loved my cap. One night, my boy Johnny Ganga and I and a couple of other guys put up some posters in Brooklyn for FACES Grand Ballroom. We noticed that all our posters were down on the floor or in the garbage. However, Ralph Mercado's posters were up instead. I got angry because we had never torn down any of his posters as a matter of respect since he was the biggest Latin Promoter in New York City. I got on the CB Radio and asked Disco Queen to tell all my guys to tear down Ralph's posters wherever they saw them and replace them with ours. I told her what Ruben, Ralph's poster guy, was doing, and she immediately alerted everyone to tear all these posters down. I knew that would start a war, but we had more guys than Ralph, and we were also much younger than Ruben and his small crew. As luck would have it, we ran into Ruben and his guys on Graham Ave in Brooklyn and stepped up to him and his guys.

We told him we would tear down all his posters wherever we saw them, and I also reminded him we had more guys and more cars than he did. He saw how angry I was, and knew not to start any shit with us, so he conceded and told us he would never do it again.

Even though he had said he wouldn't do it again, I decided to allow my crew to continue ripping down everything he had done to teach him a lesson. The following day we told David what we did; he started pulling his hair as he often did when upset.

He told us not to do that because it would start a war with Ralph, but we told him it was done, and we had also bumped into Ruben and told him what we were going to do so he would never do again. David called Ralph Mercado and told him what was going on, so it wouldn't happen again.

David called Ralph and explained what had happened; Ralph blew a gasket as he got angry that we tore all his posters down. Keeping in mind that by the time that happened, FACES Grand Ballroom events were already very popular, and I am sure Ralph had seen our posters all over the City of New York. David reasoned with Ralph, and they came to an accord.

He would talk to Ruben about it and tell him not to rip any more of our posters down, and we would leave him alone as well. As it turned out, Ralph was impressed with our work, and he would rather have us as allies than enemies, and he and David began to communicate regularly after that. David also knew that my crew was an invaluable asset to him, but more than that, he knew I had personally helped him create something he could not have done by himself.

David had already been calling me "The Machine" before all this happened, and he knew he had made the right choice when he picked me to spearhead his promotions. I took to promotions like it was something I was born to do. He involved me in all his decisions going forward, and I became his right-hand man, and he started taking better care of me financially as well.

In December of 1978, David Maldonado collaborated with Eddie Rivera, President of IDRC, the Best Record Pool in New York. We established a new precedent in how Disco Parties were done in New York.

They rented Roseland, a club in New York that held over 3,000 people and promoted a jam there with Lolita Holloway, First Choice, and Love Committee.

We also added four great DJs to the mix, which included "Tom Savarese" Carlos Ramos, Donny Lawrence, and Angel Rodriguez. The turnout was a packed house that night, and we all made a lot of money.

By 1979, all of our Jams using the Faces Grand Ballroom name were always jam-packed events, and we were the talk of the town in terms of promoters who did the best Disco Jams in New York City. I was making a lot more money now, but the best was yet to come. I often thought about my beloved Hustle and Rock, which I always continued to do but not as a performer or competing in contests. Those days were over now, but they would forever remain in my heart and fondest of memories. One night, Carlos Ramos, my cousin JR and I were coming back from putting up posters in the City using his car, and there was a big traffic jam as we were going over the Willis Ave Bridge into the Bronx. There was only one lane open, and to make matters worse, a driver was going so slow, everyone was cutting in front of him, which made things even worse.

We were heated because we still had work to be done in the Bronx, and we wanted to go out that night since it was a Friday night. When we finally got to the end of the traffic jam, and the other lanes opened up, I told Carlos to pull alongside the driver who was causing that jam, and I told my cousin we were going to pull two full moons on whoever was driving.

We both pulled our pants down and stuck our asses out the window as Carlos drove by them slowly and honked his horn. My cousin and I could not see who was driving the car because our asses were sticking out of the window.

Carlos was the only one who could see their reaction, and when he did, he broke out laughing so hard he almost crashed his car into the wall that separates the off-ramp to the Bruckner Expressway.

Carlos had to stop right there on the spot as he came to an abrupt halt with our asses still sticking out the windows, and my head banged into the front windshield, and I let out an Ouch. Carlos was laughing so hard he couldn't talk right away, but we started asking him what the reaction was. When he finally composed himself enough to talk, he told us it was a very old couple in their 80s, and the driver wore thick glasses. I guess he good look at our asses sticking out the window, and the look on both their faces was one of shock and disgust. Either way, Carlos showed us the look they gave as we startled them. We all broke out in relentless laughter, and keep in mind that we had smoked a joint on the way back from Manhattan on the FDR, which made things even funnier for us. Then my cousin told us his face almost crashed into my ass when Carlos stopped so fast; he had to apply his brakes. When Carlos told us how the older man lost control and his reaction, I thought it was a good thing he was not driving fast.

Carlos and I had become the best of friends, and we did a lot of fun stuff together; and he was in high demand as a DJ, so wherever he played, I was there.

Even at the gay clubs where you had Drag Queens walking around strutting in their outlandish outfits, I was there.

Some of them looked like real women, so I thank God for the Adam's apple. One of my cousins didn't have the same eye I did, and we once caught him making out with a Drag Queen at People's Park on 141th St. between Brook and St. Ann's Ave during a jam done by Frenchie, who was a rebel without a cause. When we told Tarzan that he was making out with a guy, he didn't believe us, so he called him over and grabbed him by the family jewels, and he squeezed until we heard a nut pop. The Drag Queen let out a scream and ran out of People's Park, and we never saw him again. Frenchie, a Vietnam Vet, had lots of missing marbles by the time he got back home, became a revolutionary figure in the South Bronx during the early 1970s, saw it go down. He came over and asked what had happened to Lala. My cousin Tarzan said, Lala fooled me; she's a Lolo. Frenchie started cracking up, and once he was done laughing, he looked at us and said, "I could have told you that, but she's still family." "Well, you can bring your sister flowers at the funeral because I'm going to kill her when I see her again." He said it in a teasing way, and we all started laughing again. Frenchie was a real character who was stoned out of his mind most of the time, but he always showed love to his people.

Those were strange yet wonderful days in my life, especially since the violence and senseless gang killings were now over. By 1979, Faces Grand Ballroom was a name that every dancer throughout New York City and the Tri-State Area knew about, and our Jams were always filled with great dancers.

I would go as far as to say the best dancers throughout the Tri-State area frequented our jams, and it was always like a competition of new talent emerging within our ranks.

Somebody was always trying to show off and get everyone's attention, and they would get a circle going. The Latin Symbolics was always present, and we always got our circle going to show everyone who the Kings and Queens of the dance floors in New York were. There was never any animosity among dancers, but I can remember anyway. But we did spank a few dancers along the way to do the Latin Hustle with a lot more style and elegance than everyone else. Even when I became a promoter, I never stopped dancing, and every once in a while, I would take to the dance floor with my friends, and we always got a circle going, and everyone watching our every move and newbies learned new steps as they watched. I was constantly meeting new girls, but for the most part, I remained single, as it seemed to me all the girls wanted to do was get married and have babies.

In the winter of 1979, I finally met someone I liked enough to want to date instead of just sleeping with random girls I met during our Jams and when I was out promoting those events. On April 7th, 1979, we hosted a Women's Grand Ballroom Disco Party, where the ladies were supposed to ask the men to dance, and we had another jam-packed turnout.

We featured a dating contest that night, much like the dating game which used to come on TV, with the prizes being a paid night on the town for dinner with a Limo taking the winners wherever they wanted to go.

It was great fun for everyone, and when it was over, a pretty girl sitting next to the stage caught my eye. When the lights were dim down again, I approached her and asked her if she wanted to dance.

She was pretty, but I could tell she was timid and said in a lovely voice that she wasn't a good dancer, but she knew I was. I asked her how she knew I was a good dancer, and she told me she had seen me dance several times in the past. I asked for her name, and she told me her name was Rosa, and I took her hand and told her I would take it easy with her, but she made me promise I wouldn't do anything fancy or she would stop and walk away.

I started laughing, but I agreed to her terms for dancing with me. I had not seen her body since she was sitting down when I saw her; however, as we walked to the dance floor, I snuck a peek; all I could say inside my head, of course, was, "OMG, what a great body!" I was captivated by her right away, and it was more than the fact that she was a wonderful young woman. A few things drew my attention, everything from her great smile to how she spoke and the way she walked.

She had elegance, beauty, and charisma that just radiated from her persona, which is why I couldn't understand why she was so shy. As we danced and I fought off both the idea of making love to her, as well as an erection caused by her fantastic body and sexuality, I decided to play it cool and be on my best behavior. All I can say is, it's a good thing I was wearing a suit, so she couldn't see my stiffy, which might scare her off or not.

I did, however, romance her on the dance floor, which she seemed to respond to favorably as she looked at me with her beautiful hazel green eyes. When we finished our dance, I asked her to drink with my friends and me at our table. Which we always got during those jams along with a couple of half gallons of Bacardi and soda. As we approached the table, my friends noticed I was walking with this beautiful woman, and they started clapping, and I called them a bunch of idiots and started laughing. Rosa started laughing too, and it was apparent she was enjoying herself with me so far. I introduced her to my friends, and they also introduced me to females they had picked up. After I poured a drink, we sat down and talked about ourselves, but she made some observations about me first. She told me she had seen me before, and she knew I was one of the guys behind the Faces jams and how my friends were always with different women. I interjected and asked her how she knew these things about us, and she told me she comes to all the jams we do. But that didn't explain how she knew about my friends and me.

"I have observed you guys in the past; you're like the life of the party, always laughing, and you're all good dancers, so I noticed those things." I started to ask her another question, but she interrupted me and said she had questions for me as well, so I gave her the go-ahead to ask freely. As you can imagine, her first and only question was, "Do you have a girlfriend?" When the answer to her question was no, she said she didn't need to know anything else for now and was looking forward to getting to know me, so long as I wasn't a player, which of course, I was. However, for some reason, I felt this was not the type of girl you wanted to play games with, she was a keeper, so I told her I wanted to get to know her as well.

Willie and Rosa, regrets I've had a few!

We started dating, and I kept my word and didn't fool around with other women, especially since I started falling for her, and I didn't want to mess things up. We saw each other and went out a few times, but I had not kissed her yet. One day I decided I wanted her to meet my parents since I had already met her mom, so I invited her over during the day on a sunny Saturday afternoon.

She was very excited as we walked from the train station on 149th St. and 3rd Ave to my house, and I took notice, so I tried to lighten her mood by sharing some history of my neighborhood as we walked through it. All I managed to do was scare her as we continued to walk through a partially burned-down area with my stories of gang violence and frequent gang violence.

Not exactly a good way of making an impression on her, but unfortunately, as I walked through those streets, the violence and killings of the recent past were the thoughts that flooded my mind. As I think about it now, I have come to realize it was nothing short of a miracle, which had allowed me to escape the violence of those mean streets and the reason I was still here. There I was, walking through my neighborhood down the very streets that had almost claimed my life several times. Those were the thoughts resounding in my head as we walked. We passed many people I knew from the hood as we walked, and she took notice that everyone in the hood knew me, and I could tell she felt safe as she held my hand with a big smile on her face.

When we got to my house, I introduced her to my parents, who were very old-fashioned people from Puerto Rico, and they greeted her with open arms.

Especially since I had not brought a girl home for some time, so they knew she must be special. After Mom and Dad chatted with Rosa for a short while, they left us alone in the living room so we could talk, and I could tell she liked them both. My father was a charmer and a bit of a ladies' man himself, which is where I got it, so he won her over instantaneously.

She told me how he reminded her of me and how pleasant he was and my Mom; well, she was special herself, and Rosa noted that we were a close-knit family, and we were. After my parents were gone, Rosa and I talked for a while, and then she asked me why I had not kissed her yet.

I told her I was waiting for the right time, so she reached over, and when our lips met, it was like magic when her kiss took my breath away. The following week Rosa came to my house early in the morning after my parents left for work and rang my doorbell. When I opened the door, she told me her ass was frozen, so I lifted her wool skirt and rubbed her ass, and it was firm yet soft and smooth but also very cold. I took her to my room, where she took all her clothes off while I was using the bathroom, and when I returned to my surprise, she was lying on my bed waiting for me. I said to her, "I thought you were shy." She blushed a bit but pulled the covers off to give me a peek and said, "Not anymore, I'm not!"

She invited me to join her, and that's when all the bells and whistles started going off inside my heart as it also skipped a few beats when our bodies met.

We made passionate love all morning long, and by the time we were done, our bodies were full of sweat, so we took a shower together, where we kissed tenderly, and we savored that moment. I was falling for Rosa. However, I knew in my heart that I wasn't ready for marriage.

On the other hand, Rosa was, and she made it apparent in a beautiful love letter she wrote me a short while after her visit. In my eyes, we were too young, but there was no denying our incredible attraction towards each other.

I was only 23 years old, and while I cared for her, I was not ready for marriage, not by a long shot. About a month after her love letter, I visited her at her house in Queens. When I got to the door, her mother opened the door. When I saw Rosa, she had done a perm on her hair, and her mother saw the look in my eyes that said, I did not like what she had done. I didn't' stay long that day, but I told Rosa I would call her soon and that I needed time to think. She knew something was bothering me but said nothing as I left.

I started hanging out with my boys again since we were preparing for another Faces Grand Ballroom event, and staying busy also kept me from thinking about Rosa so much. When I made time to think about her, I concluded that I wasn't ready for that type of commitment, and I decided to break up with her.

I figured she would be hurt, but I would rather hurt her now than down the road years later, where it would hurt us both for a more extended period. I felt awful about having broken up with her, but I knew it was for the best because of how strongly I felt about her. I had already unintentionally hurt several girls, but to be honest, they all wanted to get married and have babies, and I didn't. Rosa was no different. She wanted to start a family with me, but I considered myself too young and immature to settle down. I went to see Rosa a couple of years later, and when her mother opened the door, she was shocked to see me standing there. She told me I had broken her daughter's heart, and she changed after that, didn't want to know about men, and became a school teacher. I told her mom I never meant to hurt her; I just wasn't ready for a commitment at the time.

She gave me the school's address where she worked, so I went to see her, but when I got there, she found out it was me looking for her, she wouldn't see me. Apparently, her mother had called the school since it seemed they were expecting me when I got there. Why would she give me the address to where she worked and then call her to alert her that I was coming, I asked myself?

Perhaps she wanted me to experience rejection, or maybe it was to prevent me from ever hurting her daughter again. Either way, I left with a bowed head and a heavy heart, and I knew I didn't deserve to see her again, not after what I had done to her.

I got into my car and drove away with tears in my eyes because I knew I would never see her again, but I also knew I didn't deserve to see her, and she was better off without me in her life. A thought that weighed heavily on my mind as I got on the highway back home to the Bronx. How could I be so stupid, selfish, and blind? Why did I not see her for what she was, an Angel sent by God to make my life happy and fruitful!

Many years have gone by, but I have never forgotten her even though we were not together for long. She left an impression on my life that I will never forget. Sometimes you don't get a second chance at love, so you have to hold on to it and never let it go once you find it. I made that mistake because I was afraid, and it has taken me a lifetime to figure out that fear can kill love, and once it's dead, it can never be resurrected, and you're left with no choice but to move on. After not being able to see her, I kept myself busy by promoting our upcoming event and hanging out with my crew.

But trouble was always waiting around the corner, and one night, as my boy Chico and I were putting up posters on Southern Boulevard, we noticed a group of four guys harassing a young guy who was waiting for the bus. One guy, in particular, seemed hell-bent on hitting this kid who was about 16 years old or so, and out of left field, he hit the kid in the face with a haymaker, and the kid ran off crying. I've always hated bullies, but I was on a mission to finish up in the Bronx so we could head out to Brooklyn, so we avoided trouble by crossing the street but stayed together just in case.

It wasn't long before they noticed us putting up posters right on the corner on Simpson St. and Southern Blvd, and they came over to us. The guy who had hit the kid recognized the poster as one for a Faces Grand Ballroom event, and he told us he would help us put them up. He was a bit intoxicated or high on something, so I told him we didn't need any help. He got angry and tore the poster down, which made me mad, so I screamed at him and his three boys to stop messing with us, or he would get hurt. The one thing street life teaches you is who you can mess with and who you shouldn't mess with, and he saw it in my eyes, and so did his boys. My body language told them all, I am not someone you should be fucking with, but there were four of them and only two of us, so they tried their luck. His three friends held the tough guy as he and Chico got into an angry exchange of words. All of a sudden, they let him go, and he came running at us full speed to fight with Chico, as it seemed he didn't want any part of me. As he approached and got closer, I ran at him, hit him with a front thrust kick to the face, and thought to myself, if he doesn't go down, I'm going to hit him with the staple gun in my hand.

Down he went when he ran right into my kick, flipped over, and landed with his face in the snow. When his boys saw what happened, they tried to bum rush me, but I back-peddled a few feet, took a Karate Stance, and said, "Who's next!" All three stopped in their tracks and put their hands in the air to say; I don't want any part of you. I could tell they were cowards in disguise as wolves, but they had met their match in me. They started asking me why I hit him, and I said to them I had already warned them, and I had seen what he did to the kid across the street for no reason. Their friend finally got up from the snow-filled ground and started looking for something in a belt pouch he had around his waist. I backed up a bit in case he had a gun, and we had to run, but he was only trying to scare us, and then he took posters I had left by the pole and started ripping them up.

I got pissed again, so I told them, OK, you want to continue looking for trouble, wait right here. Chico and I ran to the car to get bats he always kept in his trunk. When they saw us coming, they started running like the cowards they were, and everyone who had gathered around and had seen what happened started laughing, and we joined in. The streets of the South Bronx are a dangerous place, and attitudes are always present. And every once in a while, a bully gets what he deserves. I had not beaten him down, but I had put him down in front of his friends, something he would not soon forget, and neither would his friends. I am not the type of person looking for a fight, but I am not one to back down either.

I had learned how to fight as a young boy so that I wouldn't have to fight, but sometimes, you have no choice, especially when you live in the South Bronx.

It didn't matter to me that he was much bigger than me. I could use a cliché here and say the bigger they are, the harder they fall, but instead, I will just state a fact.

If you corner a wild animal, that is when he is most ferocious, not that I'm a wild animal, mind you, but that concept does apply here. It was a Friday night, and on Friday nights, we sometimes played cards at Chico's house with several other friends, where we would smoke our weed and drink our beer and just talk shit all night long. Saturday nights were always party nights, and we made our rounds to the clubs so we could also promote our events and recruit girls to help us expand by giving them flyers to hand out for us, with the promise of getting them in free on the night of our events. Faces Grand Ballroom had become a household name during the late 70s, and one day out of the blue, David Maldonado called me and told me he was joining forces with Ralph Mercado and that they were going to start doing events together. I asked him if he was bringing me in with him since I had been his right-hand man for several years now, and while his answer was, "Yes," he said it would be a while before he could bring me in, as he works things out with Ralph. I was disappointed because, in my eyes, had it not been for my crew and me, David would not be hob-knobbing with the Ralph Mercado, who was the King of New York in my eyes. My biggest mistake was not going into partnership with David and putting my name on the flyers. I had, after all, earned that right through all my hard work and dedication.

Well, I was expendable now that he was with Ralph, but I knew he would call me sooner or later since my street team was the best in the City of New York, and nobody even came close. Some time had gone by, but I got the call one day, and David asked me to go to Ralph's office in mid-town to discuss their plans, including my team and me. When I got there, I was greeted by David, who was very happy to see me, and he pulled me into his new office to bring me up to speed before I met Ralph. David shared all their plans and how he was in tight with Ralph, and they were going to be opening up a club in the Bronx together, which would be called Night-Trax. He told me it would be where Club Le Noir was currently, and David wanted me to dance there and that they would back me financially, but it would have my name on the flyer, not his. I also shared 50% of the profits despite putting up all the money.

Backstage with David Maldonado at an India concert in St. Mary's Park 40 years later in 2017

Willie Estrada
PRESENTS

THE
FIRST

Oldies Disco Party

A
Blast
From The Past.

COME & MEET YOUR OLD FRIENDS FROM

FACES'
LA BAMBA
IPANEMA
LA MARIPOSA
RED N' WHITE
BOOMBAMAKAO

STARSHIP
SPOTLITE
LATIN TIMES
STARGATE
310
ETC.

Non-Stop Music of Now & Then...

STAR SPINNER

From New York, New York Disco
CARLOS RAMOS
(FACES)

A DISCO JAM SESSION

Floor THROBBING Sound System · Free T-Shirts & Whistles
WIN CASH PRIZES ROCK DANCE CONTEST 1st 2nd & 3rd PLACE
Guest Dance Celebrities

2 Floors of DISCO FANTASY
FRIDAY, AUGUST 7 1981·9PM-5AM
Club LeNoir THE NEWEST AND
LARGEST CLUB IN THE BRONX
301 East Kingsbridge Road (off Fordham Rd.)
CALL FOR FURTHER INFORMATION 933-3015/584-9855

ADMISSION $8./$6. WITH THIS TICKET

It was apparent to me that David wanted Ralph to see my worth, which was the main reason he was doing this for me. That and the fact that he had made me wait for a few months before he brought me into work with them. I guess he wanted to establish himself first before he brought me in, and I was OK with that. He told me Ralph was very impressed with my crew and what I had done for him and was looking forward to working with me.

The moment to meet with Ralph had arrived, and I was excited about meeting the King of Latin promoters from New York.

Ralph came from behind his desk to shake my hand and welcome me on board, and he was charming. I thought to myself how classy and elegant he was, and I could tell he was a man of great stature within the Latin Music Industry. I took a liking to him right away. He shared some of the things David had already told me, but he also made it a point to tell me if I messed up, I would never work for him again. I didn't take offense to that because I was very confident in what I brought to the table, and I made it a point to let Ralph know.

I can honestly say Ralph took a liking to me from the moment we met as he made it a point to tell me that is the way he got started as well. The most remarkable thing about going to Ralph's office was seeing all the Latin Stars I had come to love since I was a young boy. I'm talking about Celia Cruz, Hector Lavoe, Willie Colon, etc. They were always really nice— especially Celia Cruz and her husband Pedro, amicable and down-to-earth loving people. Ralph asked me to give Hector a ride uptown, and I was honored to comply. I told Hector about the first time I saw him in person at a club in my neighborhood in the Bronx called El Ceromar Casino on 149th St. and how I helped them bring in their instruments, and he was amused.

Hector was one of the Kings of Latin Music in my book, and to be working alongside Ralph, who pretty much made them all Superstars when he signed them all to his label RMM Records, was like a blessing to me.

I knew I would like working for Ralph, and meeting my favorite artists was a big bonus.

The plans shared with me were exciting, and the fact that they both made it clear I was to be in charge of all City Wide Promotional efforts was huge to me. Everything from opening new clubs to big concerts at Madison Sq. Garden was now my responsibility to promote on the streets. The year was now 1981, and I was already pretty well known for all I had done to date with David as a promoter. I had made my mark, but the best was yet to come. I had already worked on a couple of concerts with David and Ralph, but they wanted to see how I would do independently. David told me I would be promoting it on my own with no Radio, just posters and flyers, and he would pay for everything and split the proceeds with me.

I, of course, saw this as an opportunity to write my name in stone as a club promoter and jumped at the opportunity right away. I decided to make it an Oldies Reunion Party and invited everyone who attended all the best clubs from the 1970s to party with old friends. I also hosted a Rock Contest with cash prizes, and the turnout was a full-house with a line of people outside that stretched down the block. David and Ralph were very impressed with what I had done, and we all made money that night, so I guess that's what they were happiest about, especially since they had the bar. Trust me when I tell you, they were not as satisfied as I was.

I mean, it was not only a great turnout, but I had also done my first event on my own, and all my friends were there to show support as I made my mark for the first time, and they came to dance.

Eddie Ramundi and Sara Silver (Latin Symbolics) were among the best during the early days of the Latin Hustle. We were all the best of friends back in those days, and 49 years later, we still are.

At the Faces Grand Ballroom with Nilda in 1978.
During the Disco Days, Rappers had started doing their
thing, and Hip Hop was on the horizon.

Promoter
Willie Estrada

Nilda was an amazing Latin Hustle dancer and one of my
favorite dance partners of the 1970s.

The key to being a good Latin Hustle Dancer is getting
good at doing spins, and flowing with the music, without
looking at your feet!

CHAPTER TWENTY-THREE: WORKING FOR THE KING

By the time I started working with Ralph Mercado, I had upgraded to a better car that had been customized with a great paint job, 60-inch deep-dish Craggier tires, a Bose Sound System, swivel seats, and the engine had been modified for more speed. I now had two cars, one for work, a 1972 Chevy Impala, and a 1975 Monte Carlo, which was, of course, for going out with the ladies. Ralph was expecting big things from me, so there was no way I would disappoint him, considering that I wanted to be just like him, and I knew he would make a great mentor. My boys and I always went out to the clubs to promote his events and dance and meet girls.

We usually headed to the Ipanema on Tuesday nights because it was Latin night, and they always brought in well-known live bands to play. That night, Hector Lavoe and his band and I were there with all my boys, Blue, Junbug, Tony, and Willie Whip. At the time, I was also selling cocaine to make extra money, and I got it for a low price, so I always made a killing at the clubs, which is not something I am very proud of. We were always strapped with our guns during those days, and that night was no different. I left my friends at our usual table and went to the bathroom as the MC was calling for Hector to take the stage, but he was always late.

Hector was arguing with another drug dealer over money when I walked into the bathroom. I liked Hector and didn't like that some dude from Uptown was raising his voice at him and treating him disrespectfully.

I couldn't stay quiet while this dude, whom I didn't like to begin with, was being disrespectful to him, so I raised my voice and asked him what the problem was. He could tell by the look in my eyes I was not in the mood to be messed with. He calmly proceeded to tell me how Hector had not paid him for a gram of coke he took on credit the week before at Barney Googles after saying he would pay him after his session. Hector left that night without paying the guy, but he was usually so stoned by the end of his meetings that he probably just forgot. However, that didn't matter to me, I told him that I didn't give him the right to be disrespectful and scream at Hector like that, and he gave me a hard look, so I got in his face and told him to get the fuck out. I was angry and had a 38 special tucked in my belt, and the last thing this guy wanted was for me to pull it out. He knew who I was, and he knew who I rolled with, and the last thing he wanted was to have a problem with us. After he walked out, Hector told me he couldn't go on without a few hits, so I asked him to relax and took him into the bathroom stall. I pulled an ounce of Coke from my jacket pocket, which made him open his eyes wide and said, "Diablo." I asked him to take out a bill to give him some, and he told me he was broke until he got paid for the night.

I shook my head and pulled out a bill poured in about a gram and told him to put that away for later. We then indulged from the clear bag I pulled out, and he told me he would pay me later. I told him to forget about it but not buy anything from that other dude again and come to find me, and he agreed. We walked out, and off he went to play his set with a big smile on his face, as I went back to my table to have a drink with my boys, who had invited some girls to join us.

Hector was getting on stage as I met a couple of the girls who came to share some drinks with us and made us all laugh by saying he was not late; we were always early. He then did something I did not expect as the band started to play; he pointed to me and said, "Willie, this one is for you," in Spanish, of course, then he started singing a song called "Mi Gente."

My friends asked me what that was all about, so I told them what had happened in the bathroom. Blue got a little upset that Hector got disrespected, and since he was always a hothead, he wanted to find the guy who dissed Hector and tune him up. I shook my head and said it wasn't worth it and just wanted to have one night out without getting into a fight. We all agreed, and that was the end of it. However, it did not stop Blue from giving the guy dirty looks when we saw him later that night, but he quickly kept it moving without returning the glare.

That was only one night out of many, and those were the best times for my friends and me during an era we will never forget and hold forever in our hearts.

In 1981 John Addison and Maurice Brahms opened a colossal nightclub in the heart of Times Square called Bond International Casino. It had been a Bond Men's clothing store before they renovated it, and they kept the name Bond simply because there was a huge sign which read BOND in front of the club. After the Clash was scheduled to perform several shows there from May to June, there was a big riot outside of the club in May because the club was too full, and many people couldn't get in.

The Fire Department showed up and canceled any further shows because of the number of people who got hurt outside the club that night.

Later that year, Ralph Mercado started renting the club once a month on Friday nights to do Salsa Concerts there, and as fortune would have it, I was given the responsibility of managing the street team to promote those events. It all started on a Labor Day weekend, September 6th, 1981, where he brought in a variety of well-known Latin Recording Artists, who played to a packed house thanks to the promotional efforts of my streets team! When I got there, the guys who were a part of my street team crew were dressed to kill. Ralph Mercado, David Maldonado, and Paco Navarro from WKTU were at the top of the stairs watching us make our way towards them. Ralph called me over and told me we did a great job and shook hands with us all.

My former Rock partner Robert Rocking with Vinny

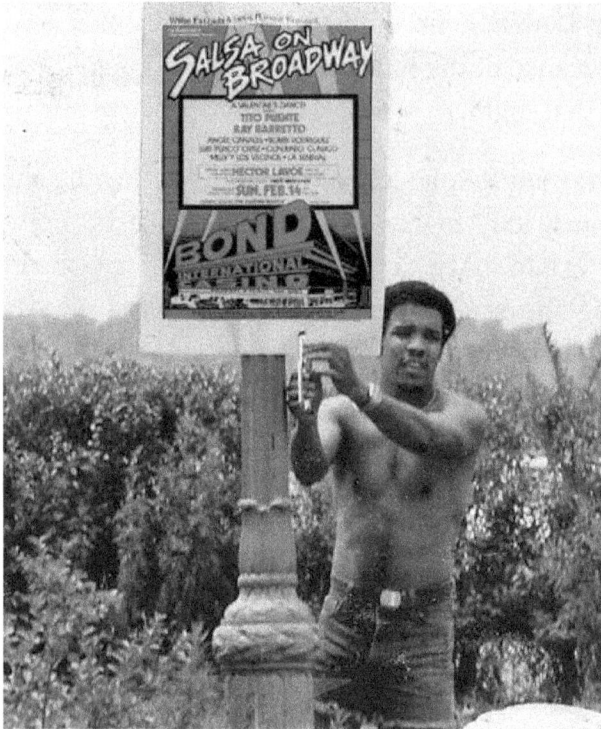

This is what I call paying my dues on the Streets!

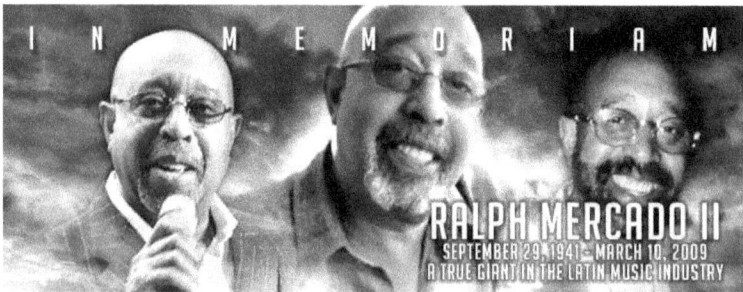

Ralph Mercado hosted the only Salsa Concerts at Bond International Casino and became my new mentor when managing his citywide promotions in late 1981. Because of him, I got the job as the Friday night promoter at Bond International Casino in early 1982.

For Latinos, Salsa came before the Latin Hustle and Rock cultures and was extremely popular in New York, where it was cultivated, nourished, and blossomed throughout the world.

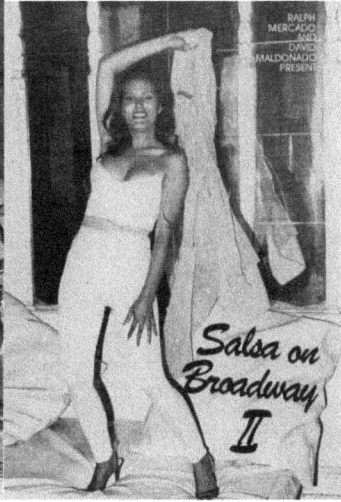

RIP Ralph Mercado

He then looked me up and down and told David and Paco, "This guy is the best-dressed poster guy I've ever seen, and damn if he didn't remind me of myself when I was his age." We all started laughing, and I took what he said as a great compliment, and I guess we all did since he told my boys we all looked dapper.

He then handed us a few drink tickets and told us to have a good time, and they walked away towards the stage area. It was still early, yet the place was already full, with a line outside stretching around the block. Later that evening, one of the guys named Jeff Levine who worked with Ralph came up to me and asked me if I had seen Paco and Ralph, and when I said no, he asked me to go on stage and make an announcement to mention all the artists who would be performing shortly.

I guess being dressed so dapperly paid off for me and was one of the reasons I was given what I considered an honor. I thought this was an excellent opportunity for me to establish myself as a promoter and a player on a bigger stage now, and I became excited. I was nervous, but I was confident, and I knew I needed to assert myself to make my presence felt. When I got on stage, I introduced myself and took the opportunity to make a couple of jokes which went over big, as I had everyone laughing before introducing the acts. It was the moment I realized I wanted to host my events with my name on the flyers!

I had been involved with many events by then, but I had never really done an event where I spearheaded the entire production and presentation.

The time for me to shine was closer than I thought, but I continued to work for Ralph and David until I could stand on my own two feet as a promoter. I went on to do several more Paco Parties at Bond International Casino for Ralph and David, and we always packed the house. David now had an office close to 14th St. in lower Manhattan, and I worked out of that office for a few months before I was approached by ABY from TKA, a very popular Freestyle Group. He handed me a cassette of a music demo by Marc Anthony. He told me Marc had tried out for their group, but he didn't get accepted because they all saw his amazing talent and knew he deserved to do his own thing.

Well, I guess they did him a favor because when I heard his music, which was Freestyle, by the way, he blew me away with his voice. The one thing I knew was music, and I knew from the moment I heard his first song that he would be a big star someday. The following day I took the tape demo to the office and had David listen to him. I made everyone sit in the conference room to get everyone's opinion on Marc and his fantastic voice. David knew if I was excited about this guy, he must be reasonable, and he was, because the minute they started listening to him, he blew everyone there away as he had done with me when I heard him the night before. David wanted to reach out to Marc and bring him in for a talk.

That same week I got a call that took me by surprise; it was from John Addison, one of the owners of Bond International Casino. I recall his deep voice as he asked for me by name, and when I told him it was I on the phone, he told me Ralph Mercado had given him my number.

Once he told me who he was and how he got my number, I gave him my full attention and asked him what I could do for him. He shared with me how he needed a promoter for Bond's on Friday nights since they were doing poorly on those nights, with an average of 150 people. That was a drop in the bucket, considering the size of that club, which had the largest capacity of any club in New York City. He told me Mike Stone was promoting Saturday nights, with an average of 2,500 people. However, they were a young crowd and didn't drink much at his bars.

He also mentioned that he reached out to Ralph because everywhere throughout New York, he saw posters of the events I was promoting for Ralph, and he was very impressed. I told him how we had the best promotional street team in New York and could saturate the entire City in just one night. He asked me how soon I could meet with him to discuss taking over promotions on Friday nights, so I told him I could be there in about an hour, and he told me he would be expecting me. This was the opportunity I had been waiting for with great anticipation for some time. I took a quick shower and dressed to impress, so he would know he was dealing with a professional and not some street punk looking to make a quick buck. If I was going to do this, I wanted to do it right and create a more prominent name for myself in the process.

It was a weekday afternoon when I jumped in my car and blasted my music like I always did. I headed towards my new destiny with stars in my eyes and the thought of being the house promoter for the biggest club in New York City on Friday nights.

It was a beautiful club with a beautiful spiral staircase that lit up in different colors at the entrance, and once you got inside, it boasted the longest bar in New York City. The club also had a spectacular light and laser show. When I finally got there, I was happy to see I was expected and asked to come right in as John was waiting for me at the top of the stairs.

The first thing that came out of his mouth when he saw me was, "Oh my, nobody told me you were such a handsome young man," in a lustful voice as he looked at me up and down. I took it as a compliment, kept my cool, gave him my thanks, and wondered if John was Gay because of what he said and how he looked at me like I was a piece of meat. When we got upstairs to his office, he asked me to have a seat and confirmed my suspicions by asking me if I had fooled around with men. I immediately got up and told him, "I only like women, so if this is what this is all about, I'm out of here." He got up from behind his desk and apologized to me as I started walking out. He told me it would never happen again, and it never did, for the most part. We got down to business and negotiated an excellent weekly salary for me with lots of perks that included unlimited drinks and guests. Once we agreed on a price and my responsibilities, he gave me an office to promote and produce events every Friday night. I only had two weeks and a half before my first event, so I knew I had my work cut out for me. I called the printer and gave him all the info, and put John Addison's name on the flyer to start with, which made him happy, as I also built up my brownie points. John was easy to work with because he left me alone to do my thing and never interfered with how I did my job.

I knew I could count on my crew to help with promotions, and they all had CB Radios in their cars, so it made it easier for us to communicate throughout the City. We set a date for March 26th, 1982, as our first Friday night party and worked hard to ensure the entire City of New York knew about it. My goal was to make Friday nights at Bond International Casino the best Party in town and secure my name as a great promoter. My crew consisted of guys and girls who were great dancers and very popular in the club scene. The girls mostly helped with giving out flyers for me, and I, in return, would give them free access to all events, even on Mike Stone nights, which was on Saturday nights. I was also provided with free drink tickets to share with my friends, so they didn't have to spend any money when they came with me to the club. One of our most significant assets was a girl we called Disco Queen, her handle on a CB Radio. She had a home-based CB Radio with a big antenna on her rooftop, so she could talk to us on our CB Radios no matter where we were throughout the City, and that was a big help as she relayed messages to us day or night.

Bond International Casino - 1982

CHAPTER TWENTY FOUR:
THE BIRTH OF FRIDAY NIGHT FEVER 1982

At a time when Hip Hop, Freestyle, and several other Cultures were starting to make an impact on the clubs in New York City, outsiders hated Disco and what it stood for. They had no idea how our Hustle culture was born or where it came from, but they hated it anyway. We had come a long way from those basement club hooky parties of the early 1970s that gave birth to a style of partying that rose from the ashes and devastation we were subjected to growing up in the South Bronx. Many people think that disco was made popular by gays in the later 1970s when Disco was booming. There has never been one mention of the Latino influence, especially after the creation of the Latin Hustle or the impact it had throughout the USA and eventually the World. So let me say we never called it disco during the early 1970s. We called it clubbing, and it had nothing to do with gays at all; however, it was part of a revolution that came out of the South Bronx during the worst of times. We didn't care who liked or disliked our partying because it was our way of coping with the hostile environment of the burning South Bronx we grew up experiencing and still living in. Gays took it to a different level, and it became wilder, so they got the credit for something they did not create but were a part of. But that's another story.

With no care in the world, my street team and I hit the streets like a tidal wave as we saturated the city with posters and fliers for what was to be the first real Friday night party at Bond International Casino. I only say that because the owner of Bonds told me the Saturday night parties Mike Stone hosted mainly were full of young people who wouldn't drink at his bar.

He went on to tell me that at the end of the night, maintenance would find dozens of empty liquor bottles all over the dance floor.

I, myself, was catering to a classier clientele whom I knew would dress to impress and drink at the bar, as well as dance the night away with a euphoric state of mind. We had fewer fights on Friday nights, considering it was a slightly older crowd, but we also had a great security staff who handled any situation with class and respect. I insisted on these measures for our security because I had already been involved with doing events where many people converged, many of whom were just like my boys and me, Ghetto Gangsters at heart, for many years. I found out the hard way when two crazy factions clash, there is always a big mess left in the aftermath, and nobody wins. That is why I thought it's always best to do things calmly and respectfully, even when the client acts crazy. Lord knows I've been in more than my fair share of all-out brawls and rumbles in my day, and I have the scars to prove it. Anyway, my team and I worked harder in the two weeks leading up to my first event at Bonds than we had with any other previous occasion we had been a part of. Of course, you work harder when your name is attached to something you hoped would serve as a catalyst for something greater. That's not to say we didn't work hard on previous events, but this one was special. All my boys were with me with a few notable exceptions who had gone their separate ways a short while before Bonds.

We were in our mid 20's now and had different mindsets because we were more mature, and we had more purpose and a strong desire to make more money. Everything was coming together as if by magic, and the stars were aligned in a sequence that radiated success for us.

By the week of the dance, the buzz was strong throughout the boroughs and beyond. My phone rang off the hook with friends who wanted to be on my guest list. I should mention that a couple of my boys and I would go to Mike Stone's Saturday night events, which was a younger Webo, Freak, and Smurf Dance Crowd.

However, keeping in mind that I had unlimited guests even on Saturday nights, I would go to the end of the long line and ask everyone who wanted to get in and jump the line by paying me, and I would get them in. Twenty or so people would raise their hands and come over to me and ask who I was and how I would get them in. I would share that I had unlimited guests, and if they wanted, I could get them in without waiting in line. The truth is that many of the security staff would take money under the table and make money letting people in regularly. Only none of them had the clout I had, so I could get away with bringing in big groups if I wanted to. The club owners figured people who get in for free would buy drinks at the bar and fill the club, giving it more allure so that it would always be packed. Mike Stone was not happy about me getting people in for free on his nights, but there was nothing he could do about it, which pissed him off. Nonetheless, we were cordial to each other even though I would catch him, giving me the evil eye from time to time when I went to his Saturday night jams.

To be honest, I could care less if he liked me or not, my crew and I were on a mission, and nobody could stand in our way since we were of that old school mentality, mess around lay around. In other words, if you mess with the bull, you get the horns.

Bond's Disco Masquerade Party - June 1982

But the truth of the matter was, we were known throughout the club scene for many years, and it wasn't only because we were among the best dancers in the city, but because we had that ghetto street gang mentality as well, and everyone knew we were not to be messed with. The day of my first event at Bond's was finally here, and the excitement of what was to come that night was high with expectations and promise for the future. I had put together an extensive list of special guests comprised of the best dancers in New York City, all of whom were my friends.

On the ride into the city that night, several of my friends in tow and their cars were full of those who helped promote this event. Including girls who had helped put up posters and hand out fliers. We wanted to make a grand entrance, so we got there fashionably late, and when we got to the street around the corner from Bond's, there was a long line of people waiting to get in.

It brought a big smile to all our faces, and we began to revel in our success as we walked past them. When we got to the entrance, the bouncers at the door knew who I was and opened the security gates for my crew and me, and we got high fives on the way in, accompanied by great big smiles. We had not even made it inside, yet we knew this was a great turnout with only two and a half weeks of promotions.

I recalled the last time I was there for an event. It was for Ralph Mercado and David Maldonado, but this time it was different. This time it was my own event, and the feeling that came along with it was much better for some reason. This time, John Addison was waiting for my arrival and that of my crew, who had worked very hard to make this night a great success. We took our time walking up the spiral staircase as John waved to us. We had big smiles on all our faces, but John's was more significant, and I wanted to enjoy that moment. When we finally got to the top of the stairs, John came over and picked me up with a bear hug, so I asked him to put me down and stop the homo shit. He was so excited he paid me no mind. He put me down but hugged me again and then introduced me to Curtis, who was the club manager, and told me I could write my ticket, and I did.

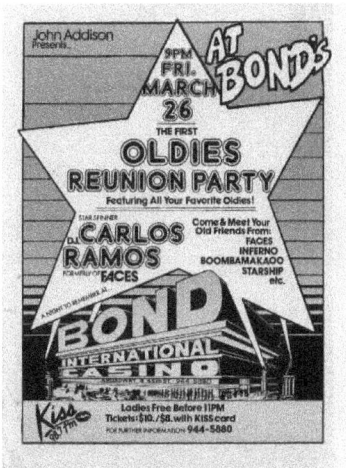

DJ Carlos Ramos is doing his thing, and if you look closely, you will see me in the background behind the two artists in the middle in the DJ Booth at Bonds.

Bond International Casino

When I first became the Friday Night Promoter for Bond International Casino, we used John Addison's name on the flyer; however, by the 3rd week, I added my name to the flyers, and John's name after that never appeared on the flyers again. After a couple of weeks, he was not there because he had opened a new Gay Club called Club 13, and he had no problem with giving Carlos Ramos and me all the credit we deserved for making Bond's the number one club in New York City on Friday nights.

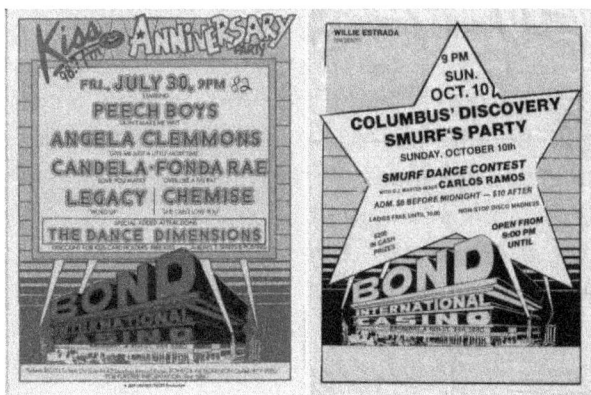

He instructed Curtis to give me unlimited drink tickets, and he handed me about 30 drink tickets and told me to let him know when I needed more. The place was already pretty full, and the line outside was still long, so John took care of my friends and me since he knew this was the beginning of something big. I had flyers for the following week's dance already printed so everyone would get a flyer on the way out that night. My great friend Carlos Ramos was our DJ, and he had his following as well since he had DJ'd at many of the best clubs throughout the City on different nights. However, he was also old school from the '70s and had been around for many years. His name was known throughout New York City. As we walked away from John and his big smiley face, my friends started teasing me about the bear hug and asked if there was something they should know about John and me. "Oh, you wannabe wise guys? Fine, no drink tickets for any of you!"

We all had a good laugh and partied the night away like we owned the joint. There's nothing like building something big with great friends by your side, and for us, it was more than just the money we made; it was the prestige and the power that came with it. We were the Kings and Queens of New York City on and off the dance floor. We commanded respect because we had earned it through hard work and perseverance in all we had gone through before reaching the top. Now don't get me wrong; we were not millionaires, but we were rich in spirit and clout, and throughout the City, our names were known. I had used John Addison's name on the posters and fliers for the first two events, but shortly after our successful grand opening on Friday nights, John purchased the lease for a restaurant named Liuchow's on 14th St. Since he was never there, I started using only my name on the flyers by my 3rd event. John mentioned it to me one night in passing, but I blew him off by pointing out that he was never there, and I was hosting all the events myself, but most importantly, he was making most of the money while I was doing all the work with my crew.

He never argued with me because I was his main moneymaker. Still, besides that, he turned the old Liuchow's into a Gay club and named it Club 13 with the entrance on 13th St. I got him to pay for everything we needed to make Friday Nights the best party in town. We started bringing in artists to perform and also Radio announcements on WKTU. That was when "Willie Estrada Presents" became a household name in New York City, as you often heard Mary Thomas from Kiss FM mention my name over the air in connection with Bond International Casino events. Our Friday night events were the talk of the town, and we started using Mary Thomas as our host more often. She was a top-rated DJ at Kiss WKTU FM, and she was always mentioning Friday nights at Bond International Casino. The promoter for Saturday nights at Bond's was unhappy about our successful Friday nights because even his crowd started dressing up and coming to my events.

One night I was at one of his events promoting my Friday nights, and as I was on my way to the office upstairs, Mike was coming up with his bodyguards with the monies from the night's take. I was accompanied by a beautiful girl I had been dating named Brenda that night, and as they came out of the elevator, one of his security staff pulled out a gun and pointed it at my head. My date and I kept cool, and I asked him to take the gun out of my face before something bad happened, and he wouldn't put it down, so I looked at Mike Stone and told him to instruct his pawn to put the gun away, or I would have him fired. He knew who I was and posed no threat to him or any of his minions. Eventually, Mike asked him to put the gun down, but not fast enough, so I went to Curtis, the club manager, and told him what happened and that Mike had not stopped it.

I was furious, and Curtis could see that I had no intention of letting this go, which is when I asked Curtis to make sure the guy who put the gun in my face got fired.

I told him if he didn't do something, my friends and I would, and that it would turn ugly. Curtis had never seen me angry, so while Mike was counting money in the next room, he called him into the office. He told him how unacceptable the actions of his security staff had been and how he would not tolerate any guns being brought into the club, and he told Mike to fire the guy responsible, or there would be problems. Mike tried to reason with Curtis and me, but we weren't having any of it; he would have to comply or would be in danger of losing his Saturday night events. The funny part was that John and I had already spoken about me taking over Saturday nights as well, so Mike was already walking on thin ice. It was behavior like his security staff, which led John to even speak to me about Saturday nights. Of course, it didn't help that Mike's crowd hardly drank at his bar. The following week, having been fired from his security job with Mike Stone, the guy who pulled the gun on me came to my Friday night event with a few of his friends looking for trouble.

I alerted our head of security, whose name was Joe, and he told me he would keep an eye on them and assign a couple of his best guys to watch my back. I told a few of my boys, and we all got together and decided to confront them since they were all giving me dirty looks and pointing at my boys and me. Joe knew it would escalate because he was a seasoned bouncer and could tell by their demeanor that they had bad intentions. One of the guys Joe had assigned to me was none other than Taimak, who went on to be the star of the movie "The Last Dragon," He and I had become friends during my time at Bond's, and he knew I was a martial artist as well, so we had mutual respect for one another.

322

We knew there was no way they had any guns on them because our security staff was very thorough in searching everyone who came into Bond's, and they didn't exactly get along with Mike's crew either.

They had come for me, but they didn't know about my security crew by way of my boys, who were bad-asses, and the regular security staff who were ready to pounce on them as well. Taimak was the first to ask them what the problem was and why they were making threats against me. All hell broke loose when the tough guy pushed Taimak and told him to mind his business. When we saw the shove, we all ran over, and fists and feet started flying all over the place, with the tough guy and his boys getting the worse of it. While I don't remember who I hit or how long it lasted, I know it wasn't long before we kicked them down the escalator that led to the ground level. Taimak kicked one guy so hard he fell over the rest of his boys, who were already heading down the escalator head first.

They didn't even know what hit them and made their way out of the club, being led by the security staff on the ground level with the head of security Joe leading the way. We all started high-fiving each other since we kicked ass and did so in a very short time, with nobody else getting hurt, except for those who came looking for trouble. Curtis found out what happened and called John to alert him, and the following night I heard he told Mike if that ever happened again, he would be out on his ass since it was his security crew who started the trouble, to begin with. When we left the club that night, we thought they might be waiting, so we walked together in a big group towards our cars, but they never showed their faces, and after that night, I never saw them again. The next time I saw Mike Stone, he didn't give me any hard looks like he usually did, and I knew right then and there that the silent war was over and that his crew would never mess with us again.

In the weeks that followed, we continued to draw tons of people regularly, so Carlos Ramos and I had decided to rent the club on a Friday night and make more money in the process. Meanwhile, back in our neighborhood, stick-up kids, as we called them, were running amok robbing drug dealers and people alike. I saw many talented people fall prey to drugs and end up dead or in jail for crimes ranging from robbery to murder. As the irrational behavior continued in my hood, my boys and I stayed focused on the task at hand, making Bond International Casino the best party in town on Friday nights. Besides the money, the best thing about running Friday night promotions at Bond's, where all the beautiful girls I got to date.

One night as I was headed towards Bond's with my best friend Tony, I was cut off by a red sports car while driving down 46th Street. Being the aggressive person I am, I caught up to the idiot who cut me off to give him a piece of my mind. As I pulled alongside, it turned out to be a beautiful blue-eyed blond who took my breath away the moment I looked into her eyes and saw her beautiful smile. She yelled out, "I like her horn," and I responded, "I like you! Where are you going in such a hurry?" She had a pretty dark-skinned girl sitting on the passenger side, which was perfect because there were two of us and two of them. She told us they were on their way to Studio 54, but I told her, "No, you're not. You're coming with us to Bond's International Casino." She said, "No way, Bond's is going to be jam-packed. They have a special event there tonight." I responded, "It's my event, I am the promoter on Friday nights at Bond's, so you don't have to pay for entrance or your drinks since you will both be my guests." "Are you sure we can get in? Don't lie to me just to get me to go with you." "Trust me, it will be fun, and I will make sure you have a great time." "OK, I'm going to trust you, so where shall we park?" We were right where we wanted to be in terms of parking, and as chance would have it, there were two parking spots directly across from each other, and I said to myself, "How convenient."

Keeping in mind that I had only seen her beautiful face, I had no idea what the rest of her looked like until she got out of her car. I parked my car and crossed the street to greet her, and the moment she opened her door and stepped out of her car, my heart jumped with joy as I looked at this voluptuous woman getting out. The first thing out of Tony's mouth was "Wow Que Tetas!" translation "Wow, great tits!"

She looked at him as I poked him on the side with my elbow but said nothing. She was wearing a short skirt, had great legs, and was just picture perfect in every way. Her friend was also beautiful, so Tony and I figured we were set for the night in terms of hanging out with two beautiful women. We, of course, made the proper introductions. Her name was Christina, and I only remember that she made it sound like Royalty when she said her name. As we started walking towards Bond's, she said, "By the way, I speak Spanish; I'm from Spain." I slapped Tony on the back of the head, and we all started laughing about it since we knew she only said that because of Tony's remark about her beautiful breasts. She assured us it was OK and said she knew she had nice tetas but asked that we treat her like a Lady. Of course, we agreed sincerely, which brought a smile to her face. It was a funny moment, but Tony was a little embarrassed but laughed it off. As we got closer to Bond's, she noticed the long line halfway down the block from the club and asked me if that was the line for Bond's. I asked some people toward the end of the line if this was the line for Bond's, and several people yelled out, "Yes." Others said it was going to be a great night. Everyone online was dressed to impress, but many women were dressed to kill. The one thing I insisted on was that people had to come dressed well, and we did not allow sneakers or jeans into the club; in other words, you had to be elegantly attired to get in. Christina asked me again if I would get them in upon seeing everyone online.

I could tell she wanted to feel special, and I had every intention of making that happen. Sometimes, I would go to the club alone, allowing me to choose someone for the night. I looked at her and asked her not to worry because she was in for a great night. When we finally got to the front of the club, big Rudy, one of the bouncers at the door, saw me walking with these two beautiful women and decided to pay me some homage.

He made the sound of a horn, and made believe he was blowing a trumpet, and announced in a loud voice, "Open the gates, the King is here! Ladies, welcome to Bond International Casino" As the security police barricade was opened, Christina and her friend were amazed at our reception, and it showed on their faces as she turned to me and said, "I am officially impressed!" Rudy bent over to give me a hug since he towered over me, and I gave him my thanks as I whispered in his ear and thanked him for making me look good. Rudy was accustomed to seeing me with beautiful women, but he also whispered in my ear, "This one is the best one yet!" I turned around laughing and walked into the club, shaking my head while thinking how I didn't' realize Rudy and the guys were rating the girls I brought to the club. Curtis, the club manager, was also waiting to greet me as I walked in, complimented me on looking dapper as always, handed me 50 drink tickets to start my night, and told me to let him know when I needed more. Christina asked me what he gave me, and I told her they were drink tickets, and she just shook her head in disbelief.

Once inside, we headed towards the DJ booth, where I hung out with the ladies and the DJ Carlos, who was one of my best friends and born the exact date I was. I gave Tony a handful of drink tickets and asked him to show Christina's friend a nice time, which of course, he didn't have a problem with.

After getting a couple of drinks, Christina and I made our way through the crowd. I went to see Carlos, who was happy to see me as he knew our first event together was a big hit, and the place was packed. My cousin JR worked the door to make sure nobody was making money by letting people in on the side, as they usually did. Carlos's girlfriend, Lorraine, was in the DJ booth as always. She was attractive but insanely jealous and incredibly protective of Carlos. She did not like that I always brought pretty girls into the DJ booth to meet Carlos, and she didn't like me very much. I could care less; she was a bit crazy and never let Carlos have any fun since she would never leave his side. I called her psycho most of the time, and Carlos would always chuckle, even when she was there, which she didn't like very much.

She just looked at Christina up and down, and I could tell she didn't like the fact that Christina was more beautiful than her, and she wasn't very receptive. On the other hand, Carlos looked at her, and his eyes said it all, but he couldn't look for long, or Lorraine would slap the back of his head. I once asked him why he was with that psycho, and his response was because she was great in bed and would do anything he asked of her. My problem with her was that she always gave the girls I took into the DJ booth dirty looks and would often say things to upset my guests, mostly about me always being with someone new. There was no way I would end up like Carlos, with a girlfriend who was always there and would not allow me to spend time with my boys.

After 10 minutes or so in the booth, I decided it was time to explore the possibilities with Christina and get the hell away from Carlos' nut job girlfriend Lorraine. We got some drinks, and I took her to the VIP room, and once we got there, I wanted to be alone with her, so I told Alex, the bouncer guarding the VIP room door, that I was kicking everybody out and not to allow anyone else in until I said it was OK. Yes, I had it like that.

The VIP room had a great view of the dance floor from the back end facing the stage on the other side. I told everyone they could come back in about half-hour, and they all left. Alex looked at Christina and bit his lip as she walked in and made funny faces at me, which Christina, of course, did not see him do. Once we were alone, she asked me what I had in mind, so I just grabbed her by the waist pulled her close so she could feel the heat of our bodies along with the look in my eyes, and she melted into my arms as we kissed.

I lured her onto the oversized black leader couch behind us where it was dark, and despite her concerns about people seeing us, we made passionate love while everyone danced below. I, of course, had eased her mind by telling her we could see them, but they couldn't see us, and in the heat of passion, she gave in and submitted to the moment, which was like magic. After we made love, she had a look of content on her face, which was pleasing. I kissed her again and told her how amazing she was. I took her by the hand, and we started walking out. As we walked past Alex, he motioned his face as if to tell me something, but I paid it no mind because now I needed a drink. She held my hand, and I could feel it pulsate with a strong vibe that said, "I like you," and I was on cloud nine. When we got back to the DJ booth, Carlos looked at my face and said, "Yo, why is your face so shiny around your lips?" My mind raced, thinking of something to say, but I looked at Christina, and she said nothing, but a small smile came across her face, along with a blush. I excused myself and asked Christina to wait for me while I went to the restroom. Carlos got it and just stood there with a big smile on his face, while Lorraine gave me a look of disgust as she shook her head. But right on time to save the day was Tony and Christina's friend, who kept her company while I went to wash my face. I left the booth with a big smile on my face, and as I made my way through the crowd, and handed out a few drink tickets like I always did.

I took that opportunity to see how we were doing at the door since I had left my cousin JR in charge to make sure everything was OK. My mistake was not going downstairs and ensuring nobody was being let in on the side, but more about that later. I went back to see Christina, and with great excitement, she flew into my arms as she was thrilled to see me. The look on Lorraine's face was not so good, especially since I had left Christina there and Carlos, being the great host, paid her some attention along with Tony and Christina's friend.

Lorraine was giving me dirty looks as I hugged Christina, and I could tell she was about to have a hissy fit, not that I cared, but I decided to enjoy the night with Tony, the girls, and hang with some of our friends. By the end of the night, Christina told me she was glad I stopped to speak to her and what a wonderful time she had had. She gave me her number and asked me if I was going to call her and I, of course, said yes! But, to be honest, until this day, for the life of me, I don't know why I waited for an entire month to call her. Her mom picked up the phone, and she asked me who I was. When I told her my name, she knew who I was. She shared how her daughter had met me when she broke up with her boyfriend and was very fond of me, but I never called her, so she went back with her boyfriend, whom she didn't like. I guessed it was the reason she told me to begin with. I was disappointed with myself, but I had girls coming out of my ears in those days, and they were all beautiful. But who's to say that was the girl for me and that I let her get away.

I will never know, but when something like that happens, and it's spontaneous and romantic, one should never take it for granted the way I did. All I kept thinking about after I spoke with her mom was telling her mom about me. I was thinking all along; she was just a fast woman, but I realized she was not who I thought she was too late. My life was based on loose women and fast cars, and the lifestyle I lived was not that of someone who wanted to settle down.

During those days, lots of good girls got away because I wasn't ready; however, the memories of those days live in my mind and some forever in my heart. In the coming weeks, I continued my Casanova ways of meeting one beautiful woman after another, and yet my life felt empty and loveless for some reason. One night at the club, I bumped into an old flame named Ivy. She was someone I have never forgotten throughout the years. She saw me from a distance, approached me as I spoke with some friends, and waited until she got my attention. My friend Tony saw her first and just said "WOW," which of course made me look and everyone else who was with us as well. As my friends all drooled over this beautiful creature standing there looking like the Goddess of Desire, I realized it was Ivy, and when our eyes met, she just smiled as she walked over and said, "Hi," she stirred my very soul, and as she got closer I felt butterflies in my stomach.

I had not seen her since our break up when she went off to college, and yet at that moment, I realized I still had deep feelings for her. I gave her a big hug, introduced her to my friends, and excused myself so that I could spend some time with her. Once we were alone, I asked her what she was doing there by herself, and she told me she wanted to see me and had heard from her cousin I was running promotions at Bond's on Friday nights. I was glad it was early, and I had not yet hooked up with anyone as I usually did, and of course, I did not tell her that. I couldn't believe that she was even more beautiful than when I last saw her. Ivy was a tan-skinned beauty with long shiny black hair, almond brown eyes, and a body beyond compare. I had met her at Orchard Beach years earlier through her cousin Doris Lopez, AKA Baby, who was one of the girls I danced the Hustle with at clubs as well as St. Mary's. The first time I ever saw her, she walked down the boardwalk with Baby, wearing a tiny white bikini in a perfect tight body.

As they got closer, all eyes were on Ivy, and the catcalls were coming from all directions, which she ignored for the most part. Baby came up and said hello; I asked her who the girl walking with her was. She told me it was her cousin Ivy and asked me to meet her. "What is that a trick question? Of course, I would like to meet her!" Baby started laughing and called Ivy over. I could tell she was a bit shy, yet she was assertive and suspicious, as I would soon find out. I took a liking to her right away, but it was not only because of her outer appearance, which was flawless, but I could tell there was something special about her. She had a smile so amazing it took my breath away, and I wanted nothing more than to get to know her better. She was pleasant and friendly; however, when I asked her for her number, she asked me, "Why?"

I told her I was interested in getting to know her and perhaps taking her out to dinner and a movie, which I only liked with girls. She immediately said, "No," so I asked her, "Why?" She told me she didn't know me and could not trust me. I made my argument and told her I was good friends with her cousin Baby, but she said: "That doesn't mean that I know you!" I was deflated, but I didn't let her see that I just said, "I understand, and it's cool. I won't bother you again, but it was nice to meet you." I smiled and walked away. I didn't want to seem desperate, and even though I was single, there was never a shortage of pretty girls, and I wasn't into groveling. I kept my distance and just observed her as one guy after another went over trying to talk to her. She looked over in my direction a few times, but I ignored her, and at one point, I just walked away without telling anyone I was leaving. The following week I had a show with the Latin Symbolics at a club called "La Mariposa," After we performed, I went to the bar for a drink, and Baby came over to say hello. She says, "My cousin Ivy is upset with you!" I asked her why? "Because you haven't gone over to say hello." My eyes opened wide, "She's here?"

"Yes, she is sitting right over there waiting for you to come over and say hello." I started laughing and told her how Ivy blew me off the day she introduced me to her, but Baby assured me she did like me, took notice when I disappeared, and asked where I went? That brought a big smile to my face. Ivy was sitting in a dark corner of the club where it was hard to see her, but as I got closer, I saw the face that launched a thousand ships, and she smiled at me. "You've been ignoring me, so it's about time you came over to say hello." I laughed and told her, "I didn't even know you were here. Sitting in this dark corner makes it hard to see you, so it was you hiding from me. Or perhaps you just wanted to spy on me to see if I was with somebody else. Or maybe, I just didn't recognize you with your clothes on."

She laughed, and she knew she had my undivided attention and was enjoying it as much as I was. I will admit it was a magical moment for me when I took her hand for the first time; suddenly, she was the only one I could see like everyone else around us became a blur of shadows mixed with beautiful music. Ivy and I became inseparable after that night, and we saw a lot of each other during the summer of 1978. In my heart, I knew she could be the one for me because she was not only beautiful, she was intelligent and had a great sense of humor which mixed well with all her other great attributes.

The strange part is that I was falling for her, but I knew very little about her or her plans on attending a college far away from the City and me very soon. It was what led up to our breakup because even though she loved me, I couldn't bear the thought of holding her back and keeping her from her dreams. In the end, we were both left heartbroken and longing for each other, and yet I knew I had done the right thing. I let her go because I did not want to interfere with her education.

Especially since, at the time, I was not thinking about educating myself, and all I thought about was dancing and having fun. Nothing had changed until I saw her on that fateful night at Bond's, and I spent the rest of that night speaking with her instead of lusting after other women.

She was on summer break but told me that she had a boyfriend even though she came to see me, and they were planning on getting engaged soon. It was just like I had seen it in my head the year she left for college, she would meet someone else, and I would lose her because I was not there, and he was. She told me had I decided to wait for her, she would have remained faithful, but deep inside me, I knew she was better off without me in her life, and I still believe that to this day.

I drove her home that night to El Barrio, where we parked and talked for a while. I told her I would never forget her as we said our final goodbye, and as she walked away, I wondered if I would ever see her again. Many years later, I searched for her again, and it was apparent I had never forgotten the amazing time we shared during the summer of 1979. My search finally came to an end in February of 2015, and just when I thought I had finally found her through a friend. My good friend Mambo Mario Diaz gave me the bad news that she had passed away some years after I last saw her from Breast Cancer. I will admit I broke down, as the news hit me hard, and even though she had died during the late 1980s, for me, it was just yesterday that we were in each other's arms with love in our hearts, and the thought of what could have been was gone forever.

RIP Ivy Leon until we meet again.

A couple of weeks later, I got another surprise visit to the club from another ex-girlfriend whom I cared a great deal for, Elba (Kitty). She walked into Bonds with her sister Nilda looking for me, and when I saw her, I got flashbacks from a few years back, when we finally became dance partners and chose "Touch of Elegance" as the name we would dance under.

We did a few shows together, but something always got in the way for her, and at the time, I had no idea it was her drug use, which was getting in the way and one of the reasons we eventually broke up.

I eventually found out it was her sister Nilda who got her into doing drugs and one in particular, which I hated the most. Although her addiction was unknown to me because she had never done it in my presence, it came in the form of a highly addictive drug known on the streets as Heroin or Dope. I once loved her very much, but so much had happened during her absence in my life, and I felt like I no longer knew her, and she was not the same girl I had fallen for just a few years earlier. Nevertheless, it was great to see her again and her sister Nilda, a beautiful young woman herself. I was hanging out with my friend Chico that night and introduced them to each other, and after partying that night, Chico and I drove them home. A week later she called me, and to my surprise, she asked me to marry her.

I asked her why she wanted to marry me after all this time, and she told me I was a good man and wanted me to help her get off drugs. I told her that it was not a good reason to get married and that she needed to do it for herself, not because she depended on someone else to do it for her. I know that sounds a bit harsh, but I was expecting her to say she still loved me or something to that effect, not that she was looking to use me as a crutch, which was basically how I understood what she said. Or, perhaps it was the way she said it that bothered me most, or maybe it was the fact that she started dating someone I knew, who I liked when we broke up. But, I guess I held that against her and may have been the single most important reason I said "No" to marry her. It could have also been because I cared more for Ivy and had a closer relationship than Kitty.

I still had a feeling of great sadness in having to say no, to marry her, so I told her I was honored that she asked me and how sorry I was for having to decline her marriage proposal.

Either way, our encounter was not as meaningful to me as was having Ivy visit me, even if it was just to say goodbye. I couldn't tell her that because I still cared about her. However, the love I once had for her was gone now. Too much had happened. It was the last time I would ever speak to her, and I found out some years later she died of an overdose and how that news made me so incredibly sad. For a long time, I thought it was my fault for not marrying her, and it took me a while to come to terms with it, but eventually, I did.

Elba (Kitty) Santiago RIP

During a Magical time in History, with two of my best friends, DJ Carlos Ramos and Tony Febles, at Bond International Casino Disco Masquerade Party on June 11, 1982.

@ Bonds International Casino

CHAPTER TWENTY-FIVE:

1983 THE DEATH OF BOND INTERNATIONAL CASINO

After seeing Ivy that night, my mindset changed, as I started to realize even with all my success as a promoter, my life was still empty because I didn't have a good woman by my side. By then, I had unintentionally broken a few hearts, which made me extremely sad but seeing Ivy again triggered those emotions. I thought about all the good girls from my past that I never committed to from fear of being tied down, mostly because I felt I was too young for marriage, which seemed to be what most girls wanted. I mean, come on, I was 26 years old and having the time of my life with my friends as well as all the pretty girls we fooled around with throughout the years.

My friends and I had been through so much together, even had life and death situations during those years. We also cheated death a few times along the way. It was a harsh world we came from, and yet, here we were, drinking champagne surrounded by beautiful women at the biggest and most fantastic nightclub in New York City, where we partied like kings. How I could be among so many pretty girls, besides my best friends, and still feel alone, is what I started asking myself after seeing Ivy. She haunted my dreams after that night, and I knew then that it was time for a change. I knew things wouldn't change overnight because I lived in the fast lane. Drugs, loose women, and cars were the norms, but my friends were getting worried about me. I wasn't enjoying those things as much as I usually did, and they noticed. There was a longing in my heart for something else, and I knew deep inside it was the company of a good woman missing in my life. Don't get me wrong; there were many good women out there; the problem was that the great ones were always taken.

On the other hand, so many great women had slipped through my fingers. I wasn't sure I would ever find another keeper.

I was tired of the status quo and living the same day over and over again, so to speak, and yet I knew many others would kill to be in my shoes. I had everything and yet nothing simultaneously, or so I thought to myself, and I realized as I was approaching my 27th Birthday something in me was changing. We continued to pack Bonds regularly, but I admit that it all became redundant after a while, and I knew something had changed. Almost as if I had brought it on by thinking about it, one beautiful afternoon Carlos and I were in the DJ Booth at Bond's, we heard a big commotion and screaming going on. Carlos and I opened the gate that gave us a view of the entire dance floor. We saw FBI agents telling everybody to get out. We didn't know what was going on, but they saw us and asked us to open the door to the DJ Booth. They asked us to leave the minute we let them in, but Carlos told them he was not going without his records and equipment. The Federal agent told us they were confiscating everything and again asked us to leave or get arrested. We asked them what the problem was and why they were doing this, and one of the FBI agents told us the owner of Bond owed the Government over 70 thousand dollars in taxes. With all the money we helped them make, we were in shock, but there wasn't a damn thing we could do about it. Carlos told them his livelihood depended on having his equipment and records and that he could not make a living without them. Finally, after going back and forth for a few minutes, the FBI agents reconsidered and allowed us to take Carlos' property off the premises. We took one last look around, knowing that was the end of an era for us.

For me, it meant finding another club to run promotions for, which was not as complicated as you might think considering what I had done at Bond's.

I was in high demand because I had a following and an excellent reputation for throwing amazing parties with huge turnouts. When we got to the car, Carlos confessed that the equipment wasn't his only the records. I just looked at him and started laughing my head off with delight. Carlos called it severance pay, but I wasn't going to see another dime, and it dawned on me at that very moment that I would probably have to move back in with mom for a while until I found something else. I was expecting money from the lawsuit against the Police and the City of New York, but that wasn't due for another couple of years. My landlord Pedro Morales knocked on my door the following week, and it wasn't for the rent. He told me he had some bad news for me, so I let him in. It's your grandmother, he said, she died overnight, and I should go see my mother. I thought about it for a millisecond, and then I just broke down and slumped to the floor as if a piece of my heart had been ripped out from my chest. Just a few days before, grandma had left a message for me to go see her, and I neglected to go even though she lived right around the corner from me. It was a massive blow for me, and it hit me like a ton of bricks as I realized I had lost my opportunity to say goodbye.

As it turns out, my sisters, whom she had also asked to go see her, actually went, and she told them she was going to die soon and wanted to say goodbye, but she also asked them to place white carnations on her coffin. I was furious at my sisters for not telling me she wanted to say goodbye, and they knew how much I loved my grandma. In the end, it was my fault for not going to see her as she had requested, and even until this day, I have never really forgiven myself for not saying goodbye to the woman who raised me right alongside my mother. When I went to see mom, she just threw her arms around me when she saw the look on my face as I tried my best to hold back the tears, but they just came like a flood in a sea of sorrow.

On the day of my grandmother's funeral, I placed white carnations on her coffin, asked her to forgive me for not seeing her, and told her I loved her with all my heart. After that, I broke down again as a flood of memories of her came rushing into my mind, and I saw her smiling face as she tried to comfort me and ease my pain. I felt the warmth of her love all around me, and I knew then that she would always be with me and that I would also see her again someday. She was the most significant loss of my life. Until that day, I had never experienced the loss of a loved one so close and dear to me, and it hurt like nothing ever had before. Her name was Juana Mojica. She was born in 1900 and died in 1983, with white doves being released at her burial. They were released as a proclamation of her passing and the love we all had for her. My biggest regret has always been not seeing her when she called for me, and I still live with the hurt of that pain today. A few months later, I celebrated my 27th Birthday and held a party in my apartment on the same weekend. I was to move out and back into mom's place.

When grandma left us so suddenly, I lost more than I realized. I had also lost my will to continue running promotions for clubs surrounded by many friends. I decided this was my last party, so I was going to make it a good one, and it lasted for two days. The one thing I had forgotten to do was ask a few friends to help me move my things back to mom's house, so on Sunday night, I slowly moved my stuff by myself. I had no help from anyone and made several trips as exhausted as I was, but even after not sleeping for two days straight. I had no choice and did what needed to be done.

At that time, I also realized I was on my own, as the change I had envisioned smacked me in the face, and I knew that the dawn of a new chapter in my life had just begun. As I reflect on those days, I can honestly say through the good and the bad; I learned lessons that will stay with me forever.

However, what resonates most in my mind are my father's lessons, and his lessons are still with me today. The most important being, "Tell me who you walk with, and I will tell you who you are!" He was saying to me in his own words to always depend on myself because people will let me down, and it took me a while, but I know now that he was right all along. Today even though I know hundreds of people from around the world and have many old acquaintances in my life, I can count my friends on one hand. I walk alone for the most part, just like my Dad did before me. I am, needless to say, more than OK with that as I continue my journey towards an unknown, but God willing, a bright future. One filled with hope and a happier place than that from which I came.

I am still here because of the power of my love for family and the resilience of my people that gave me the courage. They also gave me the strength to preserver against all the odds and through great adversity.

My family put the music in my heart, the style in my steps, and the swagger in my walk!

As the months passed, my phone stopped ringing off the hook, and while I got calls to work as a promoter at other clubs, I realized that it was time for me to move on. It took me a while, but eventually, I started a new chapter in my life. However, I will never forget the days of my youth; even though the hardship and sorrow were painful, there were also many moments of great delight and unbelievable memories, which I still carry with me today.

I must conclude by telling you, in all honesty, that for me, it was the end of a magical era, and it has been the honor of my life to share my story with every one of you. Remember always to treat others the way you want to be treated; believe in yourself at all times. Choose your battles carefully, and never go down without a fight! Most importantly, live your life in the now, never involve yourself in the foolishness of others, and lead by example! May God Bless You Always!

To Be Continued!

Author Willie (Marine Boy) Estrada

Afterword (Personal Thoughts)

In 2009, with two failed marriages behind me and 26 years later, I got a call from an old friend, Hollywood Film Director Franc Reyes, who had someone on the phone that wanted to meet me. He wanted to introduce me to Jorge (Fabel) Pabon, the Vice President of the world-renowned ROCK STEADY CREW. When he put Fabel on the phone, he immediately told me Franc had told him I was a 1st generation Rock and Hustle Dancer. When I confirmed that, he told me he was honored to meet me and asked if I would grant him an interview for a documentary he was working on called "The Untold Story of UpRock" by Pop Master Fable Pabon. I, of course, said yes, especially after he told me some guys from Brooklyn were claiming that there were no 1st generation Rockers from the Bronx and that they had created "Rocking" in Bushwick, Brooklyn. I told him they must have been high on Crack when saying something like that, especially since our style of the Rock dance was distinctively different, and they cannot claim to have created what we do.

To make a long story short, and since I plan to release a second book, which will serve as the squeal to this one, Fable shared many things I was shocked about, then asked me if I would grant him an interview set the record straight. After I said I would, he asked me if I knew of any other 1st Generation Rockers from the Bronx. I just smiled and opened the flood gates of knowledge for him by introducing him to several other dancers I knew from the early 1970s. Once I was on board, I started looking at videos on YouTube and was amazed at how far Rock Dancing and the Bboy culture had come in my absence.

Please keep in mind I had not seen anyone doing these dances for almost 30 years, so seeing it on the level it had gotten was nothing short of spellbinding for me. I was excited to bring some of the lost histories to life but a bit distressed when I started researching the culture further and took issue with false claims that the Zulu Nation brought peace to all the gangs of the South Bronx in 1974, according to KRS-1.

I started speaking out about that false history, but mostly because I knew the Zulu Nation did not exist in 1973 but came years later. The biggest reason for me was because it wiped out the real history that belonged to my generation, and all the things we did were not a part of the narrative, now being spread throughout the world. However, that was like telling me I didn't exist, which is unacceptable to me and my family and friends. What happened next? I will share another time since it's a long but fascinating story, which also needs to be told, and trust me when I say, I will tell it someday.

The other reason I had to go to war (So to speak) was to bring the truth to light and pay homage to people like Black Benjy, who died trying to make peace, and to Benjamin (Yellow Benjy) Melendez, founder of the Ghetto Brothers. They were the first to use the Ideology, which would later be used as the premise under which Hip Hop was born. It is the opinion of many that Yellow Benjy and the Ghetto Brothers were the 1st to introduce that Ideology in 1971, which would later be used in Hip Hop, and they should be given the credit they deserve for inspiring and setting an excellent example for the generation that came after them.

These are my thoughts and opinions based on the vast amounts of research I have done throughout the years. Also, I was there and served as an eye witness to that history.

We need to be put everything into the proper sequential order from the periotic timetable. Also, we must omit things that never happened, and they should be corrected once and for all. I made a promise to Benjy before he died in 2017 when he told me he didn't want his legacy to die with him. He left me all his memorabilia of newspaper clippings and photos for safekeeping, and I gave him my word that I would continue to share his story so that his legacy lives forever.

I fully intend to keep that promise before I am done, and this I swear, so you can hold me accountable for keeping my word.

The same thing goes for the story you just read and hopefully enjoyed. There is more to come in my second book, but this is all for now. Thank you for reading my story, and I hope you will appreciate the truths I shared with you all from my heart. Our history should be respected, preserved, as well as guarded so that future generations can know the truth about what happened to us and the things we did to survive the mean streets of the South Bronx as it burned down around us.

It's strange to me today that during the days of Fire and Brimstone, as well as the senseless violence, it all seemed normal for some reason, but there wasn't anything reasonable about it. As I look back now, I am amazed at the high level of our resilience and perseverance we had, and I take a great deal of pride in all the things we accomplished together as a people and the fact that we're still here!

It was the music, which led us to peace through dance, The Ghetto Brothers band was called - Beat the Street; they released their 1st Album, "Ghetto Brother Power," in 1971.

Street the Beat - Ghetto Brother Power

DJ Carlos Ramos was one of the most famous Disco DJs of the 1970s when IDRC was the best Record Pool in NYC, which provided the latest Disco and Hip Hop music we danced to at house parties and clubs during the latter part of the 1970s.

RIP Eddie Rivera Pres of IDRC. He brought us the music!

Remembering Benjamin (Yellow Benjy) Melendez

Yellow Benjy and Beat the Street with Regis Philbin and (The Ghetto Brothers)

Willie Martinez, Willie Estrada, and Tony Febles

They turned me into a cartoon on "The Get Down."
Our story is much too big to tell in one book, so I plan on
releasing a second book after we complete the
documentary we are currently working on, which will be
based on this book.

Willie Estrada and Millie Silva performing at St. Mary's Circa - 1976

Mercedes, Tony, Louie, Gladys, Mauwa, Dee Dee, Nelly Cotto, and Willie Estrada - Pioneers.

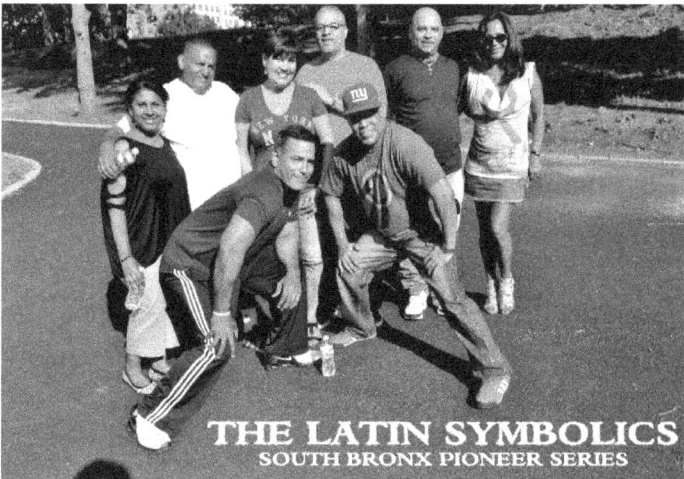

THE LATIN SYMBOLICS
SOUTH BRONX PIONEER SERIES

Reflections of the 1970s

The most significant effort in the name of peace must go to Benjamin Melendez, AKA Yellow Benjy, Founder of the Ghetto Brothers. He was followed by Henry De Sosa, Supreme President of the Bachelors. They followed his lead and finally made peace in our territory using music and dance as his weapons of choice at jams in St. Mary's Recreation Center on 145th St. and St. Ann's Avenue in 1974. While some memories have faded throughout the years, there are many scars that no amount of time will ever heal, but thanks to Benjamin Melendez and Henry De Sosa, we can now live with those scars in peace. RIP my brothers Henry and Yellow Benjy until we meet again…

Yellow Benjy and Street the Beat, Ghetto Brothers band

**Supreme Warlord - Black Spades Bam Bam with
Supreme Warlord of the Bachelors' Willie Estrada**

Once and for all, the Imperial Bachelors led the way by becoming the first gang to take off their gang colors in 1974. We requested that other gangs follow our lead to all parties without killing each other and dance with the girls at peace in our territory. In actuality, peace was made by each gang, on their turf, in their way, at their own time. Nobody can claim that any one person or gang brought peace to all the gangs of the South Bronx because that would not be true.

In regards to Hip Hop and the way we initially experienced it during the late 1970s, it was the new style of music along with the lyrics which caught our attention, but it didn't have a name as of yet, and the term Hip Hop didn't come into the picture until the early 1980s.

To be honest, many of us had never heard of Kool Herc or Afrika Bambaataa, and they never drew our attention because what they were doing was not mainstream during the early 1970s. We had our own thing going on, by way of the Latin Hustle and Rock Dance cultures and Disco music, which was mainstream by the mid-1970s.

I'm still stuck on the last part of the riddle, but I will continue to work on it until I get it right. But most importantly, I wrote this book so that the truth about how peace among the gangs was really made is known by all who read it. The fact of the matter is many have taken credit for things they simply did not do, and our beloved culture, which actually paved the way for others who came after, is never forgotten! During the early 1970s, it was Rock, and then the Latin Hustle took over in 1973 and became the dominant dance into the mid-1980s.

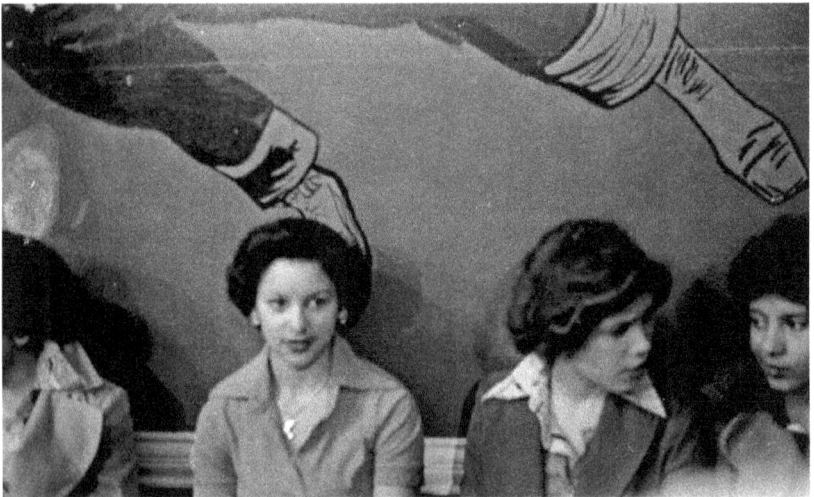

Millie and friends at St. Mary's Recreation Center 1974.

THE BIRTH OF HIP HOP FOR LATINO'S

By the time Rapper's Delight came out in 1979, DJs had already played that type of Rap music at house parties and even certain clubs. DJ Grandmaster Flash was also doing his park jams, and we would attend and dance freestyle or Hustle to the music since he also played Disco songs. The last Flash event I attended was held on the Basketball Courts at St. Mary's Park; someone started shooting, which made everyone run out of the park trampling over each other in the desperation of getting away from the gunfire.

I never attended another one of those jams as a direct result because, by that time, our culture, which was the Latin Hustle, was not experiencing that sort of thing. It was, after all, the dance we used to make peace amongst ourselves during the mid-70s. Hip Hop didn't start like that and was often violent.

The parties we attended during the late 70s always had Disco music, but the new fad was the sounds of Rap, and we gravitated towards the lyrical stories being told about our neighborhoods with great delight. Everybody wanted to be a rapper in those days, but it was more about the music combined with the lyrics that we loved and bobbed our heads to make it cool.

It was not about the dance portion, because there was no such thing as Hip Hop and there was only one dance associated with it during the early 80s, and that was Bboying/Uprock AKA Break Dancing, which is a media term, for a dance we called Rock, which had evolved. However, it wasn't until Rapper's Delight by the Sugar Hill Gang got dropped on the radio that it started gaining more popularity. However, it was still far from being mainstream, and no other Rap songs would be played on the radio for a while longer. The media also coined the term Hip Hop when it was known that the culture had no name. It was, however, LoveBug Starsky who first used that term in a song to describe the culture, or so I was told. Malcolm X also used the term Hip Hoppers during the 1960s.

However, in my experience and that of many others, the Sugar Hill Gang made it popular through the lyrics of the song, "Rapper's Delight," which was the real catalyst.

Black and Puerto Rican people cohabitated and, for the most part, got along; however, we outnumbered them in sheer numbers during the entire 1970s. We learned from each other and shared many similarities, even though we fought each other. However, we also loved each other, depending on the circumstances and the neighborhood you lived in.

My memories from the early days of Hip Hop are full of house parties we attended, where we danced several styles, which depended on the rhythm and melody of the music being played. Still, we adapted to anything that had a hard-driving beat. My crowd always preferred something with a great melody accompanied by lyrics that touched our hearts and stirred our souls and that always made our dancing spirits come out and play.

About the Author

Willie (Marine Boy) Estrada, born in Santurce, Puerto Rico, in 1956, came to New York at the age of two, where he still resides. He is a former gang leader, National IT Manager, and 1st generation dancer from the South Bronx. He started in Entertainment as a dancer in 1974, after walking away from the gang life and winning several dance contests throughout New York City.

He was recruited by George Vascones, President of the "Latin Symbolics Dance Company" based in The Bronx. He later became a Golden Member of the Latin Symbolics and leader of the Rock Team, "The Rock Master's." He was initially recruited to dance on the Latin Symbolics Hustle Team with his first Hustle Partner Maggie Solis and Later with Millie Silva.

He performed at many clubs throughout New York City in the mid to late 70s. He also danced on National TV as a member of the Latin Symbolics Hustle Team on two occasions, which was a big thing back in those days. Since conception in the South Bronx, Willie was involved with the Hustle as a simple 5 step dance done mostly at house parties, and later became one of the best Hustle dancers in New York during the early days. Willie is accredited with creating all the Rock Routines for the Rock Masters during the mid-70s.

The routines he created were shared with several dancers throughout New York City in the late 70s and, in particular, two Rockers from Brooklyn Vinny & Noel from Bushwick who would later say that some of his moves spread throughout Brooklyn and Manhattan. He is also accredited for creating the first four-person Rock Routine in New York City in 1977. After dancing with Robert Feliciano for two years, he later joined forces with Hector Berrios & Pete Martinez and were the original Rock Masters. Willie's first partner was Willie Rivera, AKA Willie Whip. They danced together from 1973 to 1975 and won many Rock Contests throughout New York City.

During the late 1970s, Willie Estrada was instrumental in making Faces Grand Ballroom the biggest disco dance party in New York City alongside David Maldonado, his mentor, and creator of Faces Grand Ballroom. He later became one of New York's biggest Club promoters and is accredited for making Friday Nights at Bond International Casino the most successful club party in New York City during the early 1980s.

In the late 1980s, he went back to school to study Computer Science, where he graduated with honors and went on to become a National IT Manager on Wall Street.

In 2009 after being out of the dance culture for almost 30 years, I got a call from my old friend Hollywood Film Director Franc Reyes. He introduced me to Fabel Pabon, Vice President of the Rock Steady Crew, who convinced me to return to the dance culture to share my knowledge in late 2009.

I was shortly after that approached by **Mr. Wiggles,** also of the Rock Steady Crew. When he saw that I was still a great dancer in both Rock and the Latin Hustle, I was invited on a European Tour with the world-renowned **Rock Steady Crew** and became the first and only 1st Generation Dancer to date to teach Hustle and Rock in Europe at the age of 55 in 2011. I am in my mid-60s now and still Rocking and teaching worldwide.

I continue to do workshops regularly, with students from all over the world to train with me since 2010, and it doesn't look like I'm going to stop anytime soon. Music & Dance saved my life; I always share with everyone, as I aspire to inspire the world's youth with my energy and love of the dance I helped to pioneer during the early 1970s.

In early 2013, I was asked once again to be a part of a European Tour with several well-known dancers, which took place in mid-May 2013, where he visited seven different countries and ended in late June. That made me the only 56 years old to do so within a Hip Hop generation dominated by dancers more than 30 years younger than me. After recently doing lectures and workshops in Shanghai, China, I was asked to come back for a more extensive tour in 2018.

Thanks to Mr. Wiggles, I have traveled the world teaching what I love, and as a result, also opened many other opportunities. Dancing with the new Queen of the Hustle Veronica Castilla below spins like a top.

With Veronica Castilla Queen of the Latin Hustle above

The cast of the Get Down, Willie, Books, Flash, and Cadillac

2015 was an excellent year for me; I got hired to be the technical consultant for the entire first season, Thirteen Episodes of **Baz Luhrmann's** NetFlix Original Series, **"The Get Down,"** which is a fictional account of the Origins of Hip Hop during the late 1970s.

I worked alongside **Jimmy Smits, Jaden Smith, who called me Triple OG, Giancarlo Esposito,** and several others from that era to ensure the authenticity of the dances, which includes the Latin Hustle the dialogue and clothing as well as the stories themselves. I have been waiting for such a long time, and I feel that God has finally opened a window for me, which hopefully, I won't have to jump out of. Meeting **Baz Luhrmann** and **Tom Kelly** were like a Godsend, giving their reception of me and that I like them both immensely. I feel blessed and fortunate to be here still and now able to have been a part of a major production that tells our story and almost got it right.

The Get Down explores the rise of Hip-Hop culture from the ashes of the South Bronx during the late 1970s and also focuses on Disco, and the Latin Hustle, for authenticity purposes of that era. When I first met Baz on the set as he was filming a scene in St. Mary's Park in the South Bronx, I was introduced to him by the Executive Producer Tom Kelly, whom I had met after seeing him cross the street from my apartment. When I told him my name was Willie Estrada, he said, "You're Marine Boy? I said, "How did you know that?" He told me Baz, and he spoke about me that very morning, and Baz was drafting a letter for me to bring me on board as a consultant to ensure authenticity that same morning. Tom then took me over to meet Baz, who was filming at the time, and when he said "Cut," Tom called him over to introduce us. When Baz saw me, he got excited and said my name out loud, "Willie" He came over, hugged me, told me he knew all about me, and then recited my entire life story, much to my surprise.

He then told me that he wanted me to come on board to help guide him, and in that instant, I felt like I was in a fairytale, and a lifelong wish was about to be granted. I stood there in shock as Baz continued, and Tom said: "He knows you better than you know yourself!" We all laughed about it as I agreed, but it got better. Tom told Baz he should put me in the poker game scene with Jimmy Smits, and Baz didn't hesitate to agree and asked Tom to have me fitted for a suit to wear during that scene. The day we filmed the scene I was in with Jimmy Smits, they decided to write my character into the script, which we filmed on July 6th, 2015, the date of the anniversary of my father's death. I got to live a dream that I once had a long time ago, in a Galaxy Far Far away, which was called the land of broken promises by the people of the South Bronx.

**Executive Producer Tom Kelly invited mom to the set,
and everyone treated her like the Queen she was!**

Executive Producer/Director Baz Luhrmann – and Actor Jimmy Smits, with Willie Estrada

Six-time Academy Award Winner Catherine Martin, Willie Estrada & Storenzo Dom

Giancarlo Esposito and Willie Estrada after a Long Day on set shooting Episode 10 of The Get Down

Working alongside Jimmy Smits was like a dream come true for me. He treated me like family!

Scene from Episode 5 – The Get Down

Jaden Smith and Willie Estrada 1st Day of shooting across the street from my house

Gang cast on the set of the Get Down below

Executive Producer "The Get Down" Tom Kelly and I

The Latin Hustle and Hip Hop

There are just too many entities who have taken credit for creating the Latin Hustle for the past 40 years. The truth of the matter is it was developed and nurtured by Puerto Rican Teenagers from the South Bronx and started being cultivated during the early 1970s. It later became the most prominent and dominant dance culture of the remainder of the 1970s, yet credit for making peace through a dance culture has always been given to those who say they created Hip Hop in 1973. Hip Hop was not the culture that paved the way to peace within the Puerto Rican community. It was Rock Dance and the Latin Hustle, which was mainstream during the entire 70s, and yet credit has never been given to us for what we created and used as an instrument of making peace in the most violent area in all of the South Bronx. We must also keep in mind that many Latino DJs, Rappers, and Bboys also helped pave the way for creating Hip Hop. That being said, there is another and more accurate account of the 1970s, which includes the participation and significant contributions by Puerto Ricans and the dominant dance culture, called "The Latin Hustle."

I've seen a couple of recent documentaries claiming it was the Zulu Nation who established peace among the gangs of the South Bronx, yet the Zulu Nation did not even exist in 1973 but were still Black Spades at the time. They got it wrong for hiring unreliable researchers and consultants, who weren't there, but pretended to know everything while attacking the truth! If someone tells me that **Kool Herc** was looping the breakbeats in 1973, that's when Bboys started doing floor moves. I would say to them, get the flock out of here with that ridiculous story; there were no Bboys during the early 1970s!

Nobody was looping beats in 1973, nor were there any Bboys during the early 1970s! There has never been any proof to substantiate those claims, but there is proof to dispute it, according to Rahiem from the Furious Five! You couldn't even purchase a Mixer at any electronics stores during the early 70s unless you had a commercial license. Most of us know those things happened during the latter part of the 1970s, but certainly not in 1973. Consequently, that was also the year when they say he started calling dancers who did floor moves, Bboys. Again, there was no such thing as a Bboy during the early 1970s, contrary to recent and reckless assertions. Or at least, not like the Bboys by today's standards. When speaking of that era, most people also neglect even to mention the Puerto Rican Rockers who were doing floor moves since the late 1960s as Outlaw Rockers, and Latino Mambo dancers were doing floor moves since the 1940s. The Latin Hustle, which quickly migrated in 1974 from St. Mary's and the 310 1/2 to New York City Night Clubs, and later Discos, became the real melting pot of its migration into other boroughs. Its roots are set in stone in the South Bronx.

Louie River, Willie Estrada, and Storenzo Dom

Author – (Kings of Dance) Luis DeJesus and Willie MB

St. Mary's Recreation Center with my old friend Sunday. As I said during my story, we had the coolest gang clubhouse in NYC!

Joseph and Abby doing the Latin Hustle at St. Mary's Recreation Center in 1974

Joseph is one of the guys who introduced the Latin Hustle to the Gay community, and he was Gay.

Honorable mention of great dancers and friends

Doris Lopez, Luis De Jesus, Gladys Rodriquez, Debra Benitez, Luis Rivera, Eddie Vega (RIP), Deb Ferro, Billy Fajardo, Sandra Rivera-Lopez, Maggie Solis, Mario Diaz, Tony Febles, Carlos Ramos, Edith Sanchez, Willie Santana, Hector Berrios, Pete Martinez, Robert Feliciano, Jacqueline Cruz, Lourdes Jones, George Torres, Bobby Morales, Tito Sandoval, Miriam Sanchez, Rafael Vega Sr., Alma Ramos, George Vascones (RIP), Sara Silva, Eddie Ramundi, Denise Florencio, Maria Vega, Ivy Leon (RIP), Elba Santiago (RIP), Yolanda Roman, Elizabeth Rodriquez, Pepsi Rodriquez, George Rivera, Alfredo Mojica, Raymond Aguiar, Tommy Rivera, Kitty Davila, Johnny Sanchez, Louie Aguiar, Charlie Aguiar, Henry De Sosa, Maria Torres,

Jackie Torres, Rosa PiJuan Leon, Mike Acevedo, Kenny Salsa, Franc Reyes, Willie Rivera, Moises Martinez, Chico Ortiz, David Pellot, Jose (Papo) Rivera, Mike Latuf, and far too many others to list here, but a big shout out to all my students around the world, far too many to mention here.

"They were the worst of times; they were the best of times!"
And I wouldn't change a damn thing!

Junbug, Willie, Ralph, Jose, Anibal, and Chico above

Three people stand out most: Luis Lugo, Father Smith and Father Mario (The Hoodlum Priest) of the Catholic Church, and most importantly, Black Benjy's mother. The meeting directly resulted from their intervention, which has been kept out of the narrative for many years now.

Thanks to the Warlord of the Black Spades Bam Bam, and a few other senior members of the Black Spades who also spoke out at our reunion, we established that the Zulu Nation did not exist in 1973 and were still Black Spades, but although the Zulu Nation came a few short years later, they have a compelling history and are renowned around the world today.

We also established that the first Peace Incentive came from the Ghetto Brothers upon the Death of Black Benjy in December of 1971, which brought a relative, but not complete peace was made among several gangs during that truce. Furthermore, several gangs, including the Royal Javelins, would not make peace with other rival gangs such as "The Turbans," and the blood feud between them and the Royal Javelins continued for a while longer. Several gangs did not make peace with some of their rivals, and gang violence continued until 1974 for many of them. In 1974, the Imperial Bachelors brought order into the most violent area of the South Bronx, considered the "Murder Capital of the United States" by hosting Latin Hustle and Rock parties at St. Mary's Recreation Center until the Death of 21-year-old dancer Rubberband.

He was stabbed to death in a dispute over a dollar with a 14-year-old teen on October 1, 1974. **RIP Jamie Rosendo (Rubberband)**

It was not gang-related; however, the killing ended those hugely successful parties attended by people from the Tri-State area for a few months before the killing. For many years now, I have been talking about the TRUE narrative of the 1970s and how different gangs made peace in other neighborhoods accordingly for various reasons at different times. In the end, it was music and dance that greatly contributed to making peace possible. However, we must also give credit to all the females who were also Pioneers of the Latin Hustle who helped establish peace in the most volatile area in the South Bronx in 1974 by getting us to dance with them. For our neighborhood, the Hustle parties the Imperial Bachelors hosted at St. Mary's made the most significant difference thanks to Henry DeSosa, Supreme President of the Bachelors. He also served as DJ for those parties. To his credit, after our gang broke up in 1975, Henry DeSosa continued to DJ at parties and clubs until he died in the early 1990s.

RIP HENRY, UNTIL WE MEET AGAIN MY BROTHER!

HENRY DESOSA SUPREME PRESIDENT OF THE BACHELORS 1976

Few friendships last a lifetime; those are the ones we call the
Chosen Few, the ones you can count on one hand! PALS!

Gang wars were primarily ended by each gang taking part in making peace, on their own turf, in their own way, at their own time.

Nobody has the right to dictate our complete story or tell someone else's story, but instead, they should share their own and add it to the collective. This story reflects how the Imperial Bachelors from St. Mary's brought peace into their territory during the summer of 1974. We were the first gang to take off our gang colors so that we could dance the Latin Hustle and Rock in peace, and we never wore them again.

Special thanks to Benjamin (Yellow Benjy) Melendez for granting me several interviews, sharing his life story with me, and being a good friend. Thank you for your contributions in the name of peace, love, unity, and having fun! SIP!

RIP BENJY 1952 - 2017, UNTIL WE, MEET AGAIN MY BROTHER, YOU WILL BE MISSED, AND YOUR LEGACY WILL LIVE FOREVER!

Benjamin (Yellow Benjy) Melendez, your journey continues in God's Kingdom now, but your legacy lives on here forever!

Yellow Benjy and Willie Estrada at the 40th Anniversary of the gang peace meeting at the Bronx Boys Club.

We need to look at all perspectives through everyone's eyes, and take them all into account, and realize we are all part of the collective, and that's the only way we will ever have the complete and authentic story of that violent yet magical era!

PICTURED ABOVE, FAT LOUIE, PRESIDENT OF THE 1ST DIVISION ROYAL JAVELINS FROM WILKINS AVE., ALBERT, RAYMOND, JAYJOE, AND CRAZY JUNIOR. WE ARE A FEW OF THE SOLE SURVIVORS. THEY ARE MY BROTHERS FOREVER!

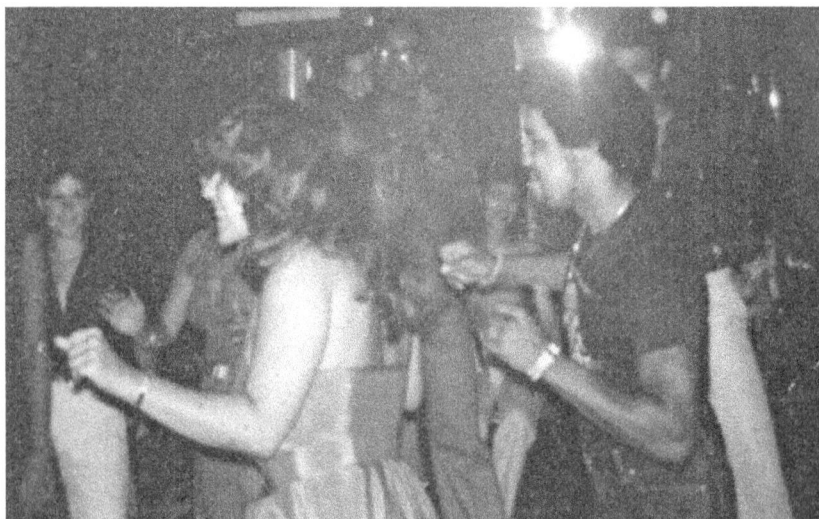

President of the Latin Symbolics with George Vacones in the background, as Lisa and I dance Hustle to Rock!

I am in my mid-60s now and still spreading our story and doing workshops and lectures worldwide. I feel blessed to do this at my age; however, I am now turning my attention towards the film industry and doing my best to get our stories told in movies and TV shows, God willing.

Our first film will be a documentary based on this book, and we feel it will serve as a catalyst that will open doors for other Puerto Ricans down the road. My partner Pedro Morales and I will be producing the film ourselves, so Hollywood doesn't screw up our story, as they have done so many times in the past. This is truly the dawn of a new era for our people, and we both have high expectations of making a significant impact on our people in the coming years.

MY FAMILY IS MOSTLY ALL GONE NOW, BUT NEVER FORGOTTEN! RIP GRANDMA, I MISS YOU!

In Memory Of Dad, Eddie Estrada, May 6, 1925 – July 6, 1998

And Mom May 30, 1936 – October 8, 2021 - RIP

THANK YOU FOR YOUR UNCONDITIONAL LOVE! ALWAYS IN MY HEART!

www.ingramcontent.com/pod-product-compliance
Lightning Source LLC
Chambersburg PA
CBHW031232090426
42742CB00007B/160